IMAGES
of America

UKRAINIANS OF METROPOLITAN DETROIT

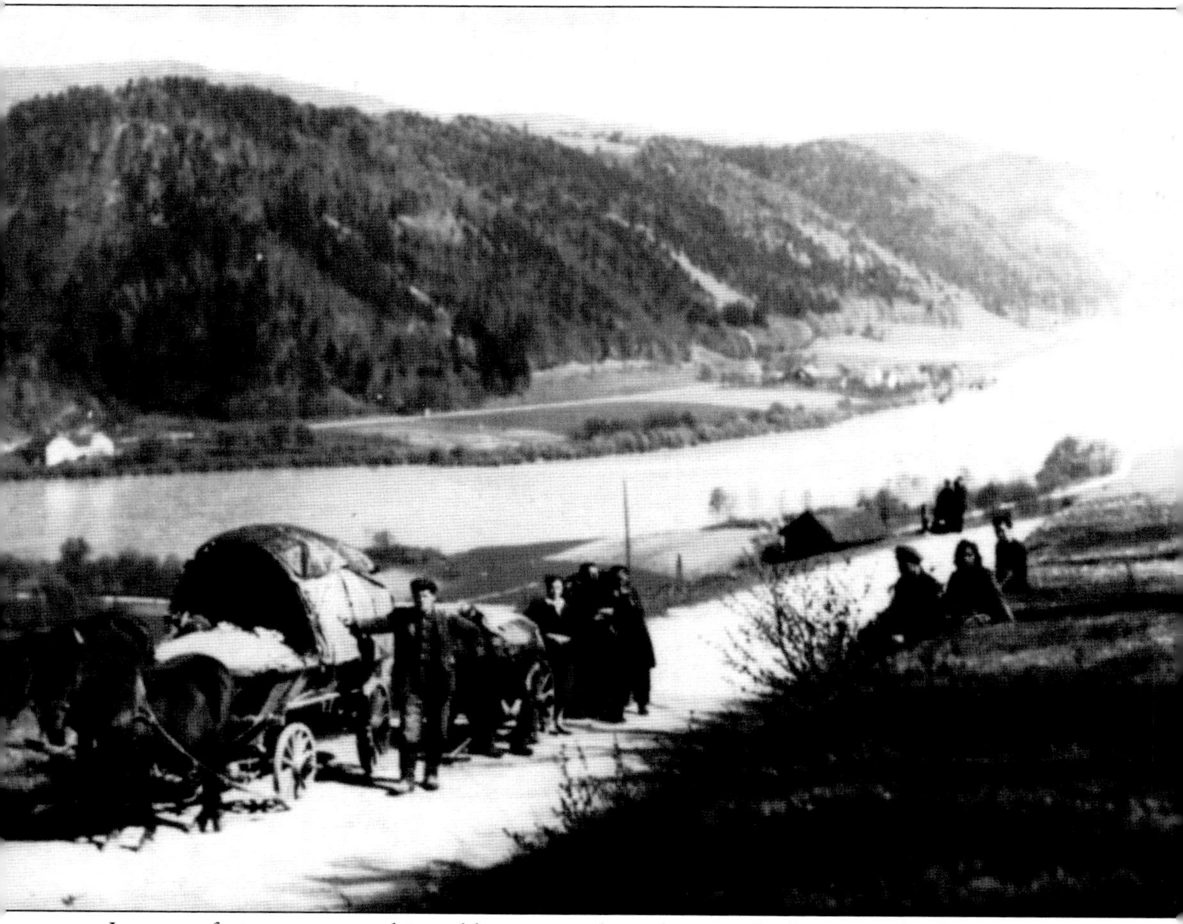

It seems fitting to open this publication with a photograph depicting the beginning of the journey to a new land. Joining thousands of other Ukrainians fleeing their homeland in the early 1940s were Gregory Symonenko, wife Anna, son Petro, and daughter Halina. Anna would pass away in Brazil, while Gregory, Petro, and Halina would make their homes in Detroit. Escaping the German onslaught, taking only what would fit in the wagon, they courageously faced an uncertain future with little hope of returning to Ukraine. (Elizabeth Symonenko.)

On the cover: Alan Elnick, a member of Echoes of Ukraine dance ensemble, performs during the grand finale of the Hopak at one of the Ukrainian Ethnic Festivals held at Detroit's riverfront in the 1970s. Joanna von Draginda-Kulchesky, director and choreographer of the ensemble, dedicated her talents to several generations of Ukrainian youth. The Hopak is often referred to as the national dance of Ukraine. (Joanna von Draginda-Kulchesky/Ukrainian Museum.)

IMAGES
of America

UKRAINIANS OF METROPOLITAN DETROIT

Nancy Karen Wichar

ARCADIA
PUBLISHING

ISBN 978-0-7385-7716-6

Published by Arcadia Publishing
Charleston SC, Chicago IL, Portsmouth NH, San Francisco CA

Printed in the United States of America

Library of Congress Control Number: 2009927922

For all general information contact Arcadia Publishing at:
Telephone 843-853-2070
Fax 843-853-0044
E-mail sales@arcadiapublishing.com
For customer service and orders:
Toll-Free 1-888-313-2665

Visit us on the Internet at www.arcadiapublishing.com

This book is dedicated to Mother, Daddy, and Grandma Wichar

Contents

ACKNOWLEDGMENTS

Thank you to my parents, Stephen and Nadia Wichar, and my grandparents, Michael and Katherine Wichar and Onufry and Ahaphia Osadchuk, for my heritage.

Thank you to all the kind people who warmly invited me into their Ukrainian homes to share family albums and stories, especially Roman Maziak, who went above and beyond the call of duty. Photograph contributors are acknowledged in the text; the remaining photographs are from the estate of Stephen and Nadia Wichar.

Historical information was obtained from the *Ukrainian Weekly Archives* and *Ukrainians in Detroit and Michigan*, 1988.

This book would not have been possible without the following: Matthew Harbron, my dear friend and mentor; Olga Dubriwnyj-Solovey, my consultant and historian for the Artistry chapter, whose dedication helped me take this project to the finish line; Emilia Vicol for her organizational skills; Karen Osadchuk for her typing skills; Cathy Koneya for her encouragement and tracking down photos that, in the beginning, seemed impossible to find; and Marie Zarycky for her incredible knowledge of Ukrainian history, her loyalty, her enthusiasm for this project, and for the many hours she devoted to this publication.

Finally, thank you to my loyal canine companions, Slava and Marusia, who patiently waited at my side with anticipation as we burned the midnight oil. I know they sensed the magnitude of the project that was about to emerge.

Introduction

I was not born in Ukraine. My parents were not born in Ukraine. Still, this enormous feeling of ethnic pride consumes me. How did this happen?

My grandparents, who emigrated from Ukraine to Detroit, certainly influenced me in many ways, especially my grandmother, Katherine Iwashkewych Wichar. I can still hear the sound of her voice as she put into words the chronicles of her childhood and then her journey to America, never to be reunited with her family or homeland. My parents, Stephen and Nadia Wichar, active members of the Ukrainian community in metropolitan Detroit, modeled a lifetime of commitment to Ukrainian culture and causes. This has become my legacy. I am grateful.

When my grandfather Michael Wichar passed in 1967, my father, Stephen M. Wichar Sr., expressed his thoughts about his legacy in the passage below.

Silent Echoes of Heritage

> As I begin this message, I become deeply moved by the death of my father. I strive to recall nostalgically some of the events in his life that had deep-rooted meaning other than that of a good husband and father.
>
> What were his thoughts in Rohatyn, Ukraine . . . in the village of Dybriniv where he made a decision to emigrate? I wonder what misgivings he had, knowing that he possessed only the barest of essentials in formal academic training, to embark on this adventure to a new land.
>
> Although the struggle for economic existence was difficult in a society that was indifferent and adversely hostile to "foreigners," he was able to transmit his ideas to a foundation of cultural, social, and political life in Ukrainian community living. It was John F. Kennedy who said that American history can, in a general sense, be interpreted as a factual episode of the immigrant's part in his own personal development of America itself. My father was such a man.
>
> Sometimes sociologists call my generation cultural hybrids . . . persons living and sharing in the cultural life and traditions of peoples . . . and we have been identified with the land of our birth and its institutions. Despite this, in the process of learning the mother tongue, the standards of morals and religion, sentiments and patterns of foreign thoughts through such media as Ukrainian schools, dancing groups, stage and other folklore, the assimilation has been successfully possible for many of us. . . .

And with the "old country ways" that my dad taught me, I have been acutely aware of the vastness of the world and its many treasures . . . and although his approach and means of intellectual training was frugal, he was able to cohesively inject into my consciousness that Ukrainians are a nationality, a group that is specific in culture.

The passing of my father is perhaps just an incidental biological expectation . . . but to him, as to many other old immigrants who passed before him, my generation owes a lasting debt . . . a tribute to those who had the courage to build pillars of Ukrainianism in a foreign land. I am humble in my tribute to a father I knew so well.

To my father I can silently say that I am proud of my Ukrainian heritage. This is my dearest legacy.

Stephen M. Wichar Sr.

I am indebted to the many Ukrainian-Americans in Detroit who opened their hearts to share their legacies through the treasured photographs that appear in this book.

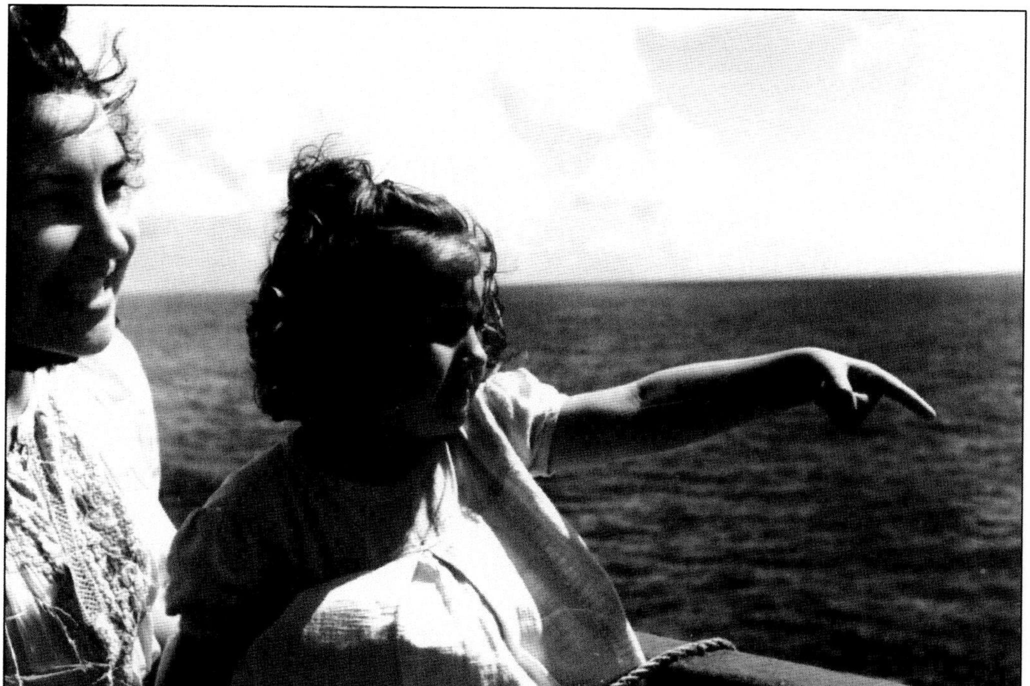

After almost three weeks at sea, Tatjana (Krawziw) Mojsiuk and daughter Tamara arrive in New York on June 24, 1950. Husband and father Myroslaw Mojsiuk was also aboard the carrier, SS *Blacthford*. Carriers were used to transport new immigrants because the numbers emigrating from the displaced person camps was so staggering. The Mojsiuk family made their way to Detroit with help from their sponsor, Denys Kwitkowsky. (Tamara Petraszczuk.)

One

Family and Community

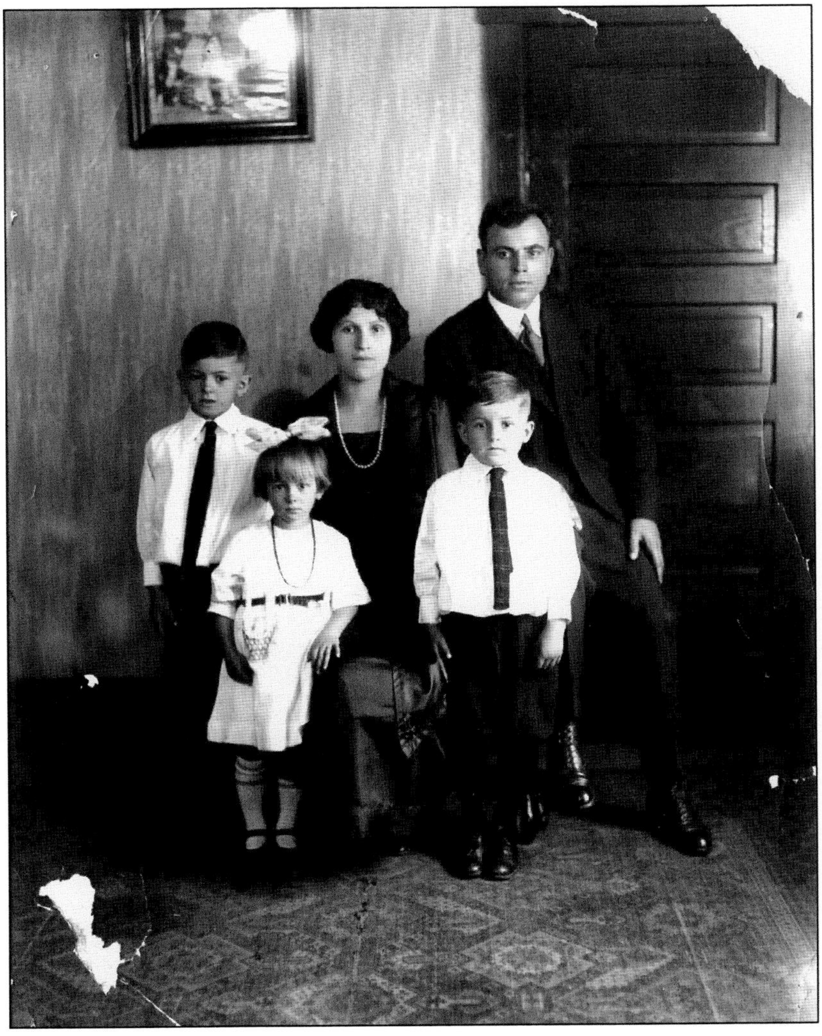

Katherine Wichar and her husband Michael pose for a family portrait with their three children, from left to right, Eugene, Stella, and Stephen, in 1924. It was customary for Ukrainians to dress in their finest clothing and utilize a professional photographer to preserve family memories.

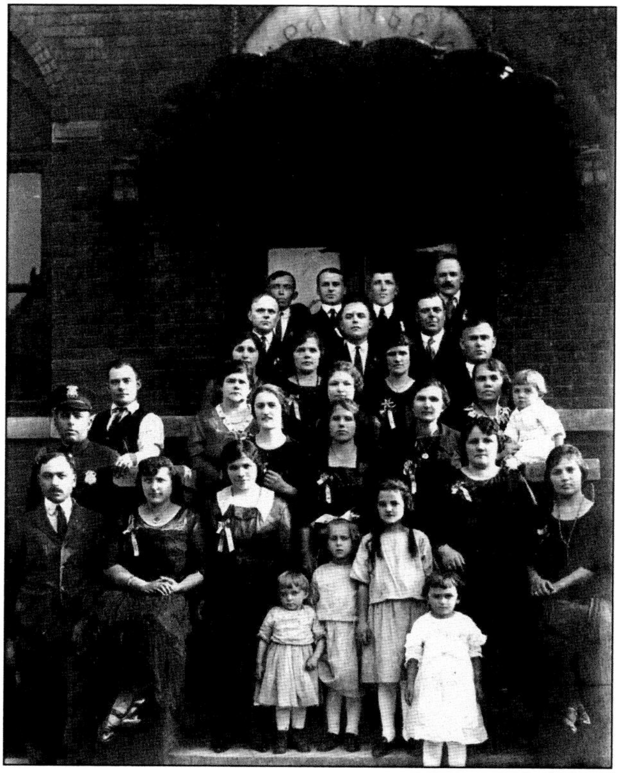

New immigrants (1918) gather in front of the building referred to as the Ukrainian Home on Grayling Street in Hamtramck. A meeting place was essential for socializing and maintaining the Ukrainian culture. (Andrew Kruk.)

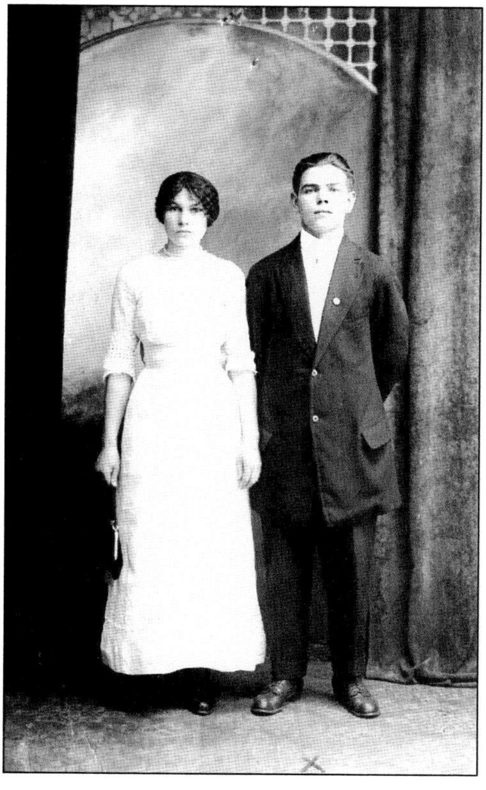

Ahaphia Kohut and her brother Petro Kohut pose for their arrival photograph in 1915. Ahaphia would later marry Onufry Osadchuk and raise three children, Mitchell, Nadia, and Stephen.

In 1929, Mary and George Tomiak are photographed with their two-year-old daughter, Olga. Olga would later marry Stephen Seniw and raise three children. (Olga Seniw.)

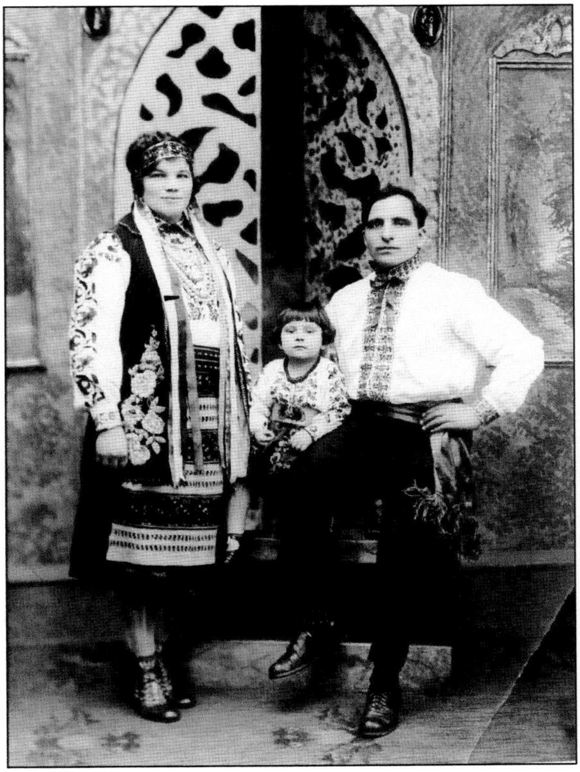

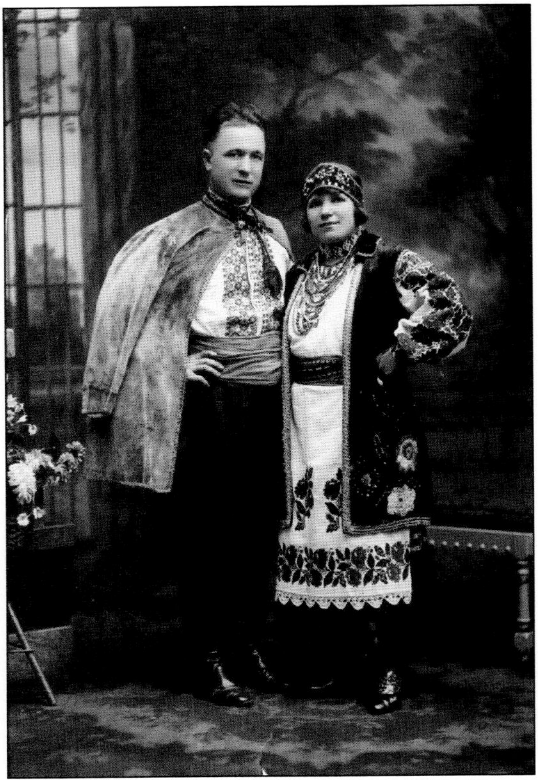

Mr. and Mrs. Dobriansky proudly model traditional Ukrainian costumes in this portrait taken in the late 1920s. (Olga Seniw.)

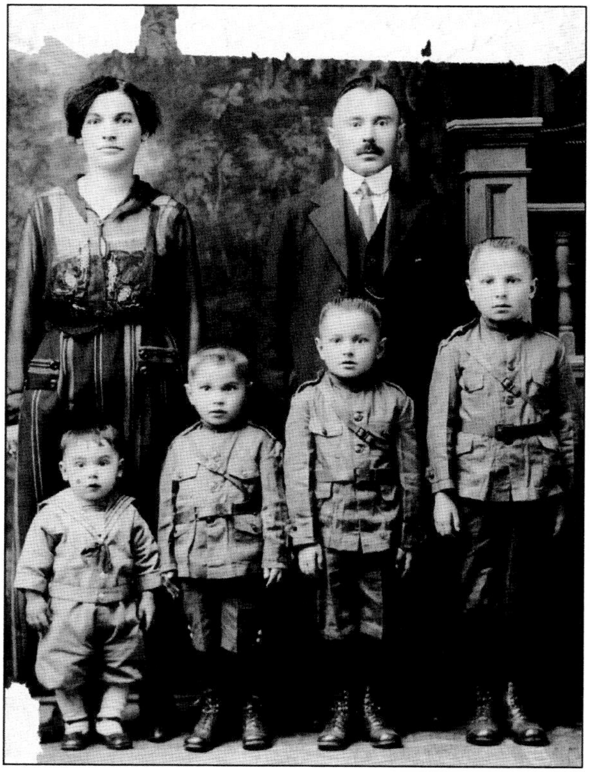

In the 1920s, Peggy and Michael Martyniuk are pictured with their sons, from left to right, Dmytro, John, William, and Peter. (Catherine Whitfield.)

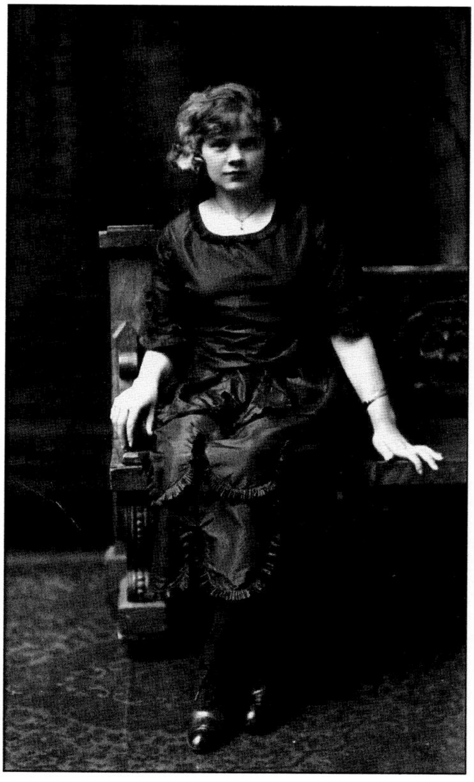

Nadia Diachun's elegant portrait is preserved for eternity in this photograph taken in the early 1930s. (Nadia Stratelak.)

In the early 1930s, Sonia Romanchuk poses in a traditional Ukrainian costume. She performed in many theatrical productions at the Ukrainian American Center. Most of the intricate costumes were hand-stitched by women in the community. (Olga Seniw.)

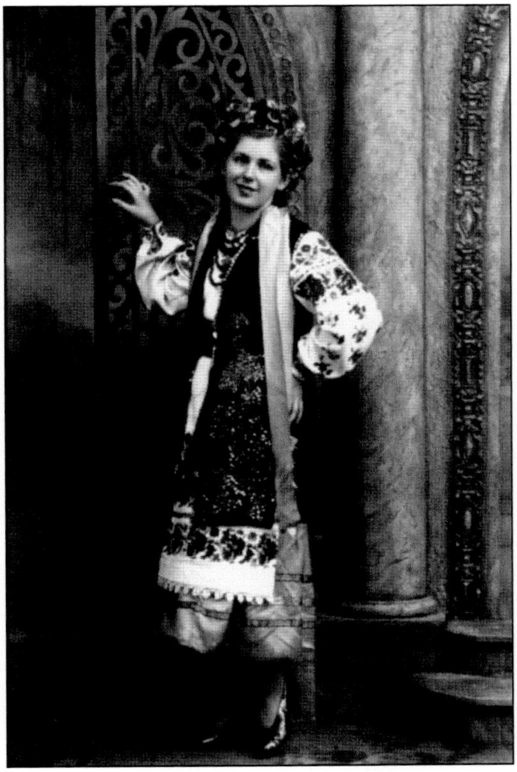

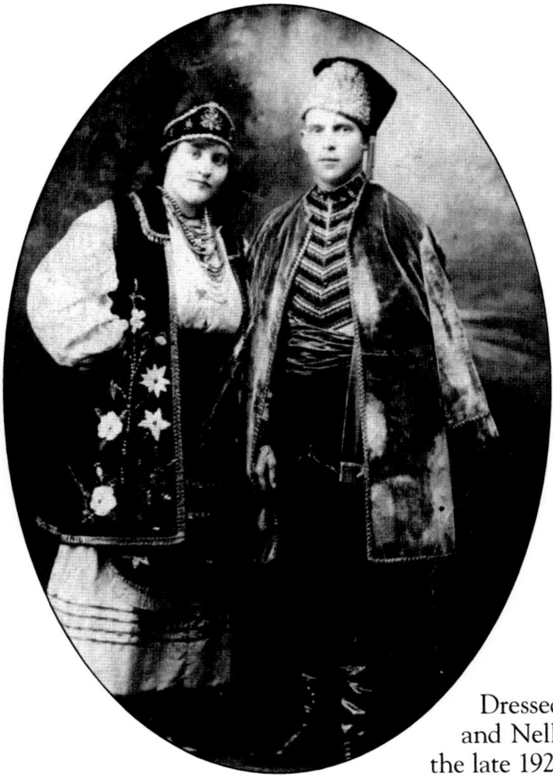

Dressed in traditional Ukrainian costumes, George and Nellie Feifer demonstrate their ethnic pride in the late 1920s. (Olga Wasik.)

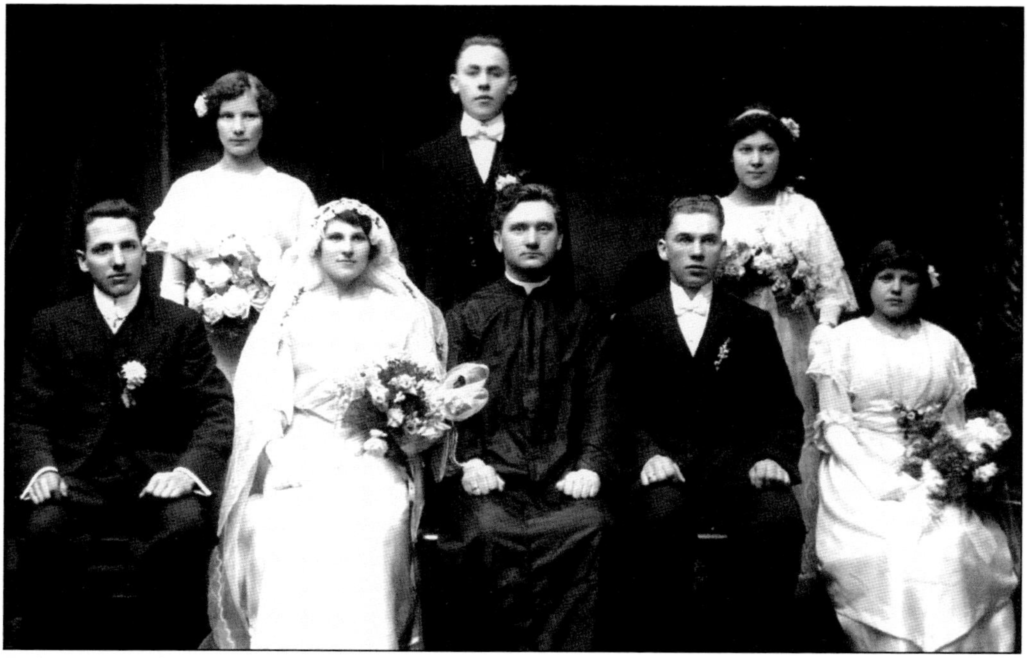

Father Sterniuk of St. John's Ukrainian Catholic Church performed the marriage ceremony for Mr. and Mrs. Wojtowicz in the late 1910s. It was considered an honor to have the priest pose with the wedding party. (Olga Solovey.)

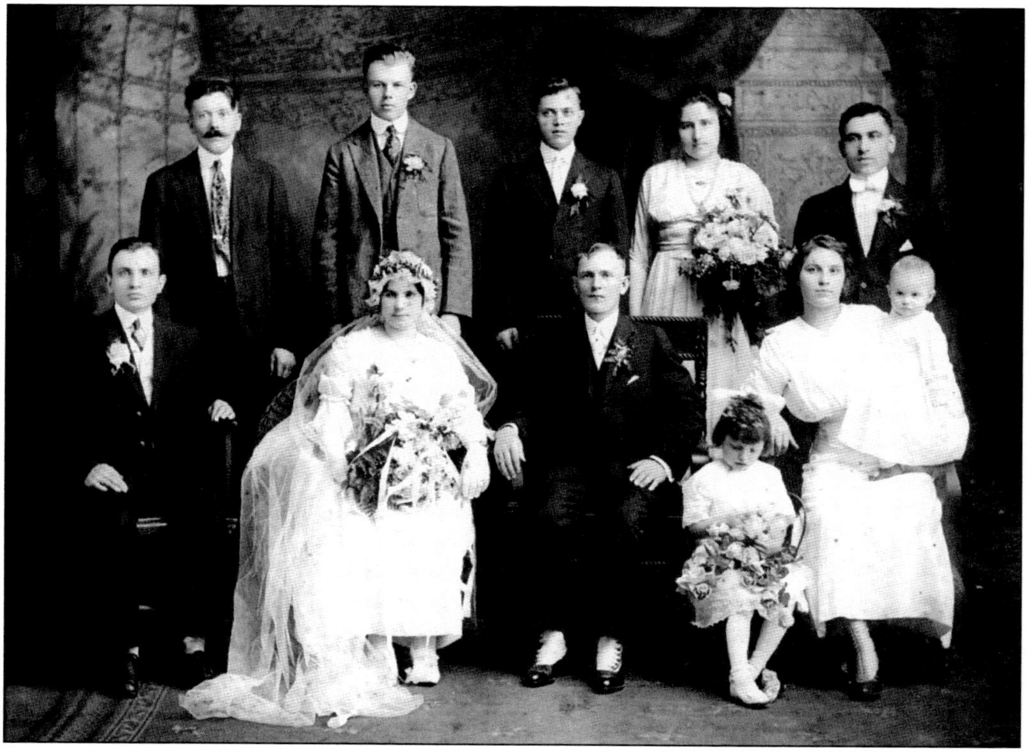

Anne Czuchraj and Michael Meges were wed in the late 1910s. The tradition of including children as part of the wedding party is still practiced today.

Peter and Wasylyna Marfey married in Toronto but settled in Hamtramck in 1924 where they would, along with many other Ukrainians, build a new life and raise their two children, Zinovia and Walter. (Zinovia Ogrodnik.)

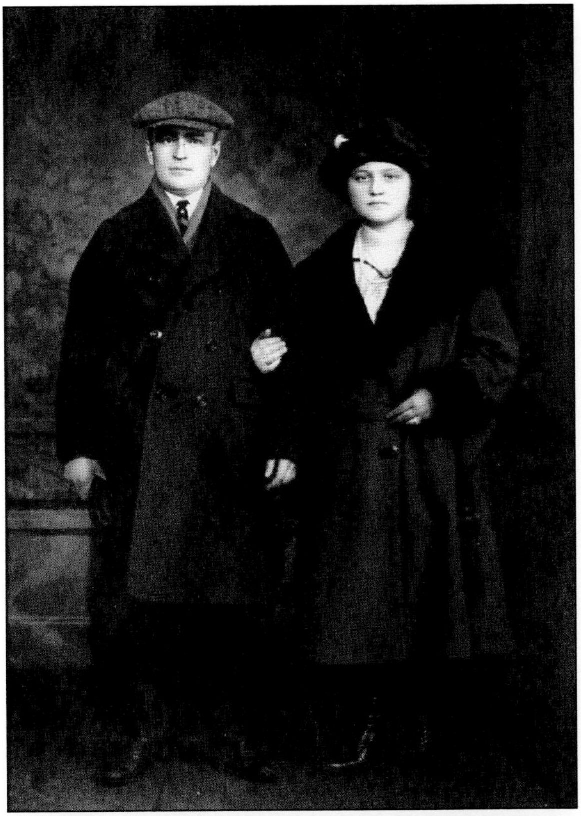

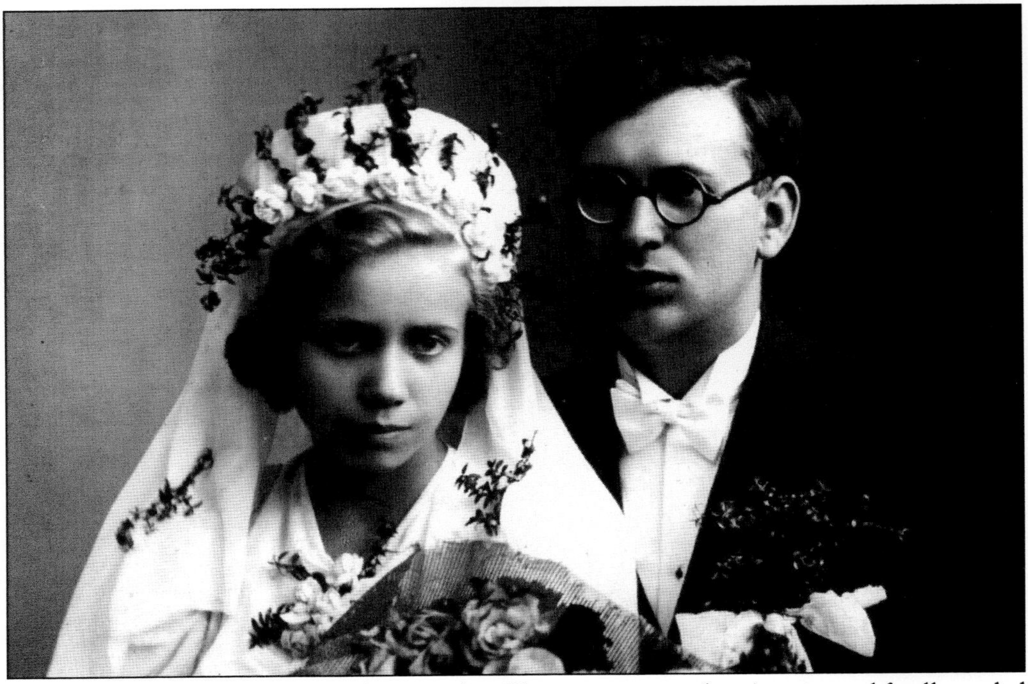

In 1937, Anastasia and Leo Maziak married in Ukraine, emigrated to Austria, and finally settled in Detroit. (Roman Maziak.)

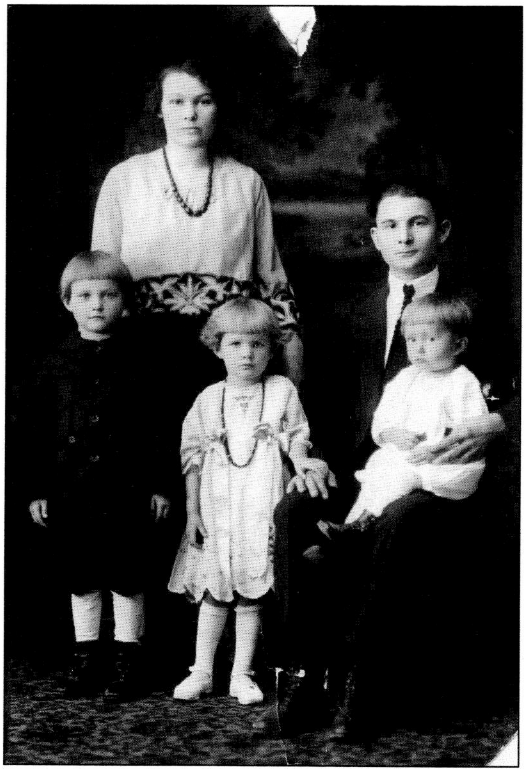

This Osadchuk family portrait was taken in 1924. Ahaphia and Onufry pose with their children, from left to right, Mitchell, Nadia, and Stephen.

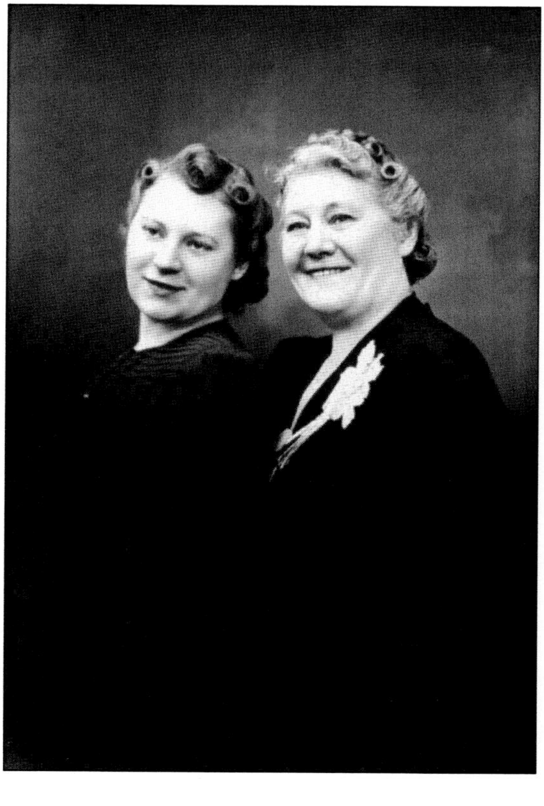

This mother and daughter portrait of Tillie Ogrodnik and Evdohia Ogrodnik was taken in 1940. Both women were active in the Ukrainian community. (William Dowhan.)

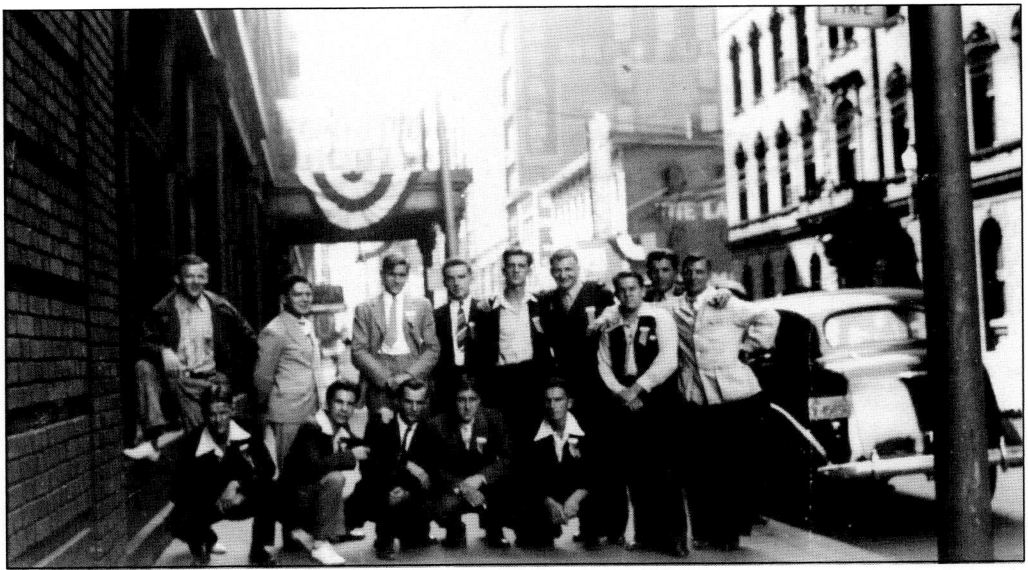

Detroit's youth attended the national convention of the Ukrainian Youth League of North America (UYLNA) in the late 1930s. In 1941, Detroit would host the national convention at the Leland Hotel. UYLNA was founded for the purpose of embracing in its orbit all Ukrainian American youth to promote the principles of democracy and loyalty to this country.

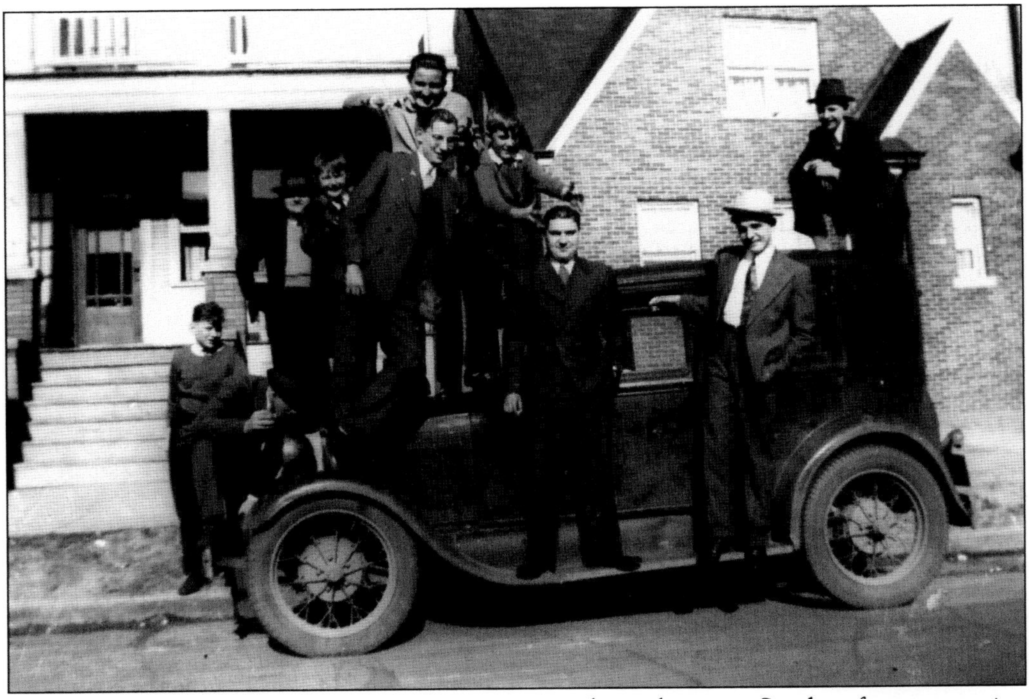

In the late 1930s, these young Ukrainian men amuse themselves on a Sunday afternoon posing on a Model T Ford in front of the Prowalny home in Detroit. The adults are, from left to right, Eugene Ogrodnik, Steve Hrynik, Walter Prowalny, Walter Solovey, Hank Prowalny, Bill Senyk, and Eddie Holowchak. Sunday was a day for dressing up, visiting friends, and in this case, perhaps getting into some mischief.

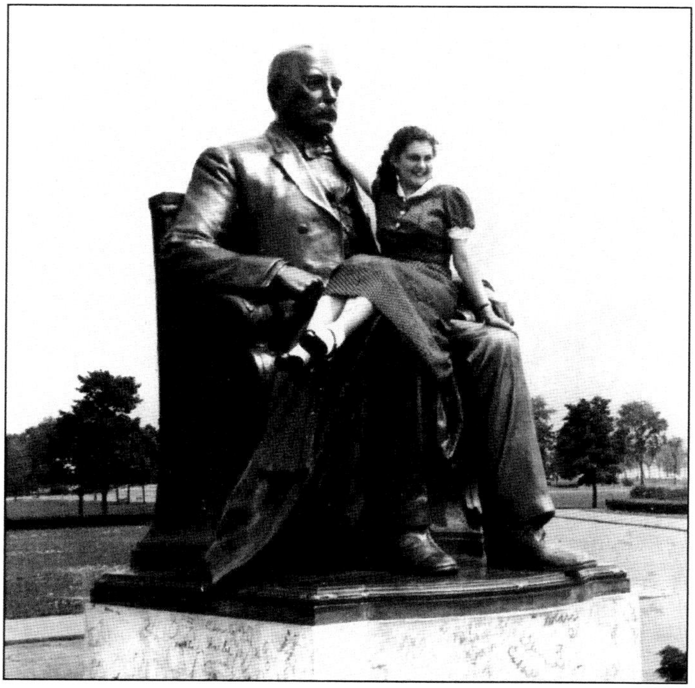

In 1952, Iryna Nehaniv made her first visit to Belle Isle, Detroit's most famous historic island park. She climbed on to the lap of one of many statues on the island to have her photograph taken. (Bohdan Nehaniv.)

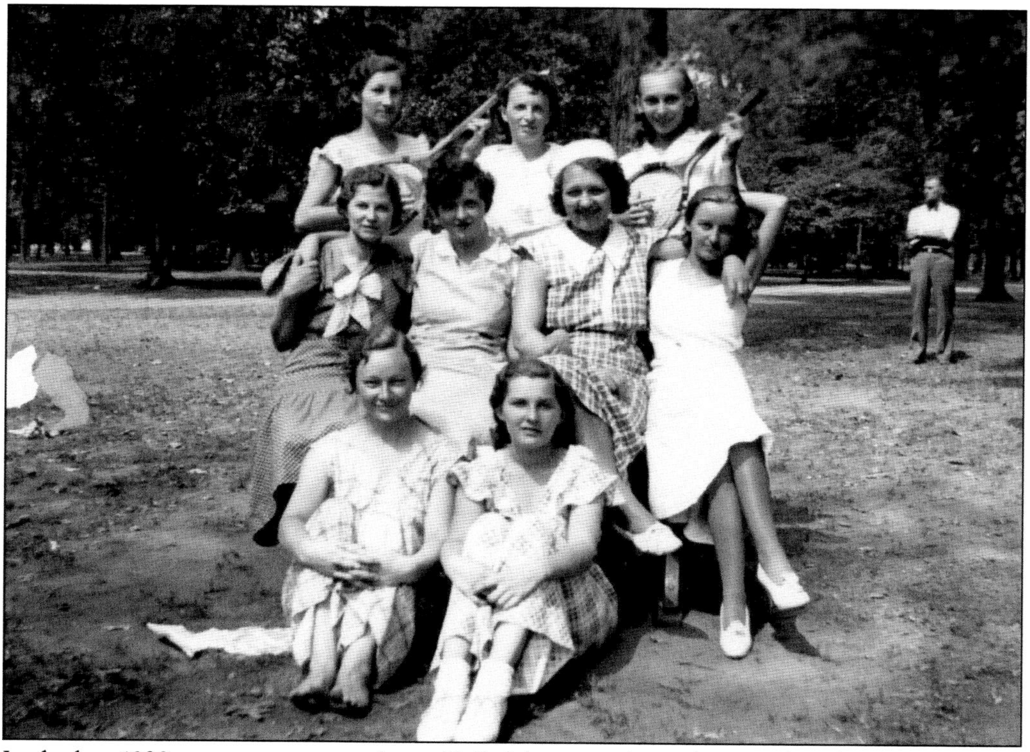

In the late 1930s, young women gather at Belle Isle, a popular gathering place for all generations of Ukrainian-Americans, for a day of fun and flirtation. Seen here are, from left to right, (first row) unidentified and Nadia Osadchuk; (second row) Alice Warrick's sister, Olga Kolomyjec, Olga Kohut, and Marie Warrick; (third row) unidentified, Amelia Kolomyjec, and Olga Predski.

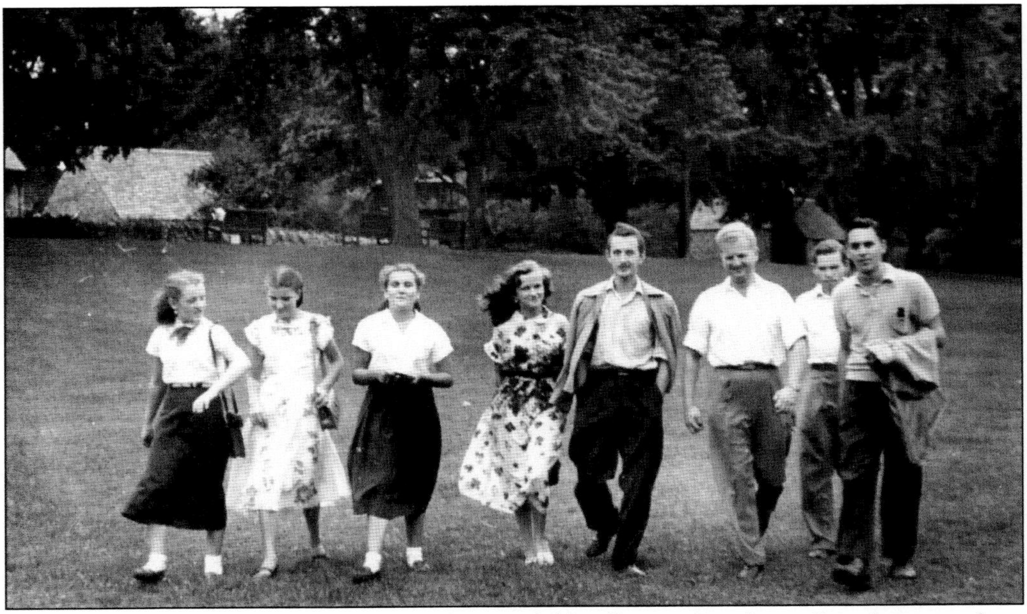

In 1954, Ukrainian Plast members visited Greenfield Village in Dearborn. Seen here are, from left to right, Dana Iwanec, Mika Kazanivsky, Halyna Cisaruk, Tamara Kuziw, Anton Sobko, Bohdan Fedash, Wasyl Kolochin, and Bohdan Nehaniv. (Bohdan Nehaniv.)

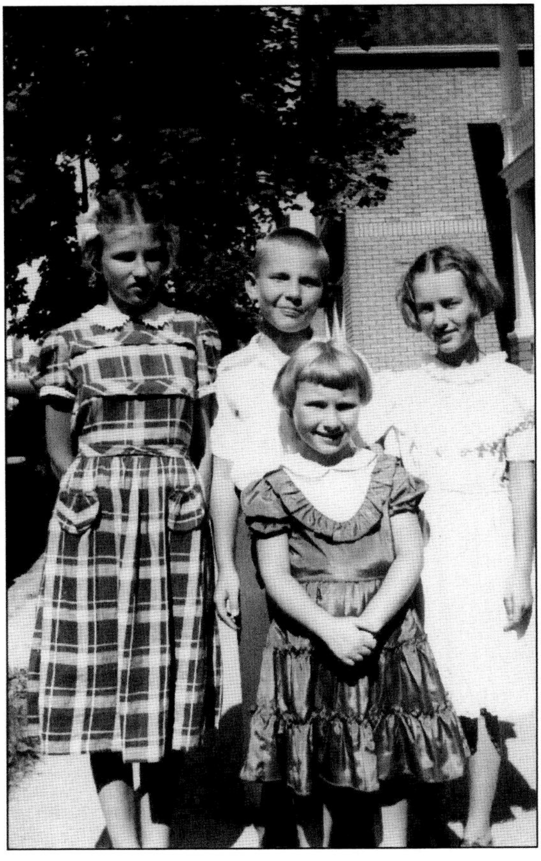

After recently arriving in Detroit, new immigrants pose for a photograph in 1951. Standing in front is Iya Zdaniw. From left to right in the back are Chrystyna Nykorak, Oleh Zdaniw, and Dzvinka Nykorak. (Dzvinka Hayda.)

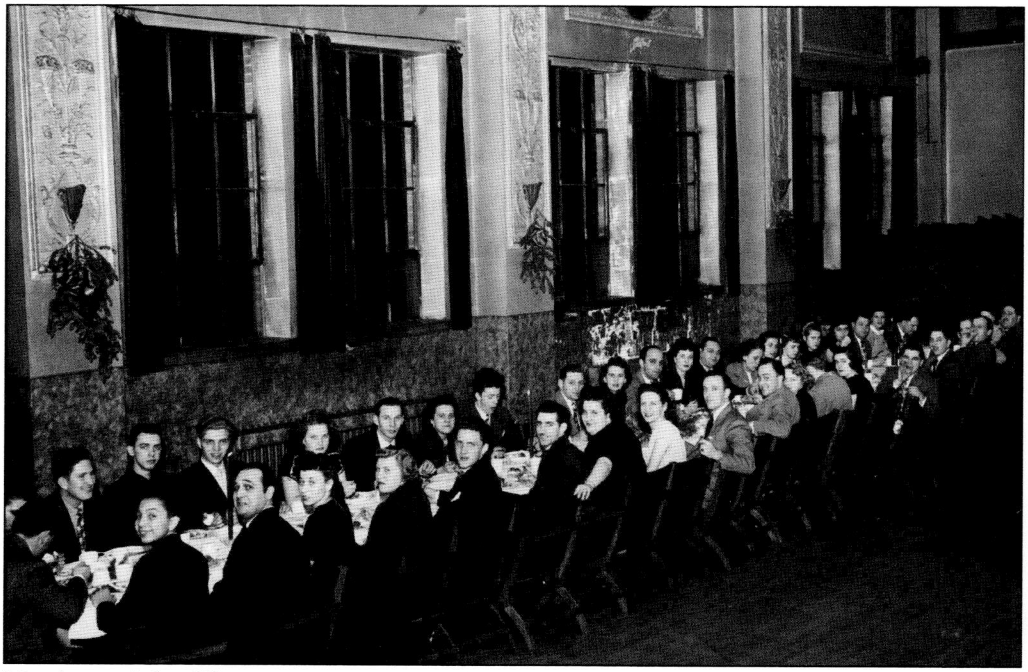

Members of the Ukrainian American Center gather for a Christmas celebration dinner in 1946. The center, constructed by the members in 1930, became the hub of east side activities until it was sold in 1984. Several years later, the Ukrainian American Center Foundation was established to honor the pioneers who founded the center and to promote Ukrainian endeavors in the community.

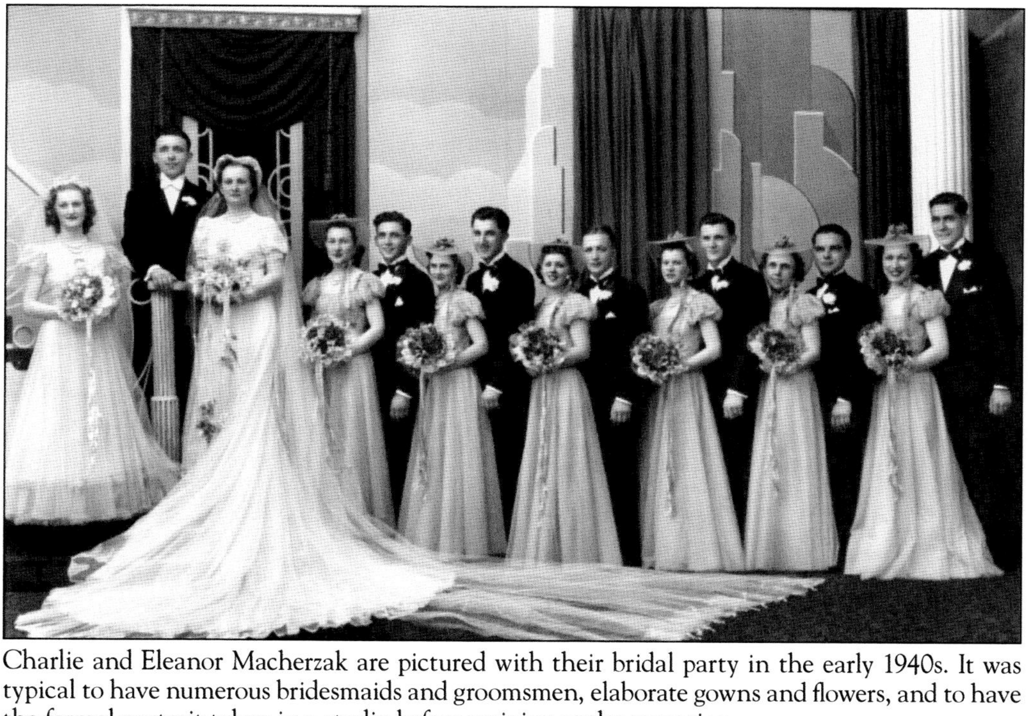

Charlie and Eleanor Macherzak are pictured with their bridal party in the early 1940s. It was typical to have numerous bridesmaids and groomsmen, elaborate gowns and flowers, and to have the formal portrait taken in a studio before arriving at the reception.

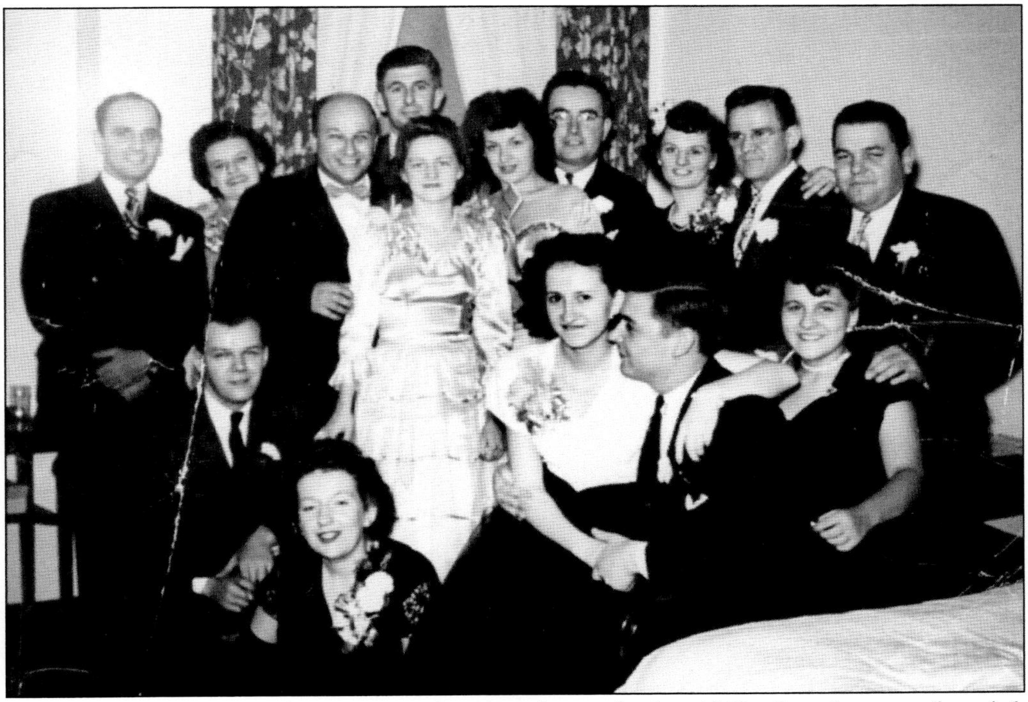

Friends gather for a special evening on the town during the late 1940s. Seen here are, from left to right, (first row) J. Kuchapsky, H. Hales, J. Sirko, G. Sirko, and F. Pakizer; (second row) G. Whitney, A. Zenivk, P. Kasey, J. Hales, M. Koshowsky, S. Polny, L. Polny, N. Kuchapsky, G. Kuchapsky, and J. Lukuwy. (Zinovia Ogrodnik.)

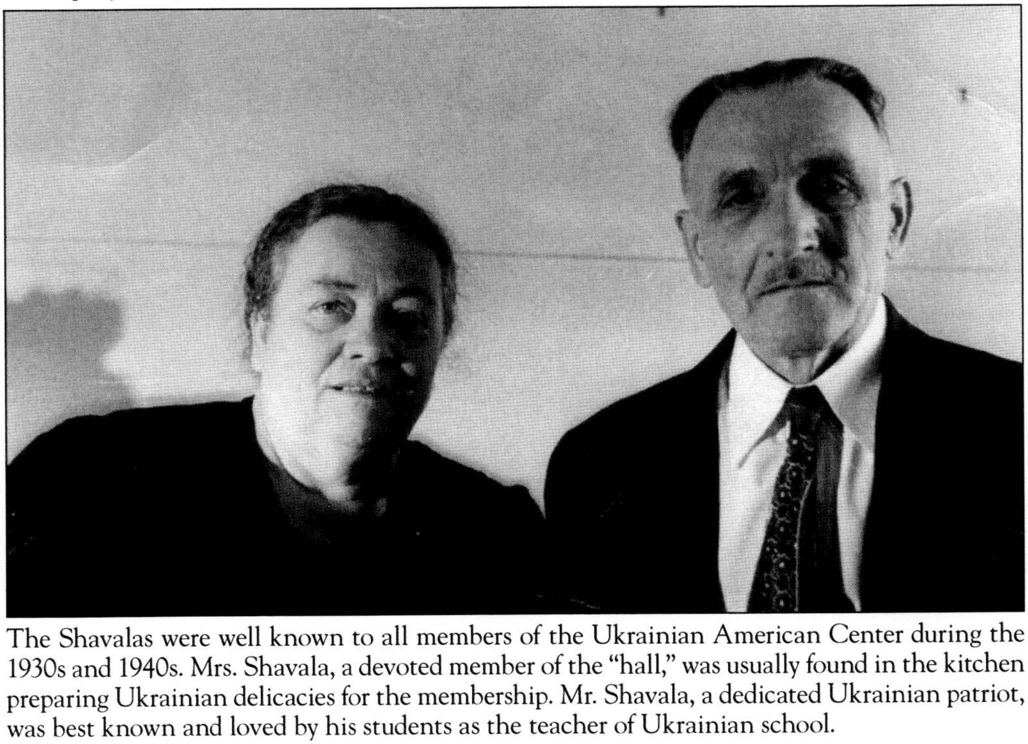

The Shavalas were well known to all members of the Ukrainian American Center during the 1930s and 1940s. Mrs. Shavala, a devoted member of the "hall," was usually found in the kitchen preparing Ukrainian delicacies for the membership. Mr. Shavala, a dedicated Ukrainian patriot, was best known and loved by his students as the teacher of Ukrainian school.

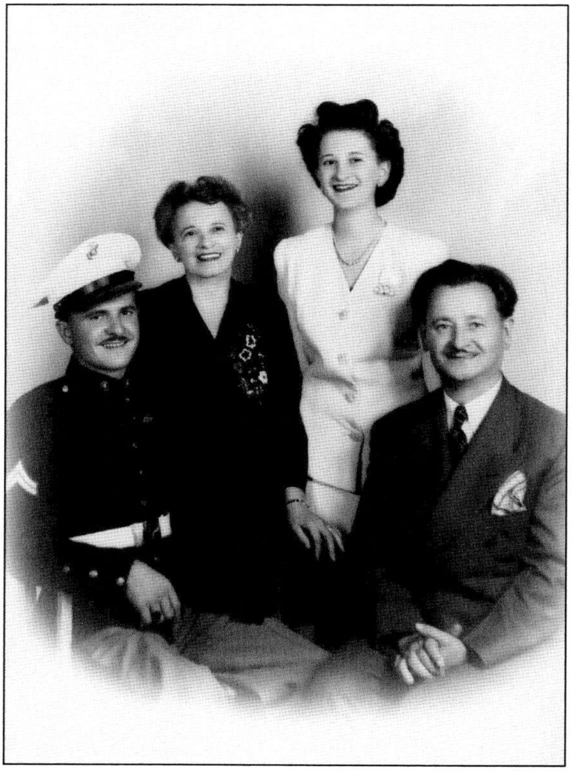

In 1942, United States marine Walter Kolomyjec posed for a family portrait with his mother Amelia, his sister Juby, and his father William while on leave from World War II.

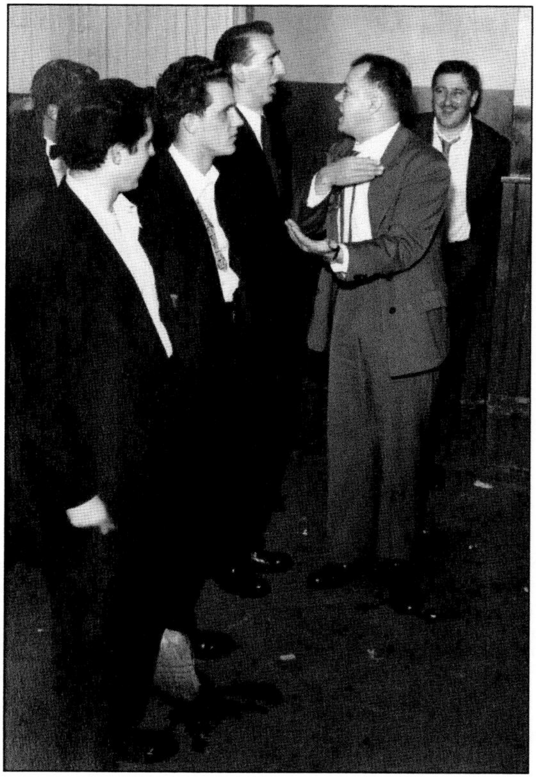

From left to right are unidentified, Bernard Solovey, John Sawchuk, John Kuchapsky, and Mike Ogrodnik engaged in some good-hearted role-playing in the basement of the Ukrainian American Center (1946). It was not unusual for the men to leave a party upstairs and retire to the basement for a bit of male bonding. (Leo Hulyk.)

Plast sea scouts practice their skills on Lake St. Clair in 1954. Plast means scouting in Ukrainian, and membership of Ukrainian youth is very popular in both Ukraine and the United States. (Bohdan Nehaniv.)

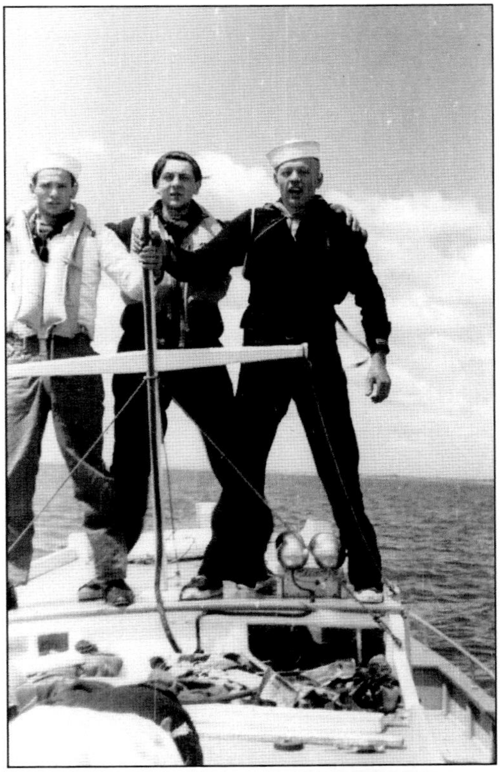

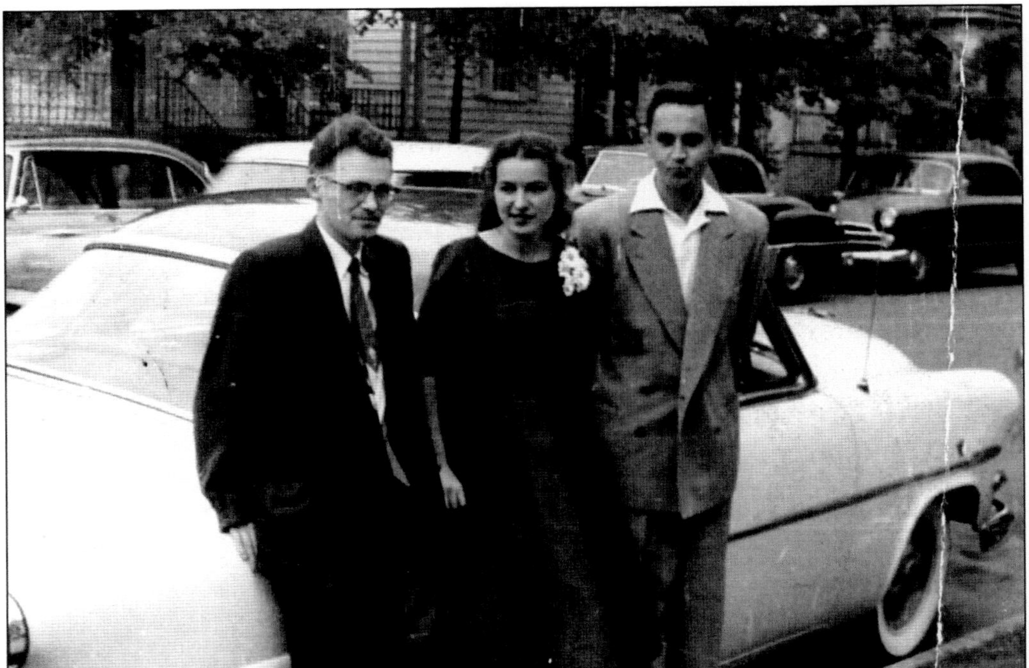

Jaroslaw Stadnyk, Chrystina Hodiw, and Bohdan Nehaniv spend a Sunday afternoon together in 1955. During their first years in America, maintaining cultural ties was extremely important. (Bohdan Nehaniv.)

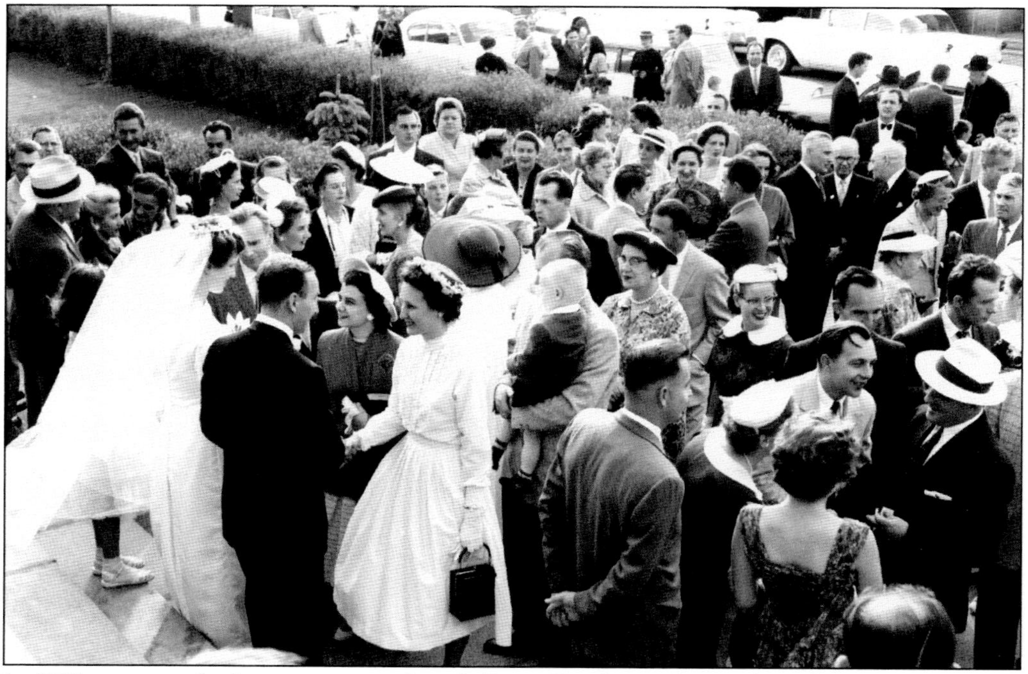

In 1955, guests and relatives greet newlyweds Roma Kniahanytsky-Hayda and Ihor Hayda on the steps of the Immaculate Conception Ukrainian Catholic Church in Hamtramck. (Marie Zarycky.)

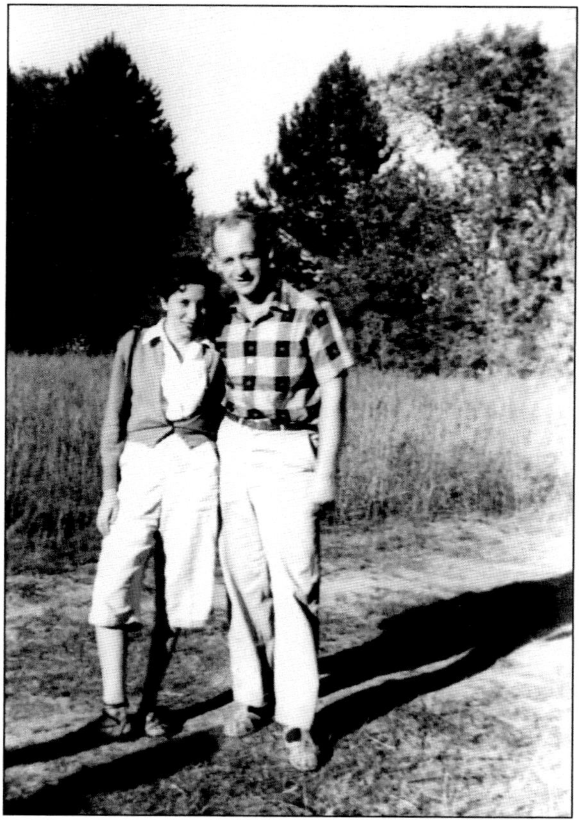

Natalie Osidach and Lubomyr Hewko take a stroll at the Ukrainian park "Dibrova" located in Brighton, Michigan. They both immigrated to America as displaced persons after World War II in the late 1940s. The activities of the Ukrainian scouting organization Plast, to which they both belonged, led to a romance and then to marriage in 1956. (Lubomyr Hewko.)

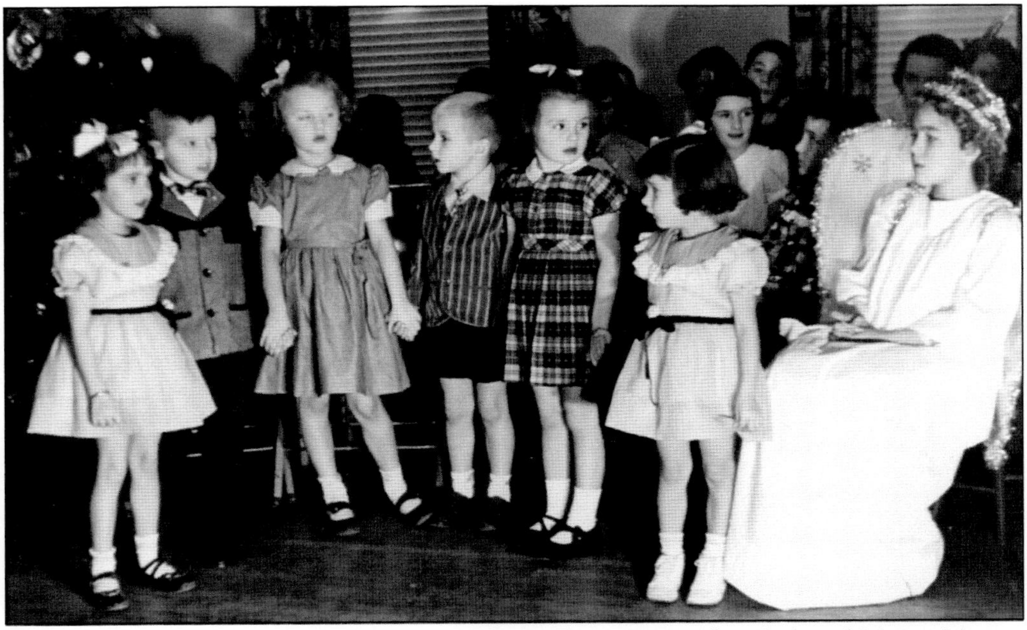

In 1952, Cathy Martyn, Jimmy Goley, Lorraine Strokon, two unidentified, and Margie Martyn meet with the Christmas angel at the annual Christmas party sponsored by the Ukrainian Graduates of Detroit and Windsor. Children of the membership always looked forward to this traditional get-together. (Cathy Whitfield.)

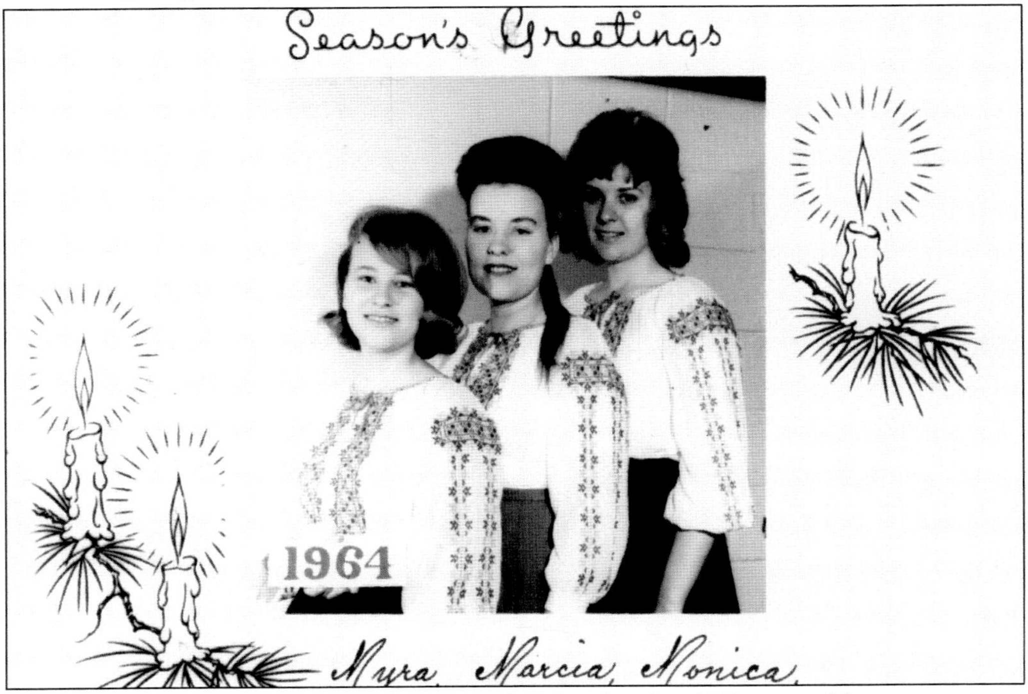

Myra, Marcia, and Monica Wichorek, wearing hand-embroidered Ukrainian blouses, appear on the 1965 Christmas card sent out by their parents Michael and Martha Wichorek. Friends of the Wichoreks looked forward to receiving the traditional card that always featured the three sisters in Ukrainian costume. (Ukrainian Museum.)

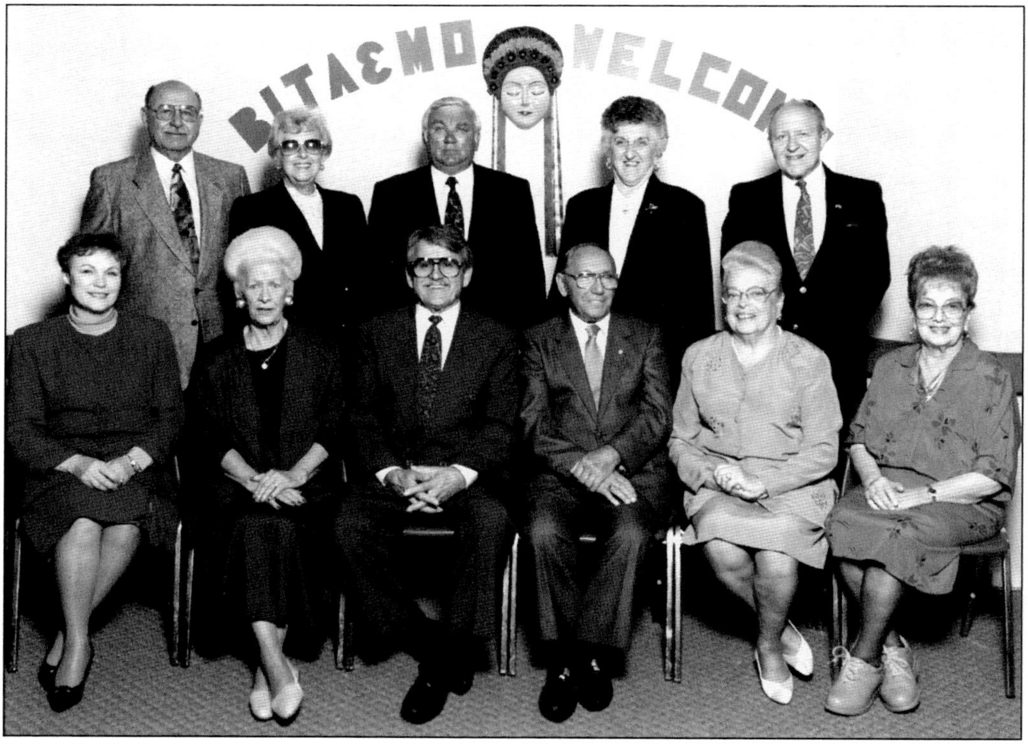

The 1992 Ukrainian Village executive board members are, from left to right, (first row) Juliana Maziak, Justine Nelligan, Stephen M. Wichar Sr. (board president), Michael Tomyn, Stefania Dub, and Olga Adamek; (second row) John Dodson, Amy Burzynski, Ihor Iwanyckyj, Kay Stoiko, and Zenon Wasylkewych. The Ukrainian Village, located in Warren, houses 146 independent living apartments for seniors in the community.

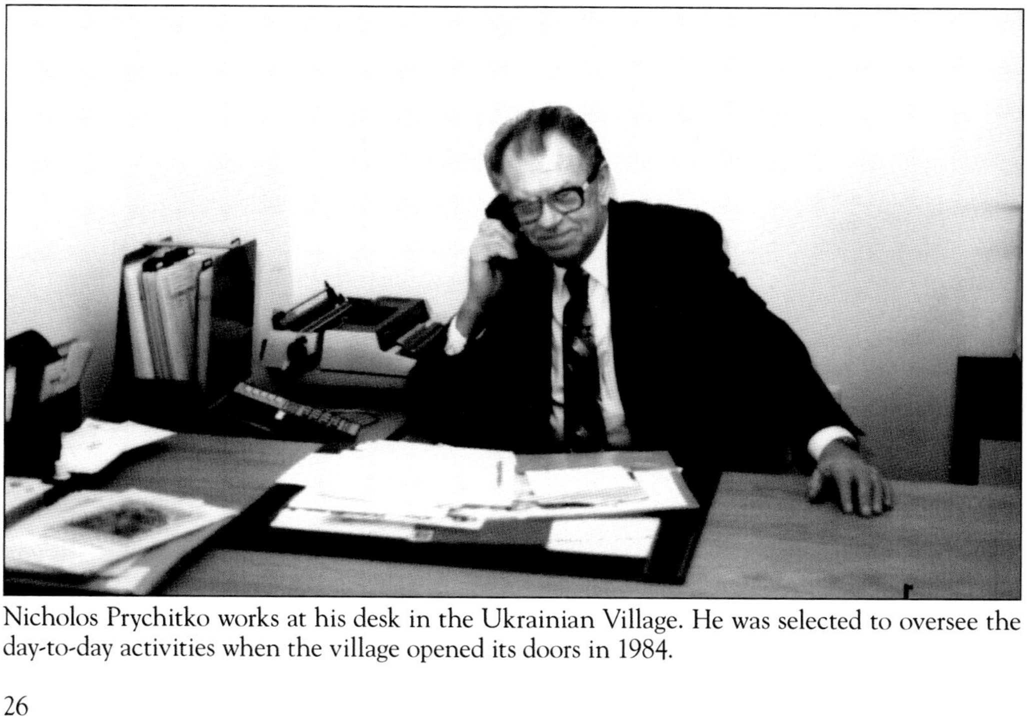

Nicholos Prychitko works at his desk in the Ukrainian Village. He was selected to oversee the day-to-day activities when the village opened its doors in 1984.

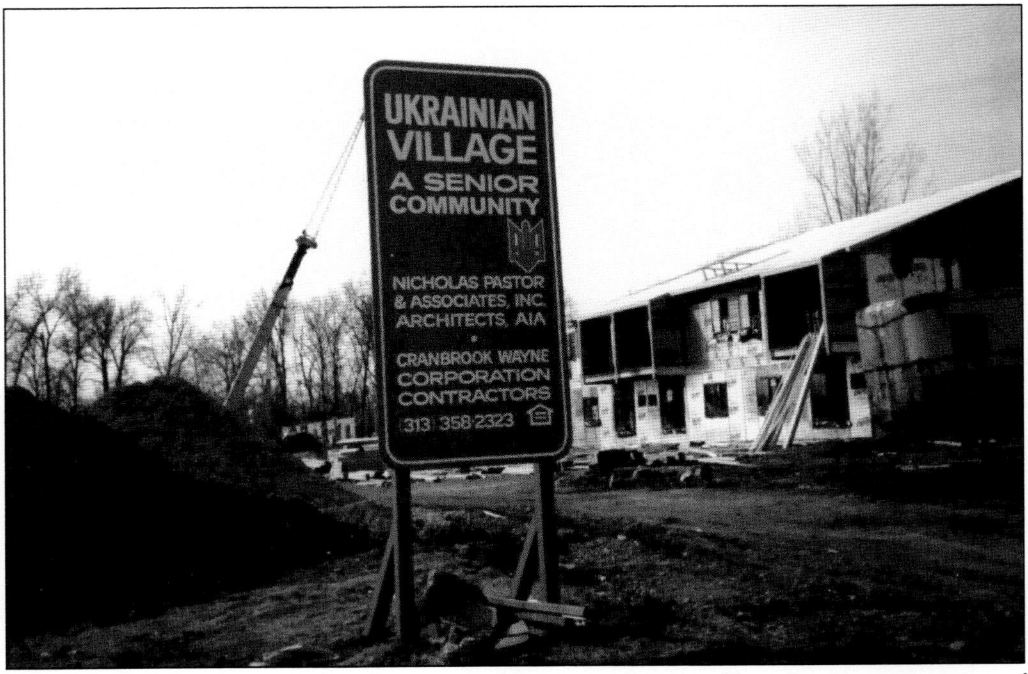

After years of persistence and perseverance, the community was able to begin construction of the Ukrainian Village, a residency for seniors, in 1982. It would take two years to complete.

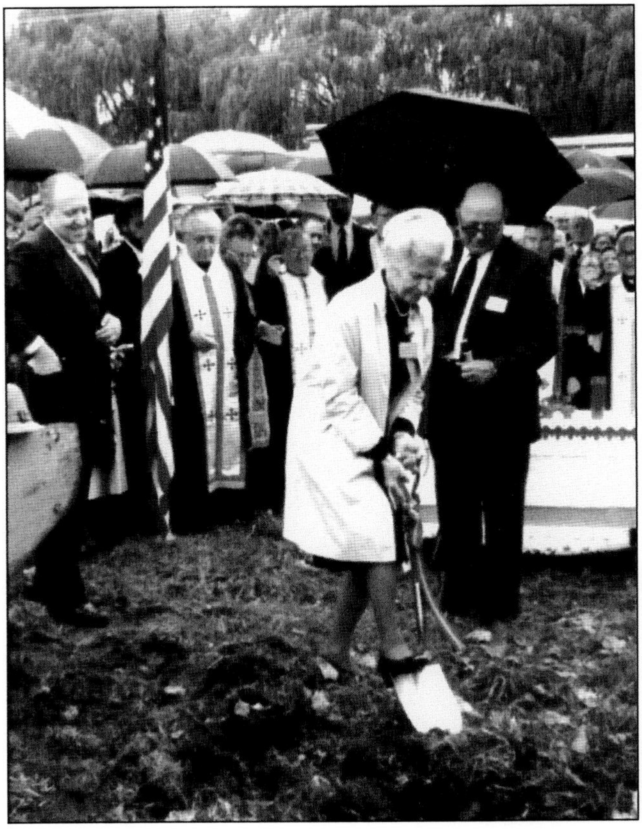

Anastasia Volker, chairperson of the building committee and the first president of the Ukrainian Village board of directors, breaks ground for the building of the Ukrainian Village in 1982. Watching the ceremony are members of the Ukrainian clergy, Zenon Wasylkewych (far left), and John Dodson (far right).

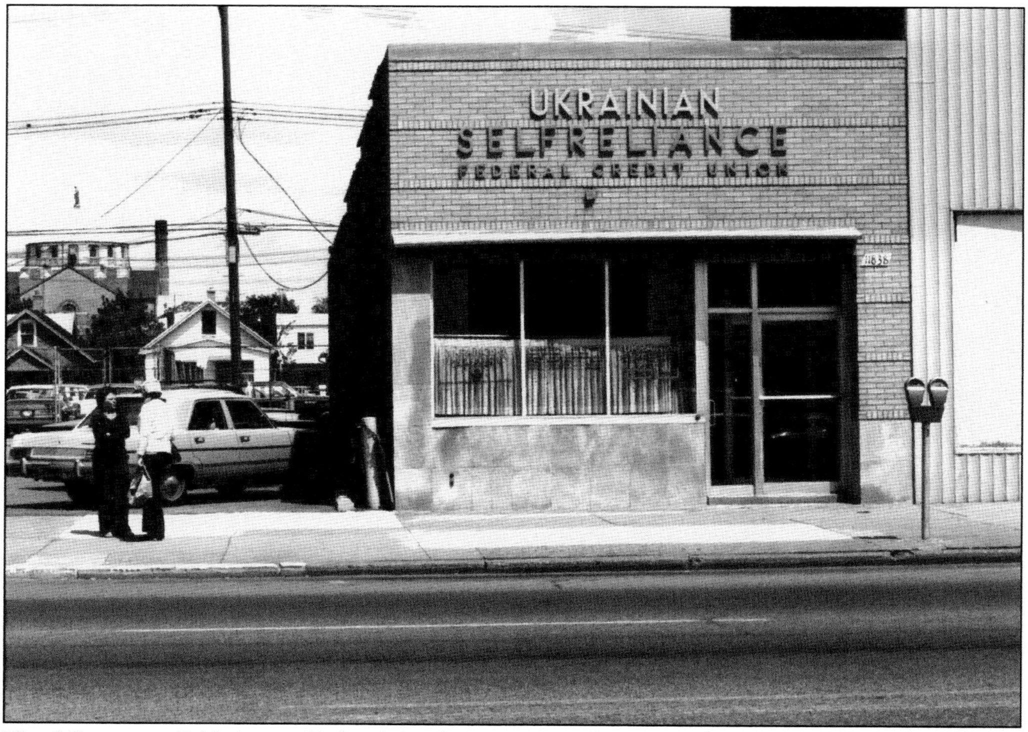

The Ukrainian Selfreliance Federal Credit Union purchased its first building in Hamtramck in 1957. The first full-time manager was Dr. W. Schkudor. A second building was purchased in 1969 on the west side of Detroit. The main branch was a new structure built in Warren and officially dedicated in 1978. (Ukrainian Self Reliance.)

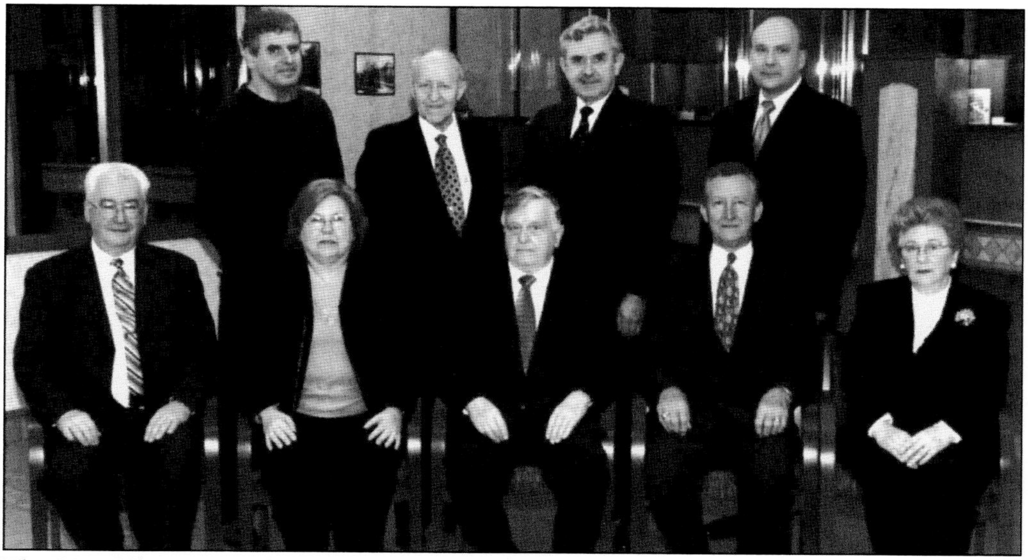

The 2009 Ukrainian Selfreliance Federal Credit Union board of directors are seen here. They are, from left to right, (first row) Bohdan Lisowsky, Sophie Koshiw, Lubomyr Lypeckyj, Bohdan Korduba, and Romana Dyhdalo; (second row) Nestor Rychtyckyj, Zenon Wasylkewych, Mykola Hryhorczuk, and Andrij Smyk. The credit union depends on volunteers to serve on the board of directors and other committees. (Lubomyr Lypeckyj.)

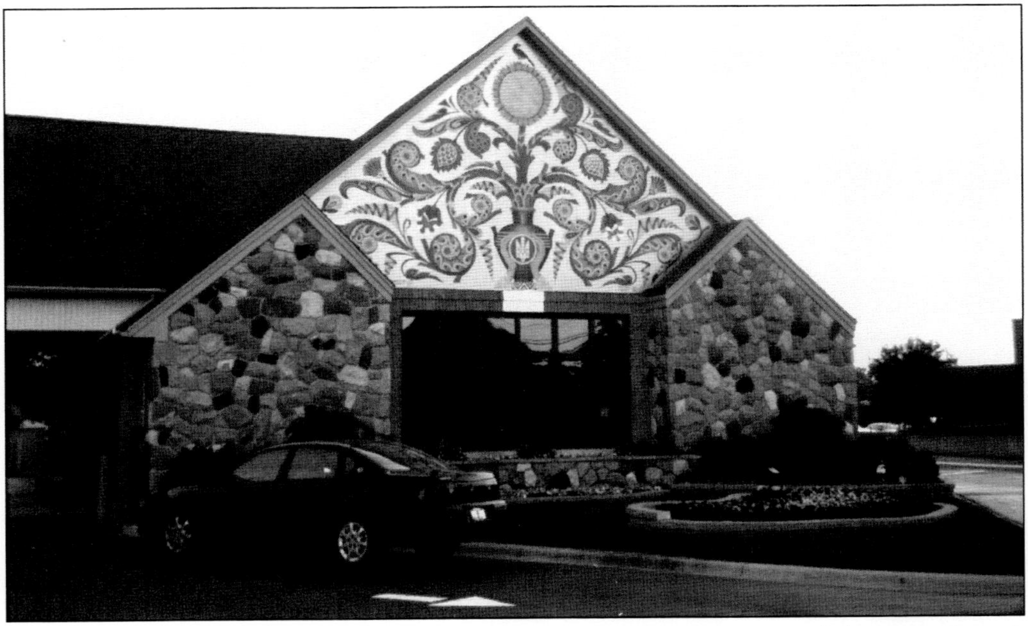

In 1988, the Ukrainian Future Credit Union began new construction of the main branch that would also house several leased offices. Distinguished artist Mychajlo Dmytrenko was commissioned to complete the folk art painting seen on the front of the building. Due to serious illness, Peter Marfey would complete the project. (Future Credit Union.)

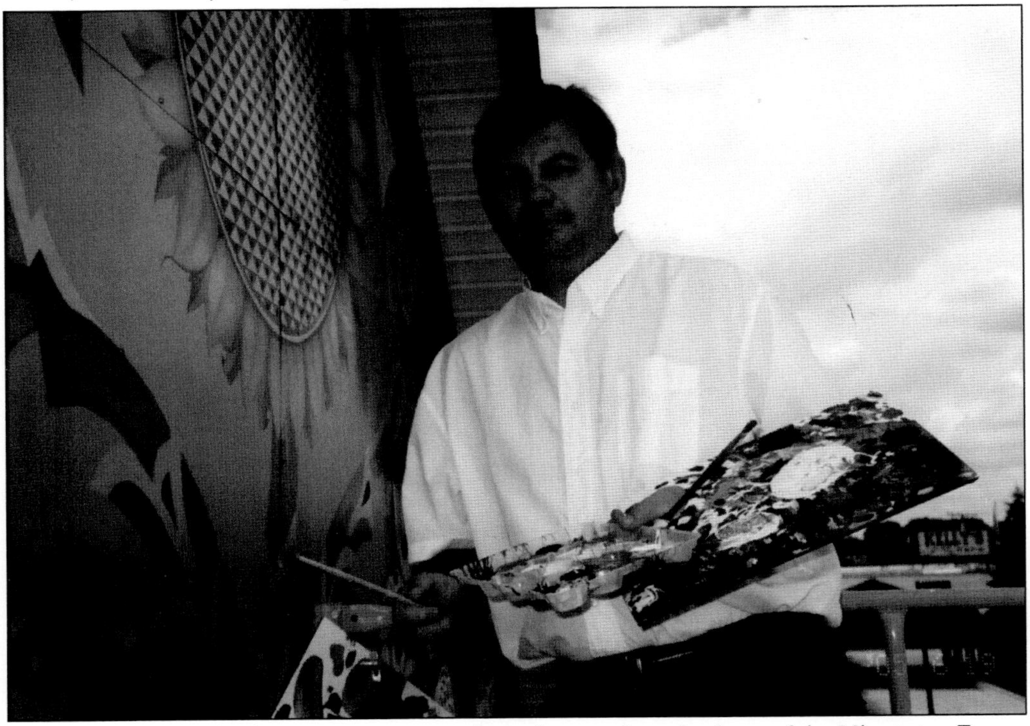

Peter Marfey, a local Ukrainian artist, completes the mural on the front of the Ukrainian Future Credit Union, located in Warren, in 2002. Marfey used the design created by artist Dmytrenko, who was unable to complete the painting. (Future Credit Union.)

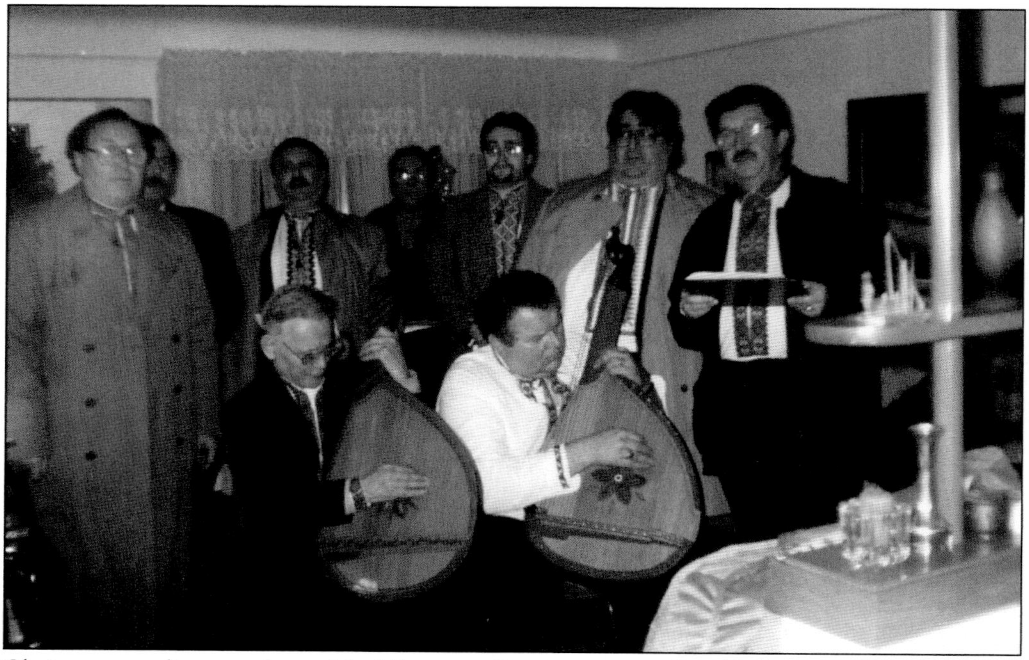

Christmas caroling members of the Ukrainian Bandurists seated in the first row are Petro Kytasty and Wolodymyr Murha. Standing in the second row are two unidentified, Alex Shrubovych, unidentified, Andrew Shrubovych, Jerome Cisaruk, and George Jurkiw (2001). It is customary for the koliadnyky (carolers) to go from home to home singing the songs of the season.

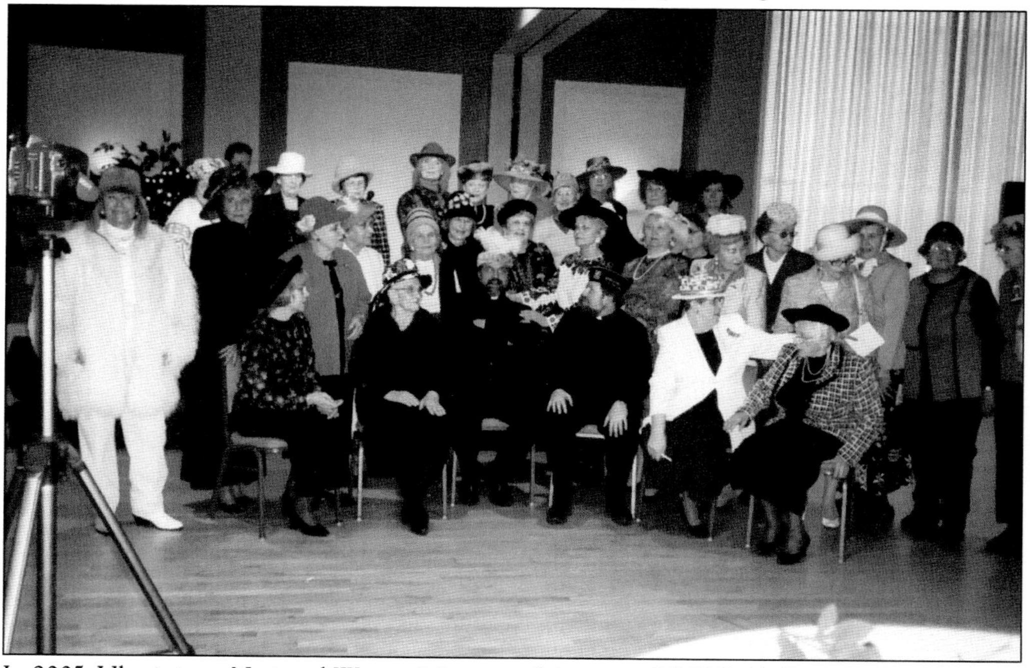

In 2005, Ukraininan National Women's League of America (UNWLA), Branch No. 36, hosted their traditional Lenten Oseledets. The ladies were asked to wear an unusual hat to the affair. Seated in the center are Reverend Philip Sandryk and Reverend Walter Rybicky, who are joining the fun. (Marie Zarycky.)

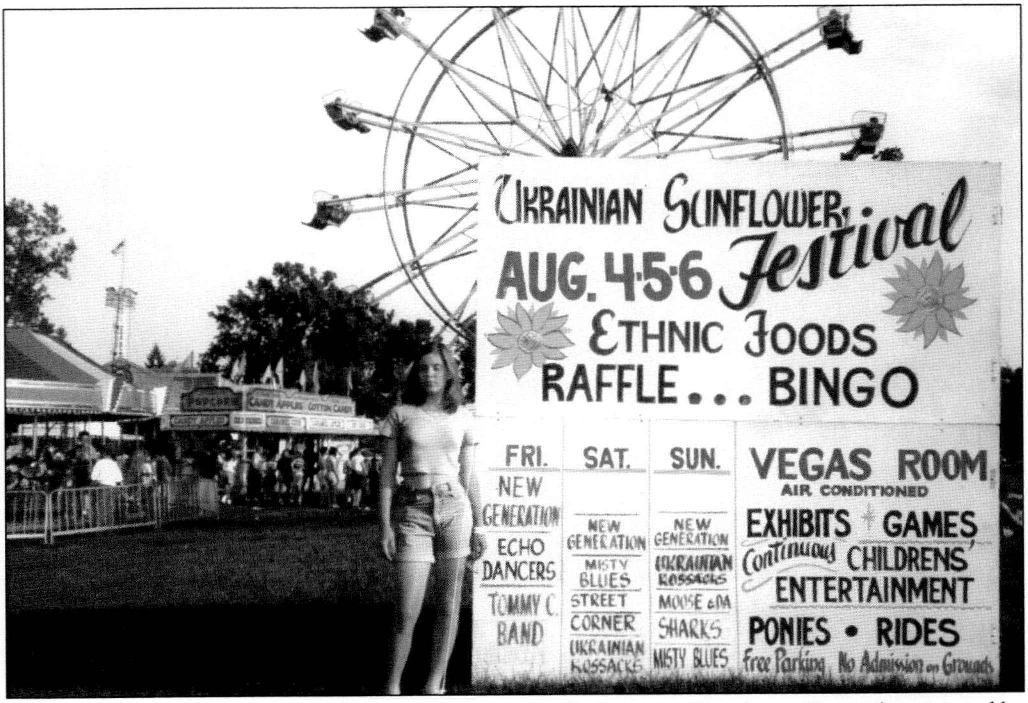

Anya Maziak poses next to the billboard for the annual Ukrainian Sunflower Festival sponsored by St. Josaphat Ukrainian Catholic Church. The festival was one of the most popular ethnic gatherings in the Detroit area, attracting more than 25,000 people each summer. (Roman Maziak.)

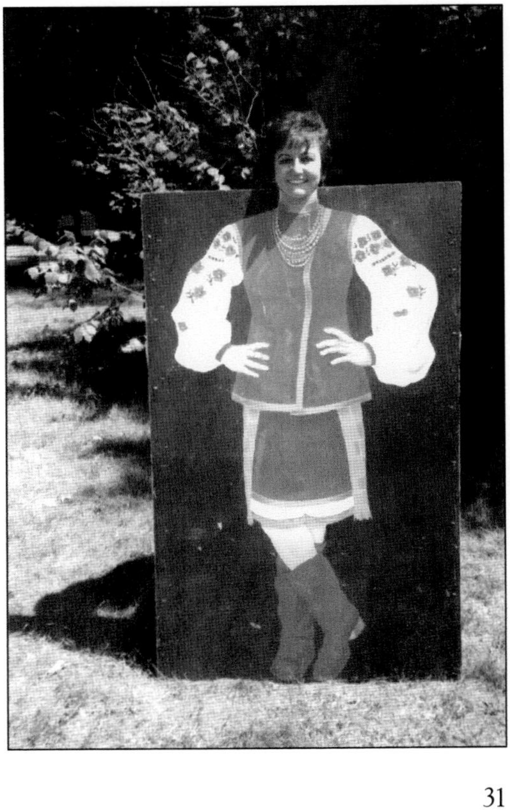

Christine Shumeyko takes time to pose for a bigger than life portrait at the Ukrainian Sunflower Festival in 1991. In addition to the entertainment, the festival also featured ethnic food, music, and exhibitions.

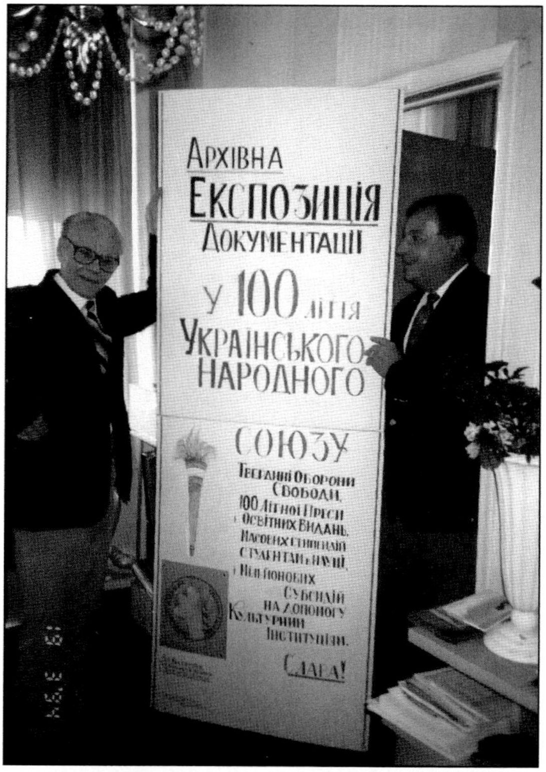

In 1991, Roman Dacko, founder and curator of the Ukrainian-American Archives Museum and Library, and Dr. Alexander Serafyn, president of the Detroit area Ukrainian National Association, display the advertisement for an exhibition of UNA publications to celebrate its 100th anniversary.

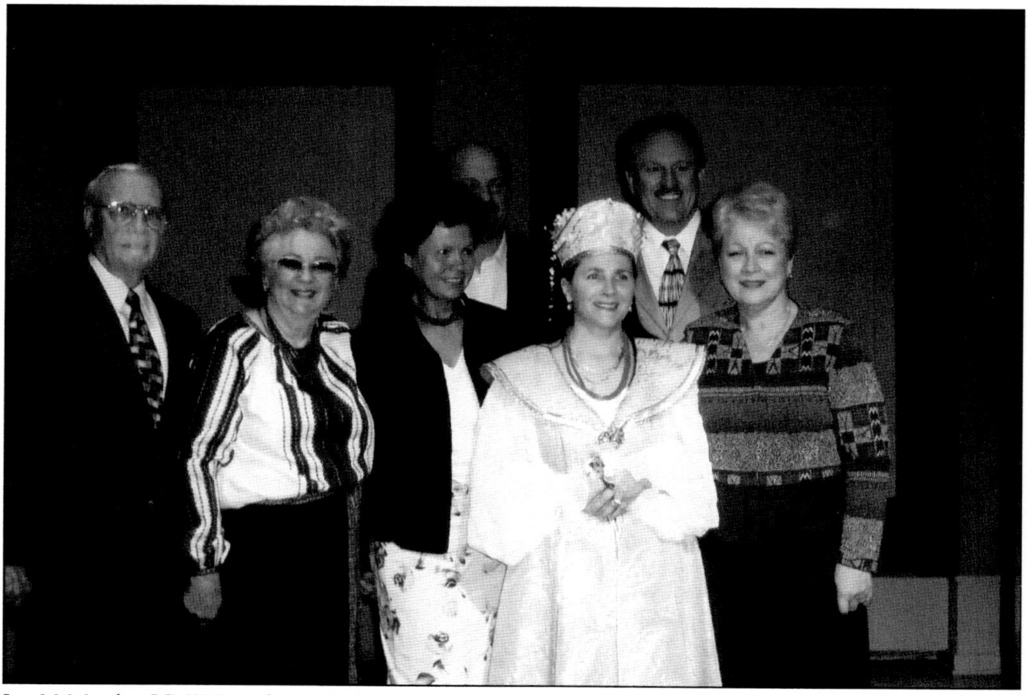

In 2006, the UNWLA hosted the famous soulful singer from Ukraine, Nina Matvienko, in Warren. On the far left are Wolodymyr Dyhdalo and Roma Dyhdalo and on the far right are Alexander Cherviovskiy and Marie Zarycky-Cherviovskiy. (Marie Zarycky.)

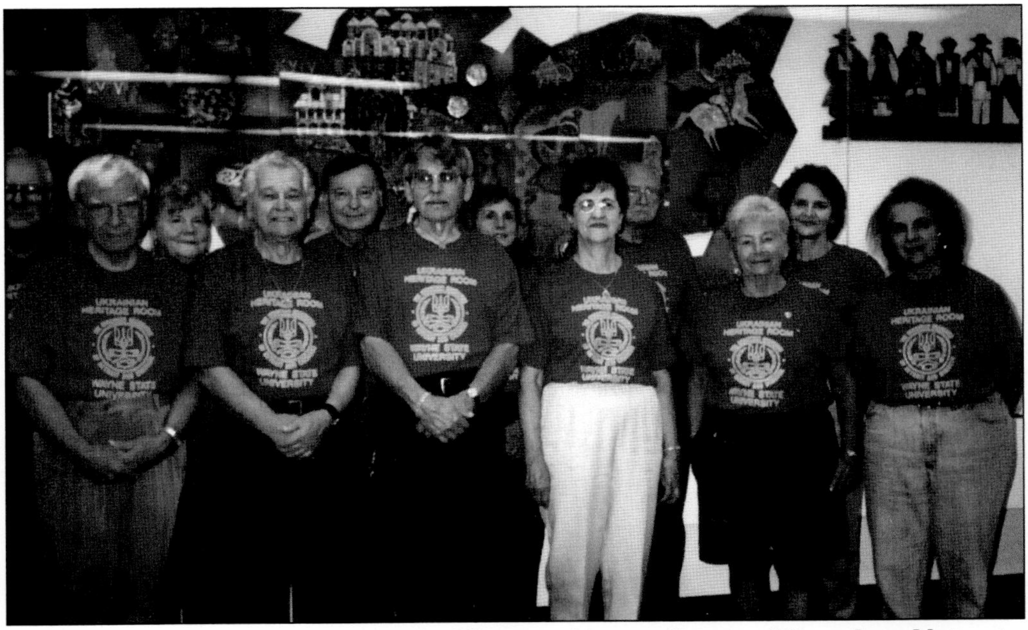

Members of the committee to restore the Ukrainian Heritage Room at Wayne State University are, from left to right, (first row) Dr. Paul Dzul, Joesph Elnick, co-chair Stephen M. Wichar Sr., co-chair Olga Dubriwnyj-Solovey, Irene Torrence, and Olga Meyer; (second row) Oleh Cieply, Alberta Cieply, Dr. Alexander Serafyn, Catherine Koneya, Tom Meyer, and Lydia Taraschuk-Nehaniv. The first Ukrainian Heritage Room was created by a committed group of Ukrainian Americans and dedicated in 1976. The restoration and addition to the room was sponsored by the Ukrainian Graduates of Detroit and Windsor and dedicated in 2003.

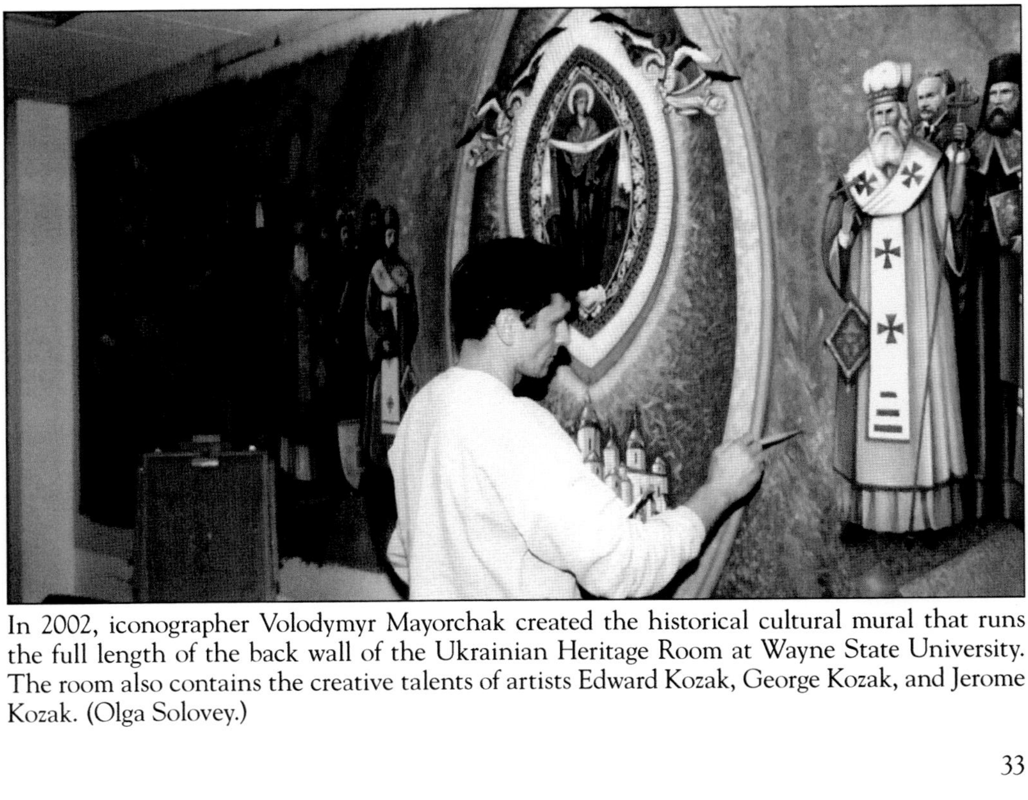

In 2002, iconographer Volodymyr Mayorchak created the historical cultural mural that runs the full length of the back wall of the Ukrainian Heritage Room at Wayne State University. The room also contains the creative talents of artists Edward Kozak, George Kozak, and Jerome Kozak. (Olga Solovey.)

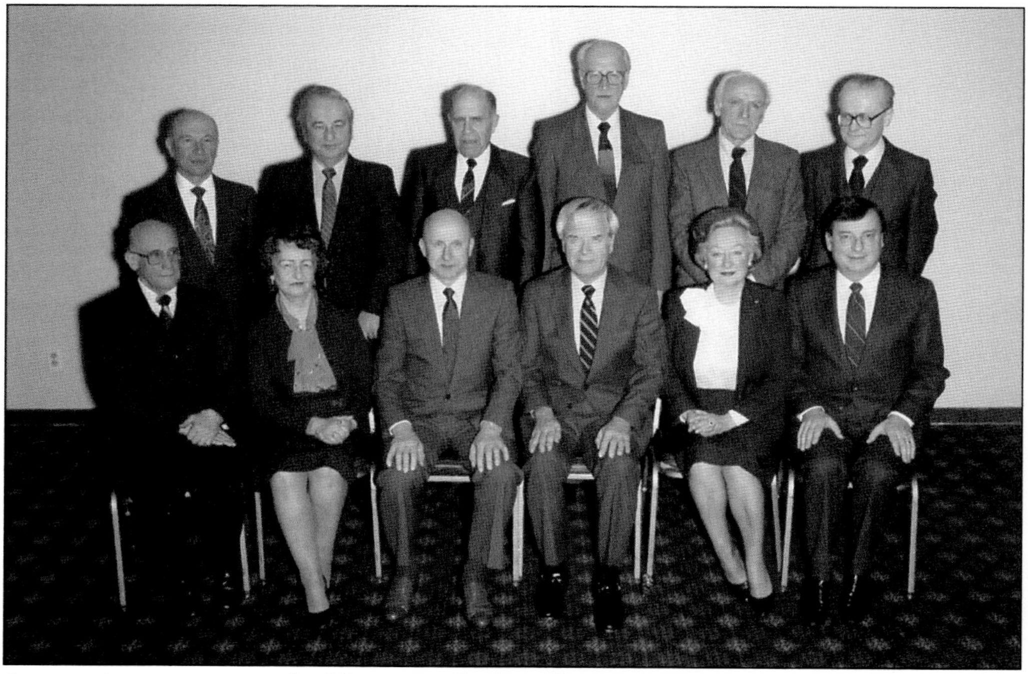

A committee to support the Ukrainian Studies Chair at Harvard University was formed in the early 1980s. Pictured from left to right are (first row) unidentified, Mrs. Kunynsky, Jaroslaw Duzyj, Dr. Paul Dzul, chairperson Olha Duzyj, and Dr. Alexander Serafyn; (second row) Stefan Fedenko, Adrian Bluj, Dr. Zenobious Stelmach, Mr. Kunynsky, Mykola Lawrin, and Peter Stasiw. (Andrey Duzyj.)

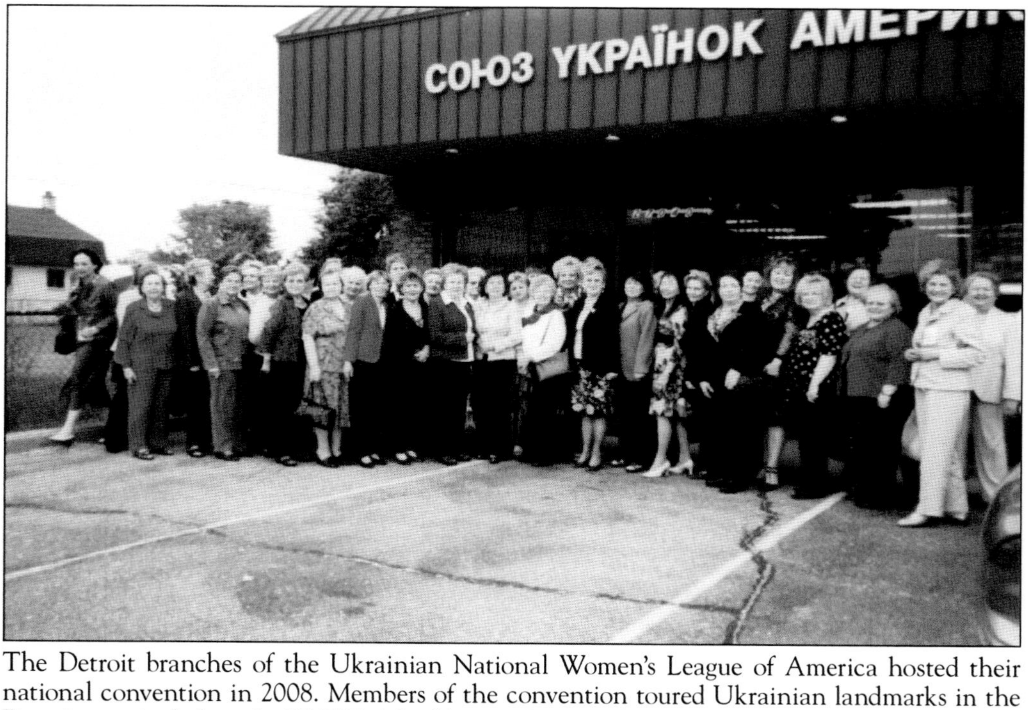

The Detroit branches of the Ukrainian National Women's League of America hosted their national convention in 2008. Members of the convention toured Ukrainian landmarks in the Detroit area including the UNWLA building in Warren. (Lydia Taraschuk Nehaniv.)

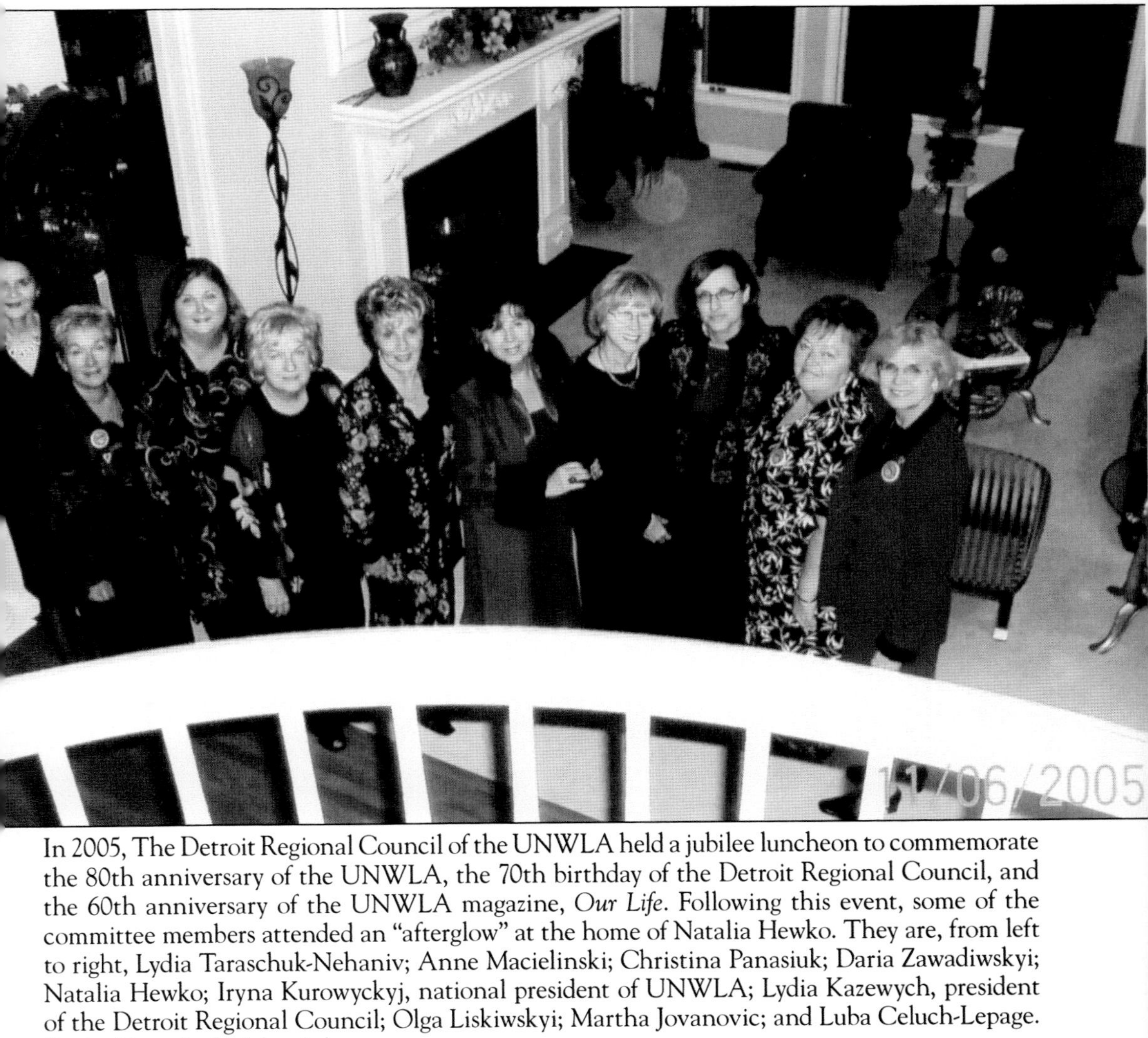

In 2005, The Detroit Regional Council of the UNWLA held a jubilee luncheon to commemorate the 80th anniversary of the UNWLA, the 70th birthday of the Detroit Regional Council, and the 60th anniversary of the UNWLA magazine, *Our Life*. Following this event, some of the committee members attended an "afterglow" at the home of Natalia Hewko. They are, from left to right, Lydia Taraschuk-Nehaniv; Anne Macielinski; Christina Panasiuk; Daria Zawadiwskyi; Natalia Hewko; Iryna Kurowyckyj, national president of UNWLA; Lydia Kazewych, president of the Detroit Regional Council; Olga Liskiwskyi; Martha Jovanovic; and Luba Celuch-Lepage. (Lydia Taraschuk-Nehaniv.)

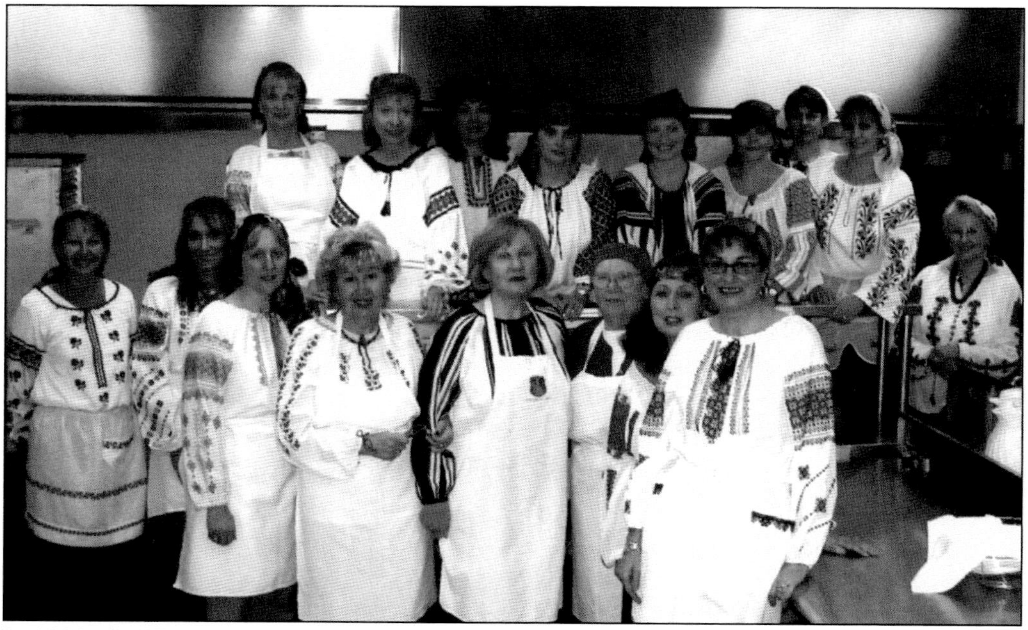

In 2008, the UNWLA Branch No. 115 participated in a cooking seminar focused on the art of Ukrainian bread "bulka" baking. The class was conducted by Maria Derkacz (front row, sixth from left), well known in the community for ethnic culinary talents. The ladies experienced all the steps of bulka baking and went home proudly with a loaf to share with their loved ones. (Annie Buhay.)

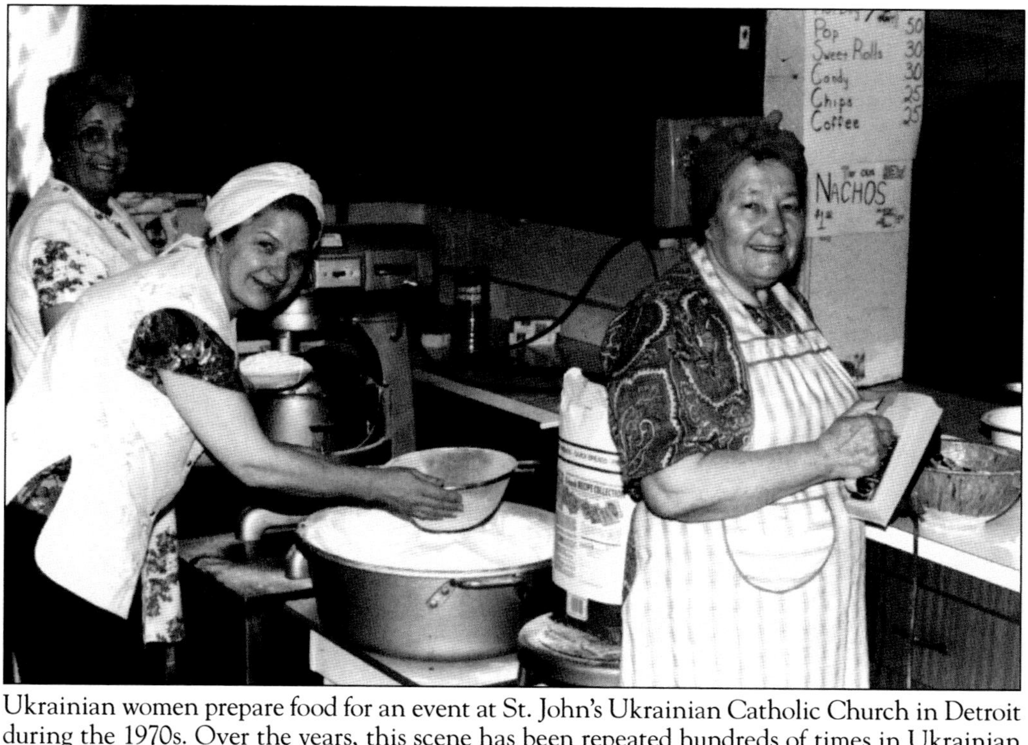

Ukrainian women prepare food for an event at St. John's Ukrainian Catholic Church in Detroit during the 1970s. Over the years, this scene has been repeated hundreds of times in Ukrainian churches and institutions throughout the city. (Joseph Szafranski.)

In 2003, Nadya Sepell stands behind her display of Ukrainian Easter eggs (pysanky) at the Henry Ford Centennial Library in Dearborn. Sepell has been sharing her Ukrainian pysanky displays for 33 years. (Nadya Sepell.)

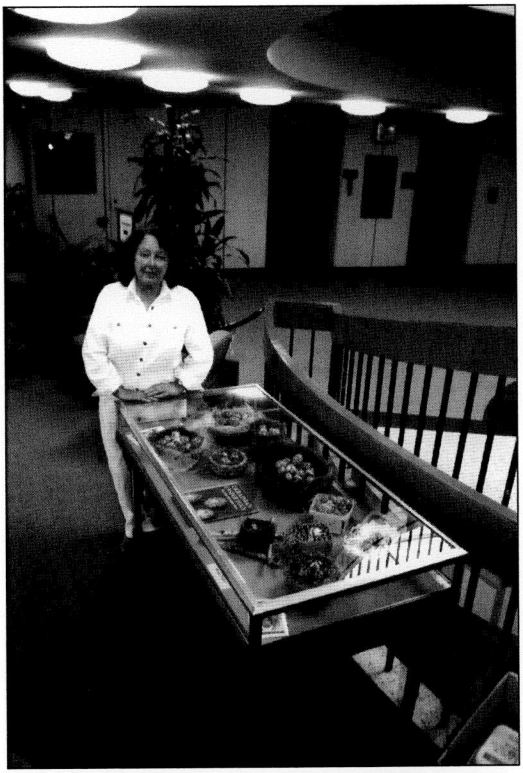

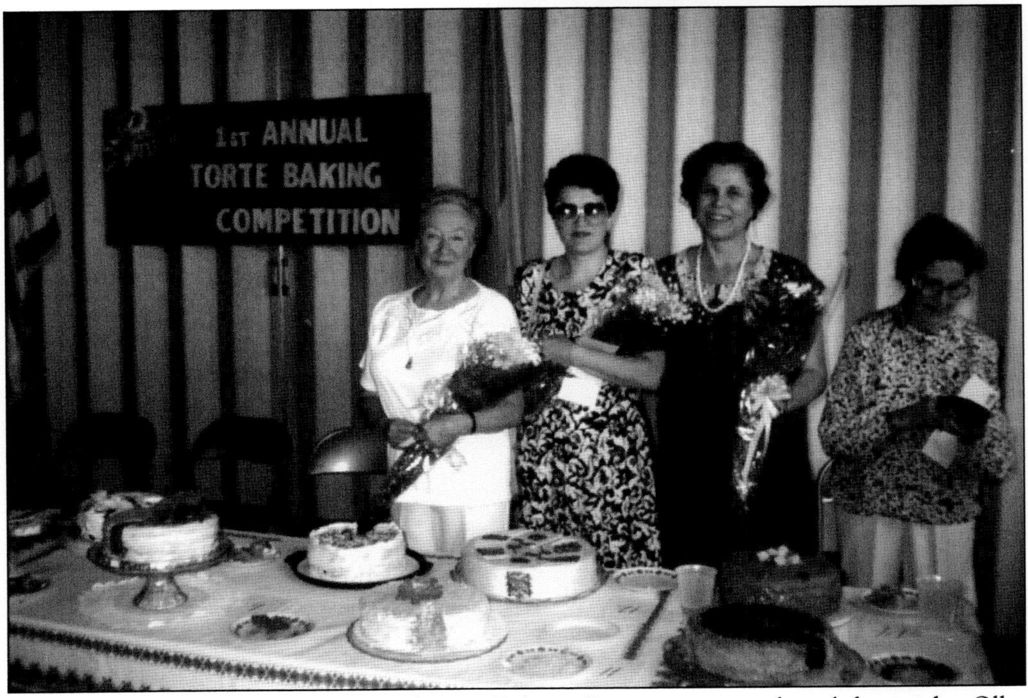

The proud winners of the first annual Torte Baking Competition are, from left to right, Olha Duzyj, Irene Gogoska, and Irene Pryjma. No Ukrainian festivity would be complete without a table filled with various types of delectable tortes. This image is from the 1990s. (Roman Maziak.)

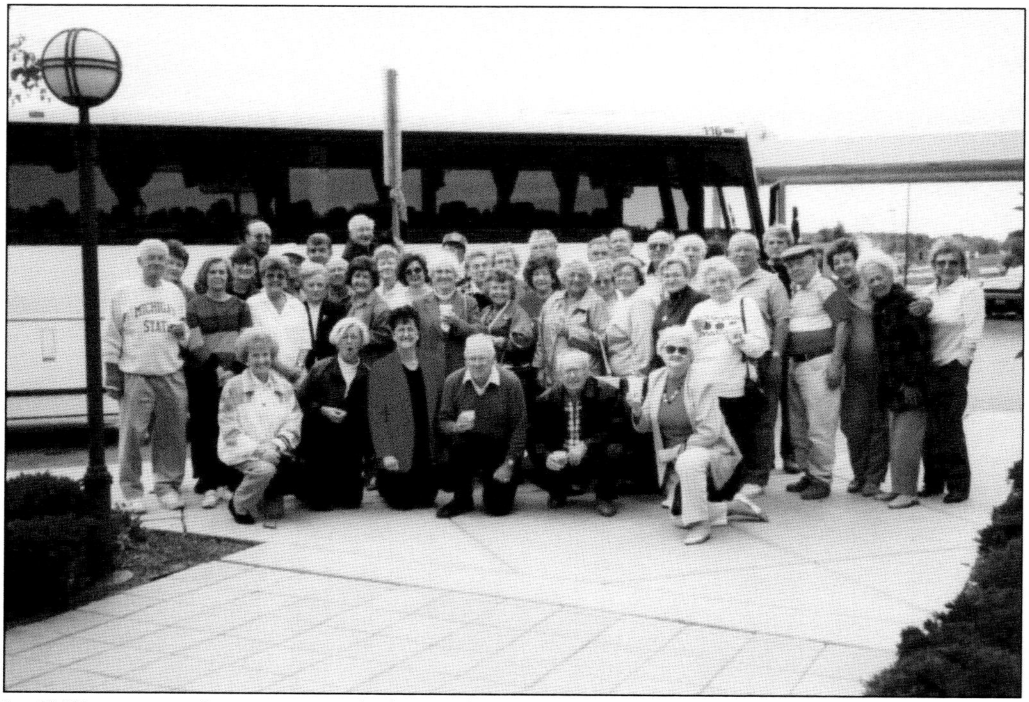

In 1987, a group of seniors poses before embarking on a fun-filled trip to the Ukrainian resort, Soyuzivka, in the Shawangunk Mountains of upstate New York.

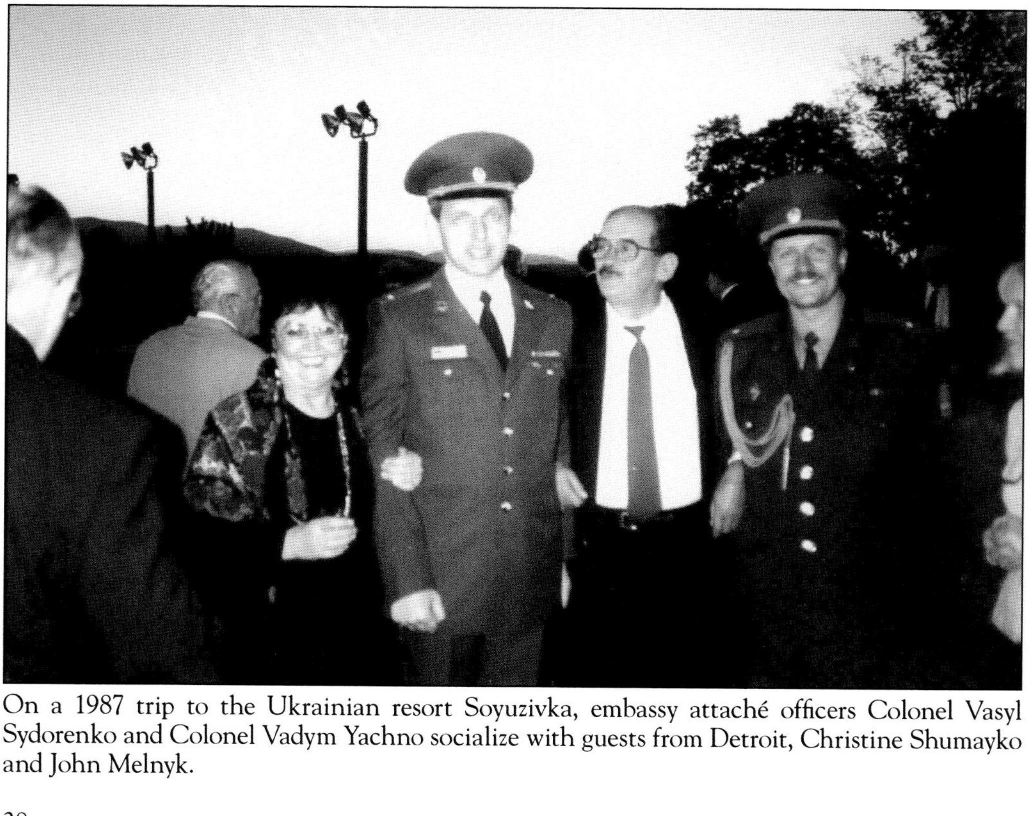

On a 1987 trip to the Ukrainian resort Soyuzivka, embassy attaché officers Colonel Vasyl Sydorenko and Colonel Vadym Yachno socialize with guests from Detroit, Christine Shumayko and John Melnyk.

Two

Religious Life

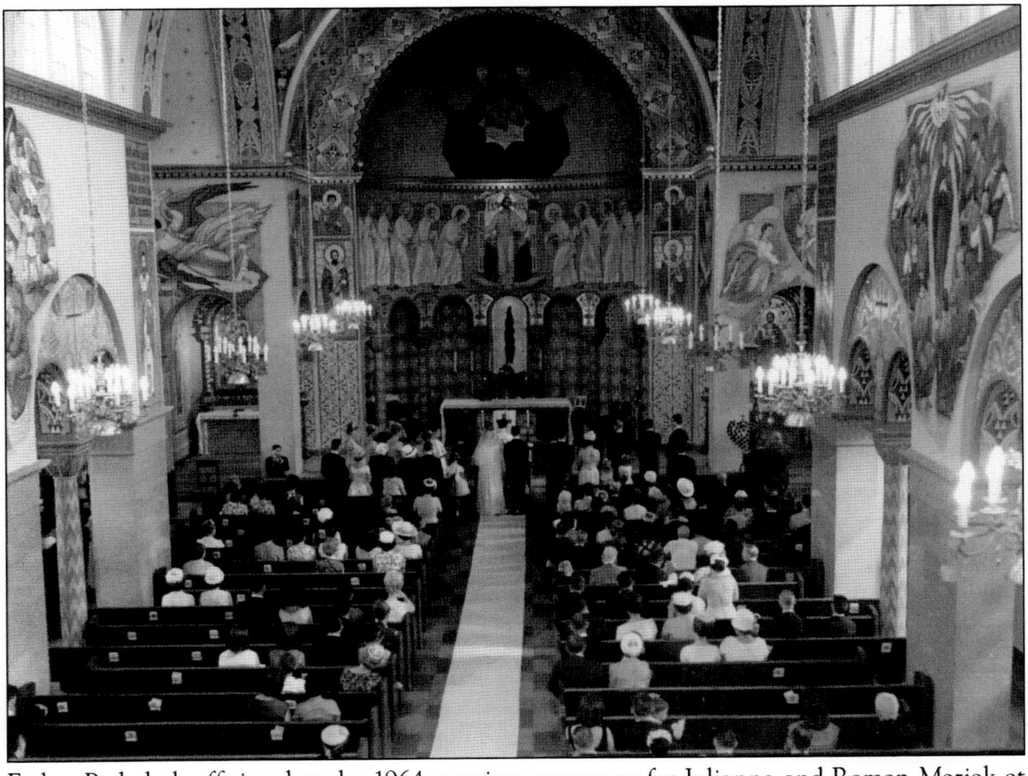

Father Pashchak officiated at the 1964 marriage ceremony for Julianna and Roman Maziak at the Immaculate Conception Ukrainian Catholic Church in Hamtramck. The first Immaculate Conception Church was built on Grayling Street in 1913. The new church, shown above, opened its doors in May 1942 and at one time had a congregation of well over 1,000 families. In 1976, renowned artist Mychajlo Dmytrenko was commissioned to paint the mural icons as depicted in the above photograph. The iconostasis carvings were done by D. Berezowksy. There are four other Ukrainian Catholic churches in the Detroit area: St. Michael's in Dearborn, Our Lady of Perpetual Help in Dearborn Heights, St. John the Baptist in Detroit, and St. Josaphat's in Warren. (Roman Maziak.)

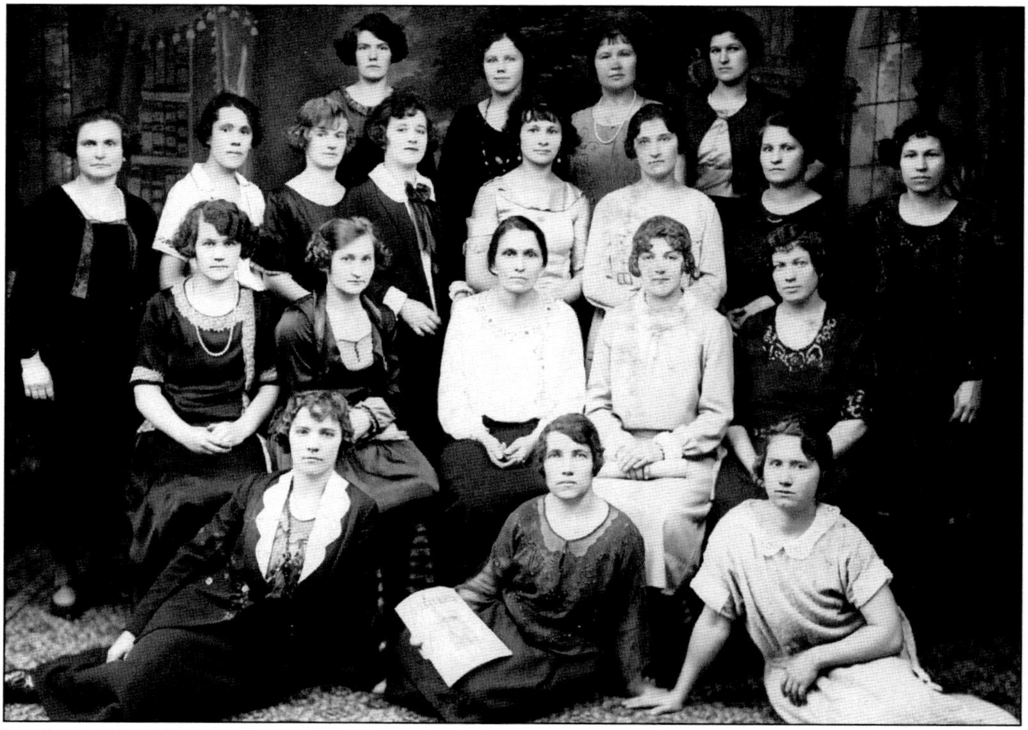

In the 1920s, Ukrainian women formed solidarity groups to raise funds and perform charitable work for the parishes. (Ukrainian Museum.)

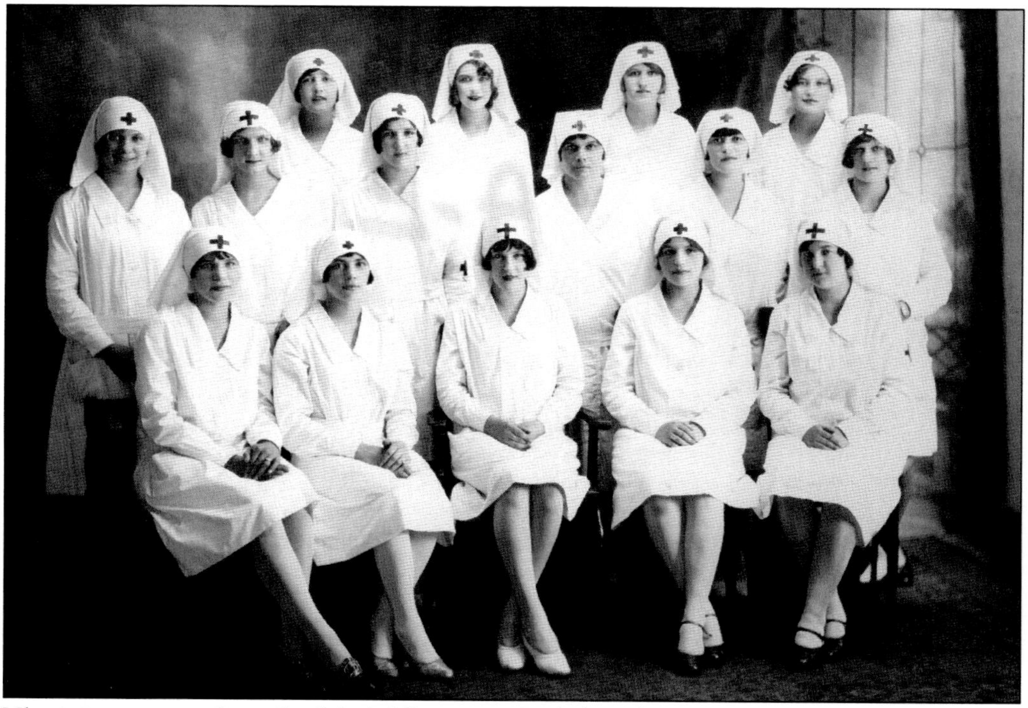

Ukrainian women from St. John's Ukrainian Catholic Church united to form a Red Cross organization during the 1920s. (Ukrainian Museum.)

In 1907, the original St. John the Baptist Ukrainian Catholic Church was established in Detroit to serve primarily the parishioners who lived on the west side of the city. (Joseph Szafranski.)

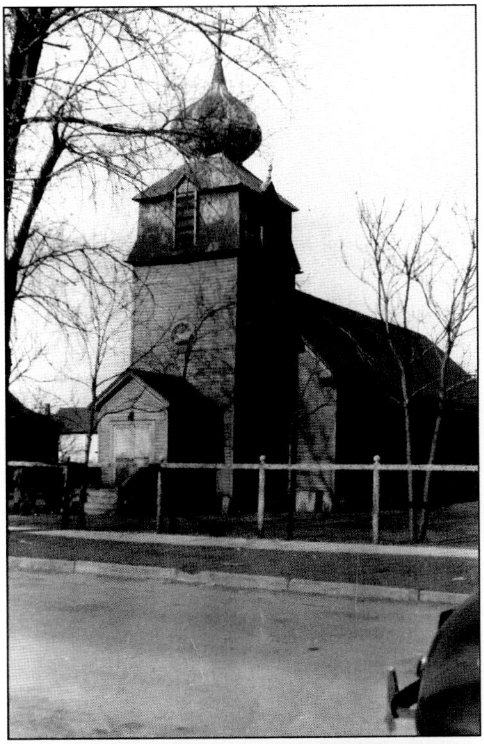

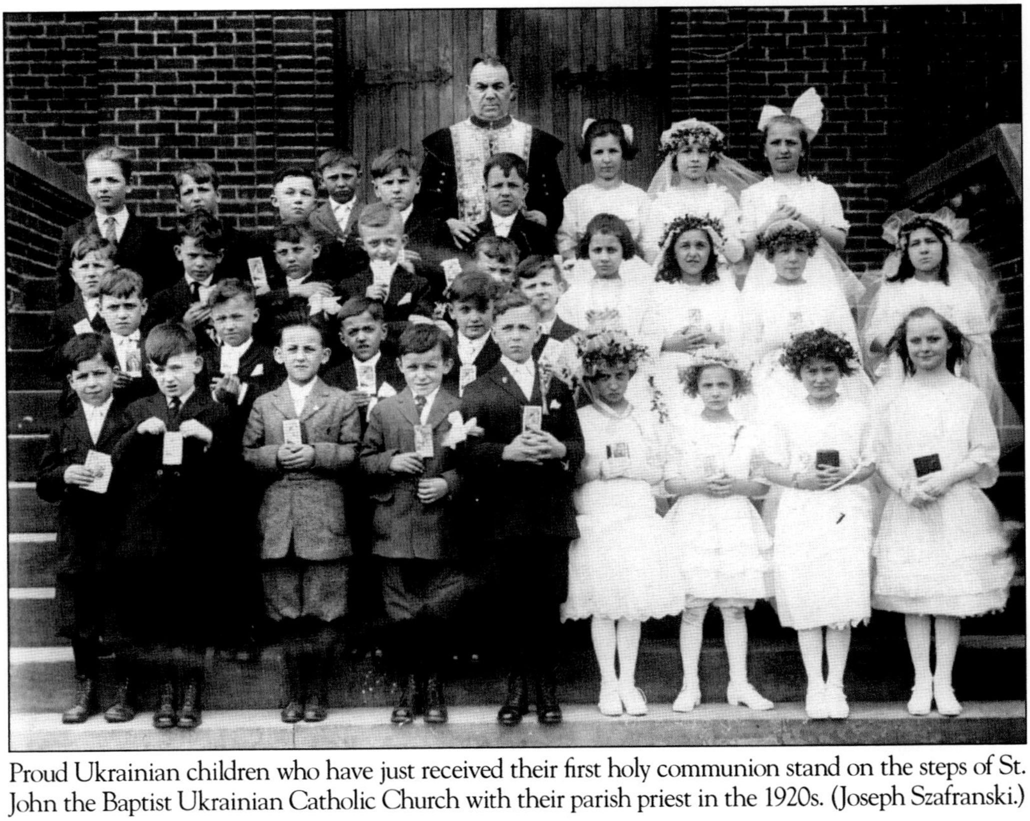

Proud Ukrainian children who have just received their first holy communion stand on the steps of St. John the Baptist Ukrainian Catholic Church with their parish priest in the 1920s. (Joseph Szafranski.)

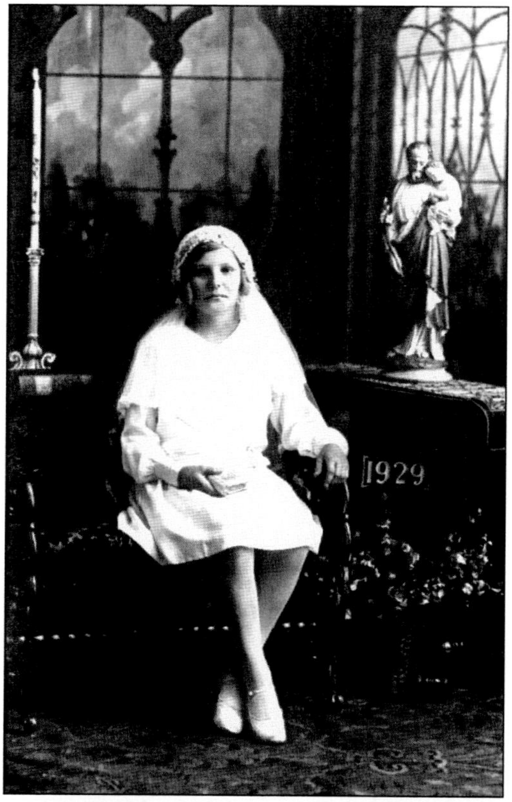

Eva Wichorek received her first holy communion at St. John the Baptist Ukrainian Catholic Church in 1929. Religious practices played a critical role in the upbringing of Ukrainian children. (Olga Solovey.)

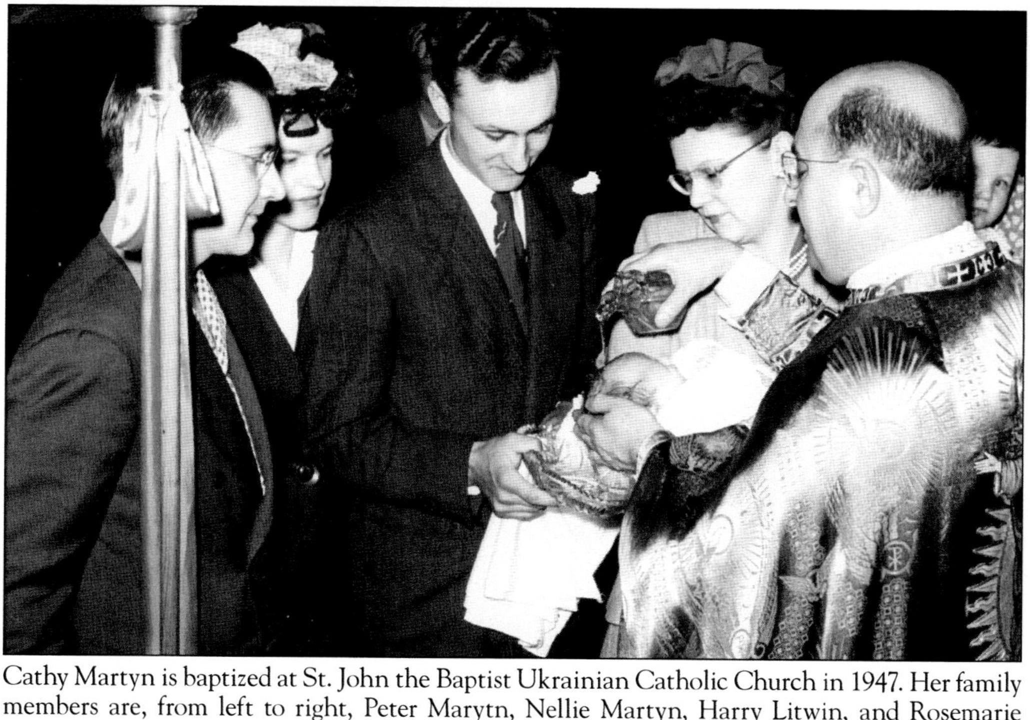

Cathy Martyn is baptized at St. John the Baptist Ukrainian Catholic Church in 1947. Her family members are, from left to right, Peter Marytn, Nellie Martyn, Harry Litwin, and Rosemarie Martyniuk, with Father Pobutsky officiating. (Cathy Whitfield.)

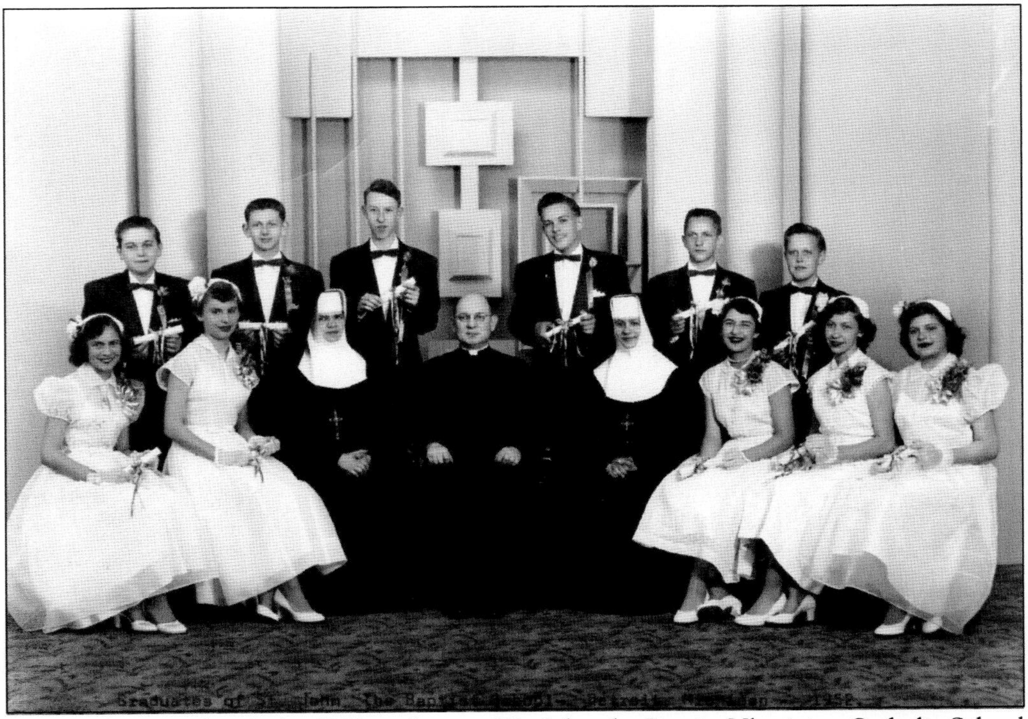

With diplomas in hand, the 1952 graduates of St. John the Baptist Ukrainian Catholic School pose with Sister Bernard, Reverend Stephen Knapp, and Sister Phillip. (Joseph Szafranski.)

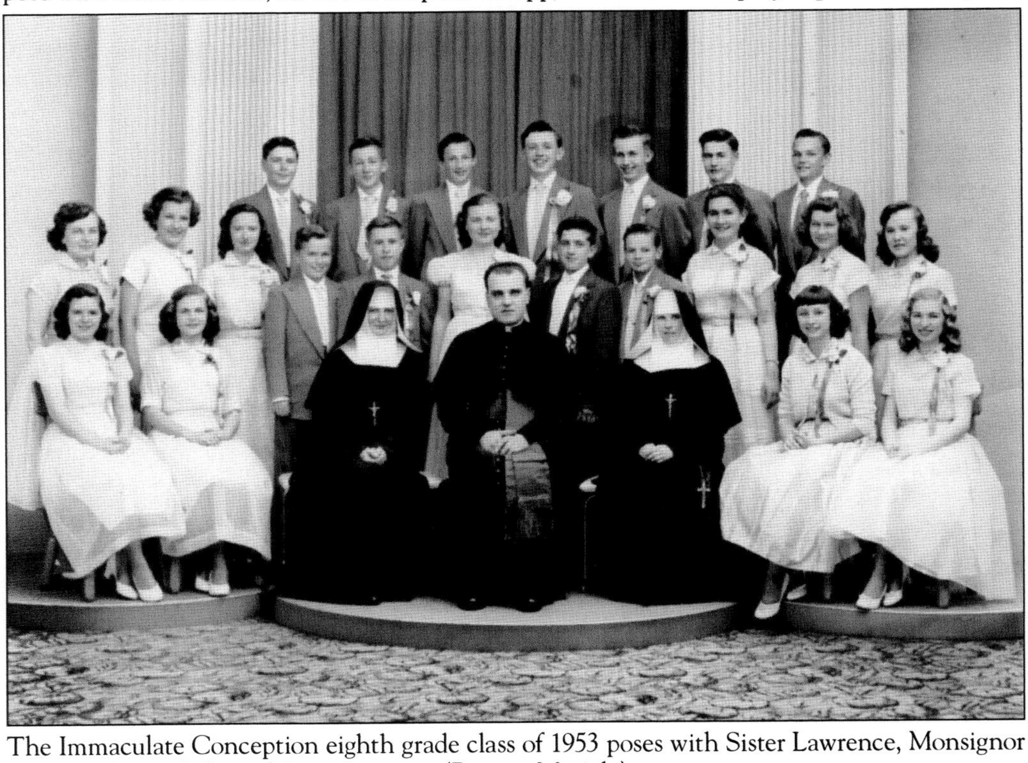

The Immaculate Conception eighth grade class of 1953 poses with Sister Lawrence, Monsignor Joseph Schmondiuk, and Sister Leontia. (Roman Maziak.)

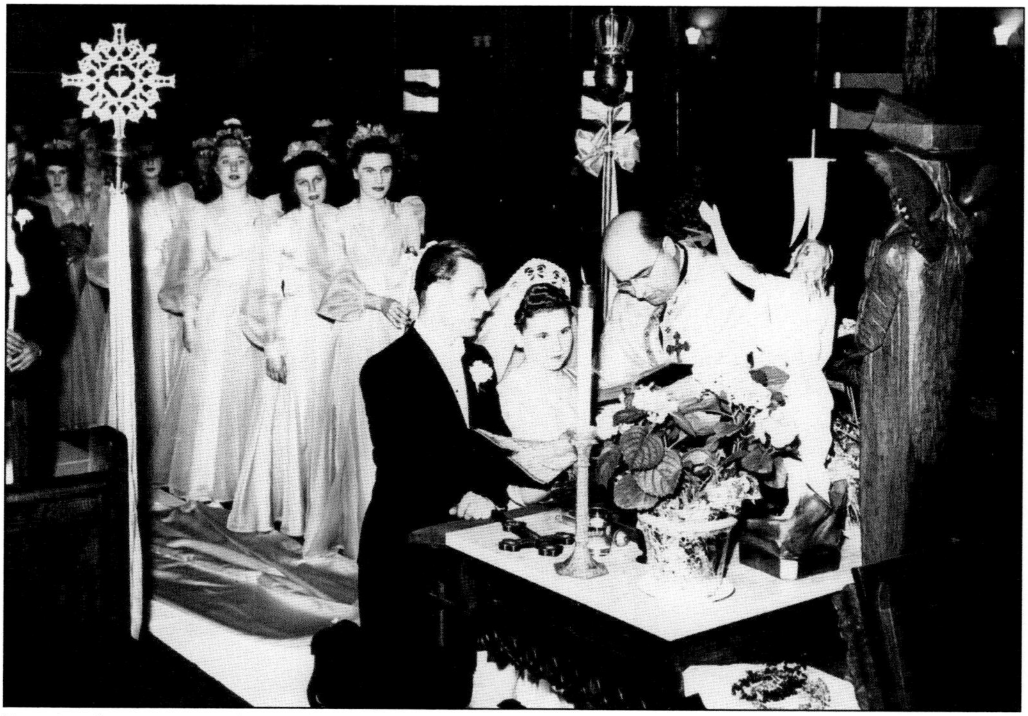

During the 1940s, Father Pobutsky officiated at the wedding ceremony for Michael Trubilowycz and Mary Wichorek in a traditional ceremony at St. John's Ukrainian Catholic Church in Detroit. (Olga Solovey.)

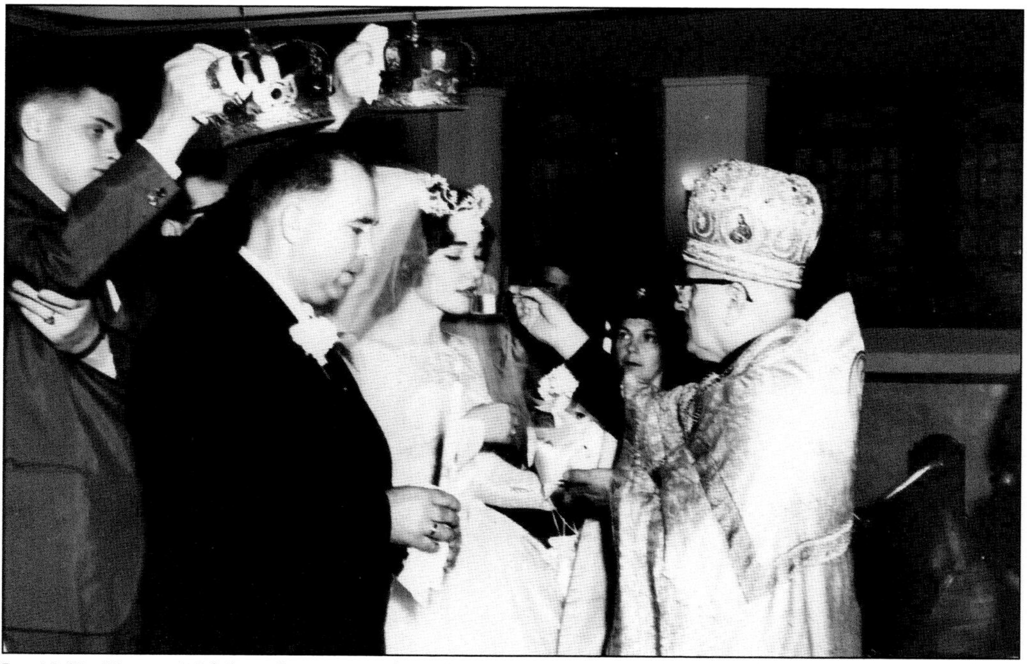

In 1962, Victor Milchynsky married Halina Symonenko at the original site of St. Mary the Protectress Ukrainian Orthodox Cathedral. Part of the ceremony includes the traditional wedding crowns. (Elizabeth Symonenko.)

In the late 1950s, St. John the Baptist Ukrainian Catholic Church celebrates the May crowning, which is a traditional Catholic ritual that occurs in the month of May when an image or likeness of the Blessed Virgin Mary is ceremonially crowned to signify her as Queen of Heaven and the Mother of God. (Joseph Szafranski.)

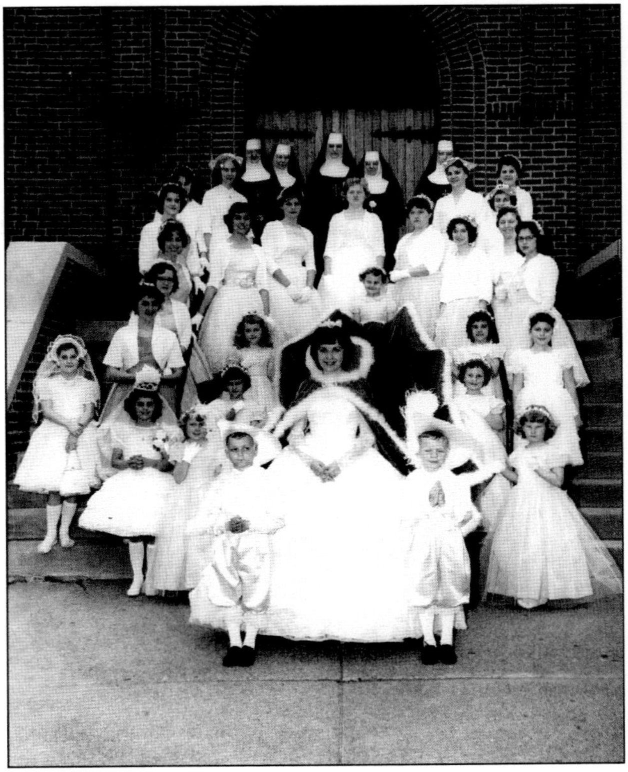

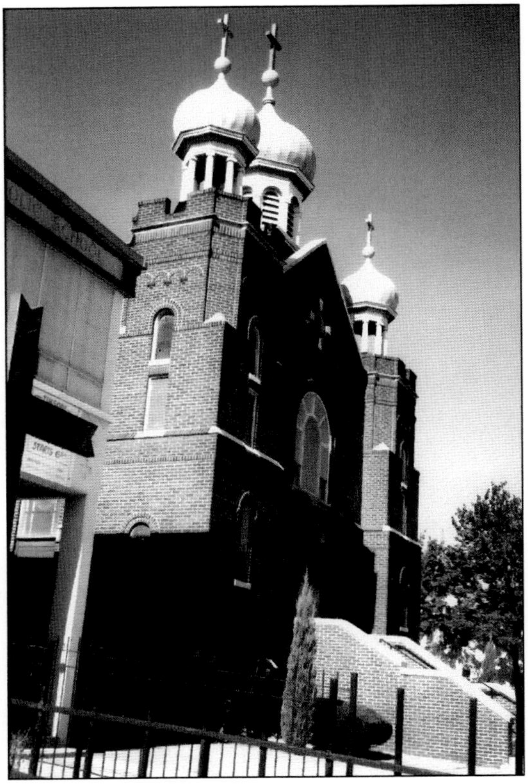

St. John the Baptist Ukrainian Catholic Church in Detroit opened its doors in 1918. In 1951, the construction of the new school building was completed. The Ukrainian community celebrated its 100th anniversary in 2007. (Joseph Szafranski.)

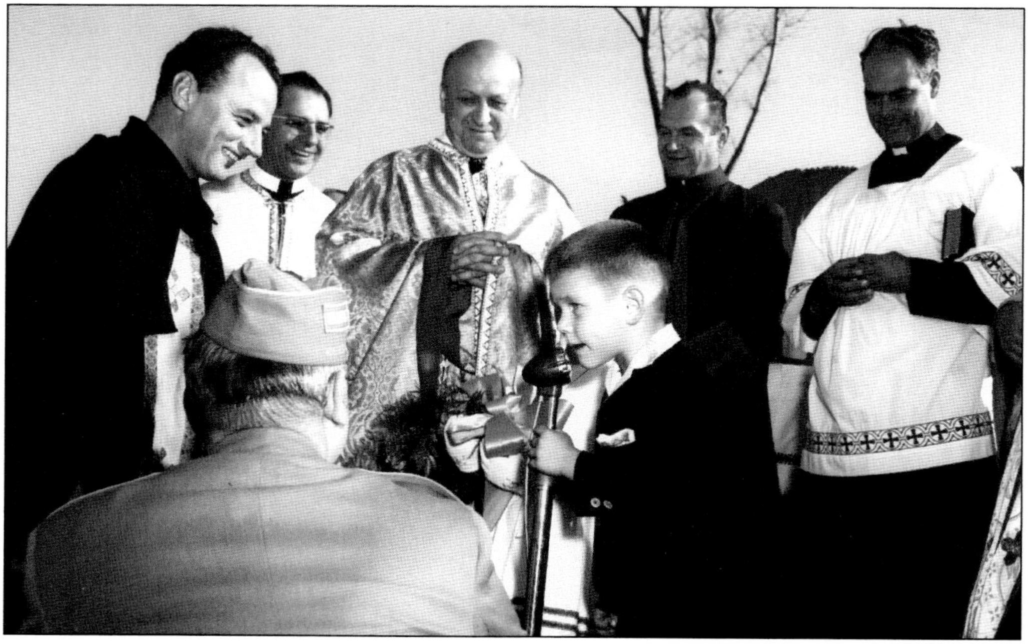

Young Roman Kolodchin welcomes the clergy to Warren in 1964. They are, from left to right, Reverend Jerome Barnych, Reverend Patrick Paschak, unidentified, Monsignor Bohnevych, and unidentified. (Lydia Kolodchin.)

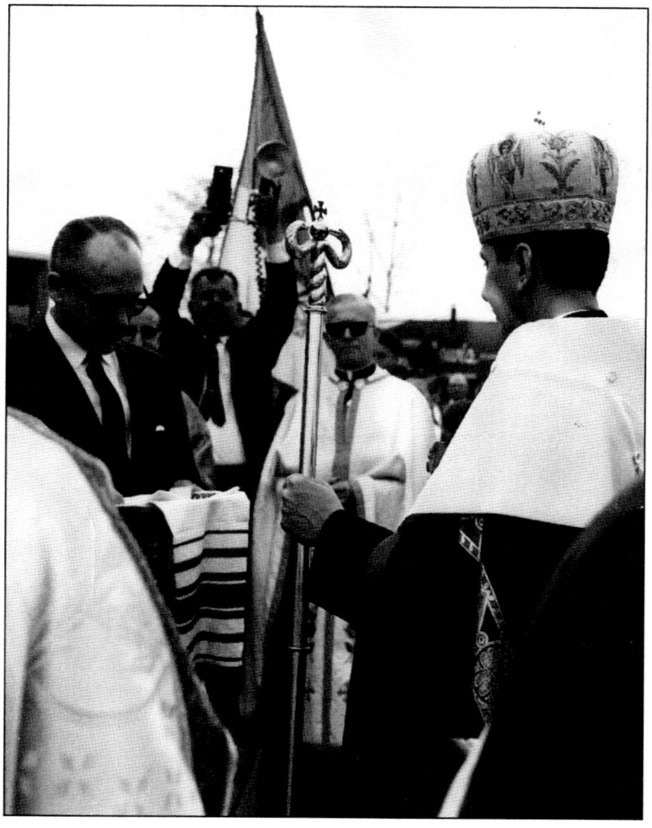

In 1966, Ukrainian Catholic Bishop J. Gabro greets Lubomyr Hewko, president of the St. Josaphat Ukrainian Catholic Church building committee, during the church's formal dedication in Warren. Assisting the bishop is Reverend Ivan Prokopovych. (Lubomyr Hewko.)

Reverend Barnych blesses the water at the Feast of the Epiphany at St. Josaphat Ukrainian Catholic Church in 1966. (Lubomyr Hewko.)

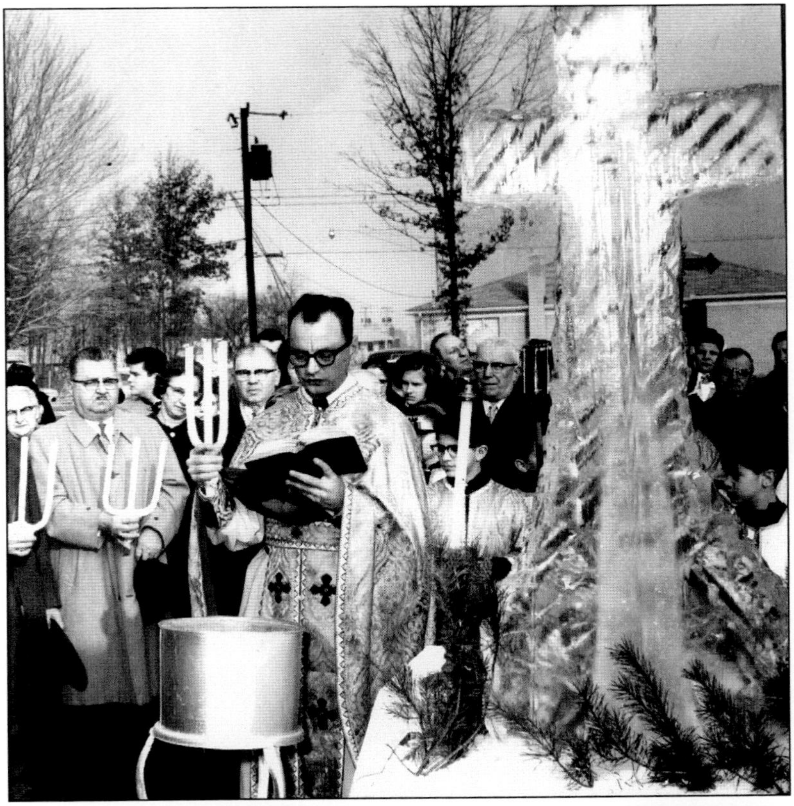

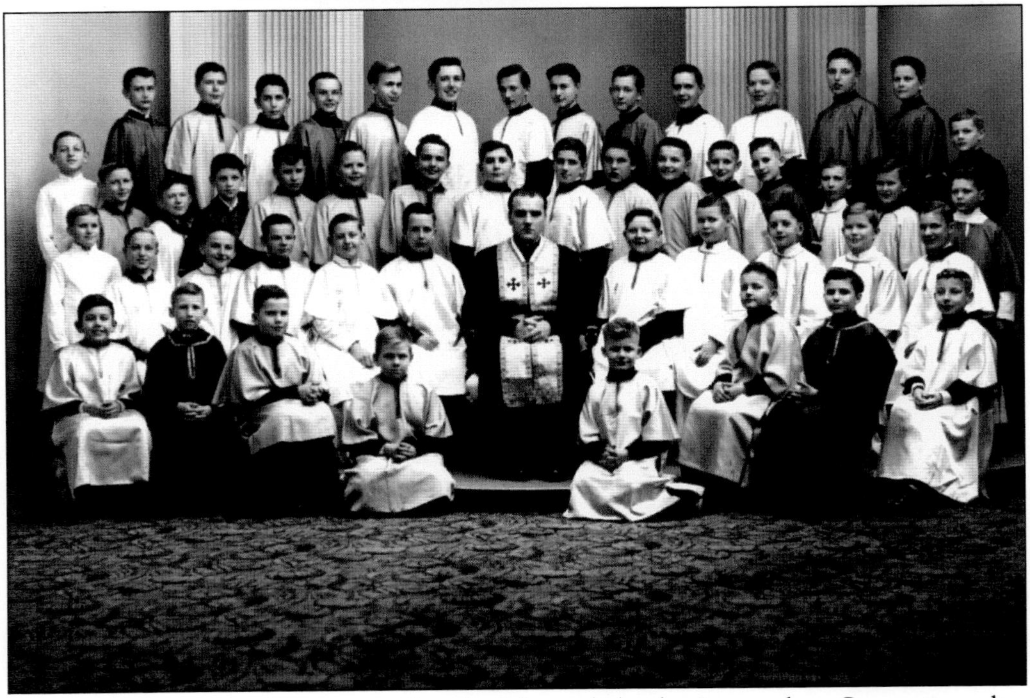

Under the direction of Monsignor Joseph Schmondiuk, the Immaculate Conception altar servers, grades five through eight, pose for their photograph in 1954. (Roman Maziak.)

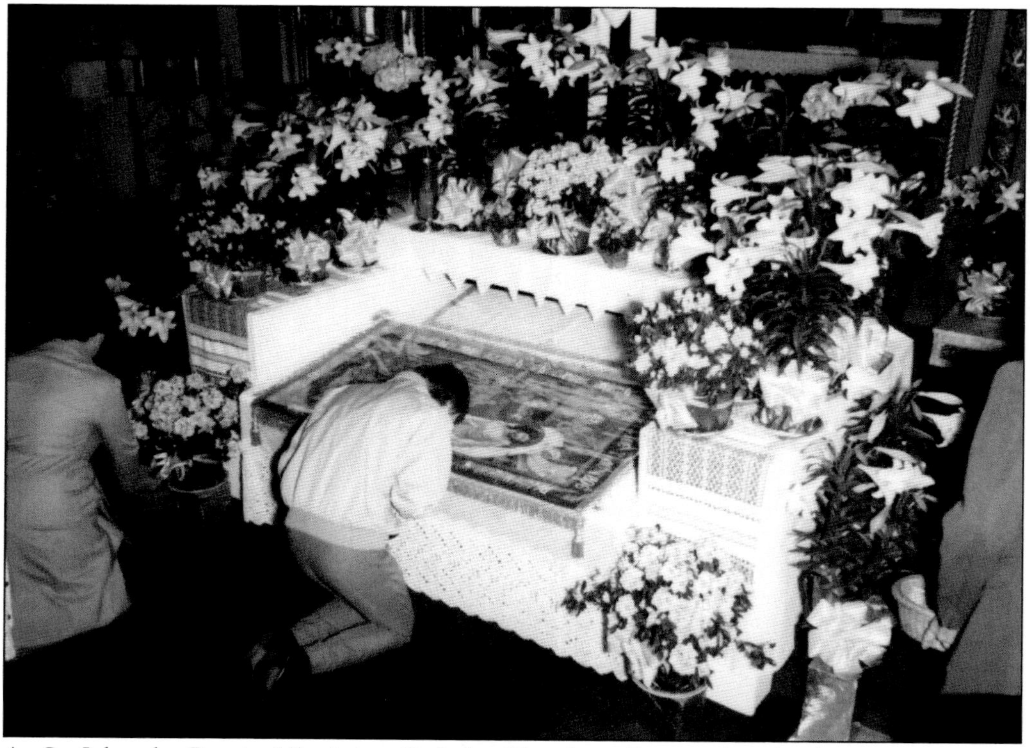

At St. John the Baptist Ukrainian Catholic Church in Detroit the Plaschanytsia (the Holy Shroud) is laid out on Good Friday and is guarded until it is put away on Easter Sunday. During this time, parishioners visit the Plaschanytsia to pray and symbolically kiss the wounds of Christ. This image is from the 1970s. (Joseph Szafranski.)

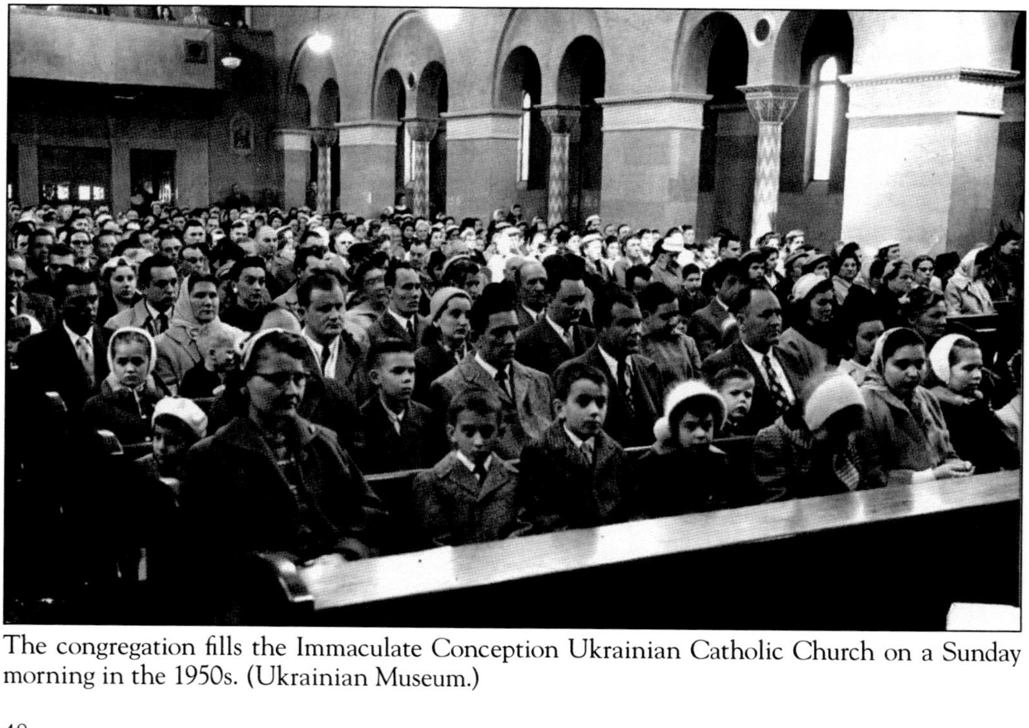

The congregation fills the Immaculate Conception Ukrainian Catholic Church on a Sunday morning in the 1950s. (Ukrainian Museum.)

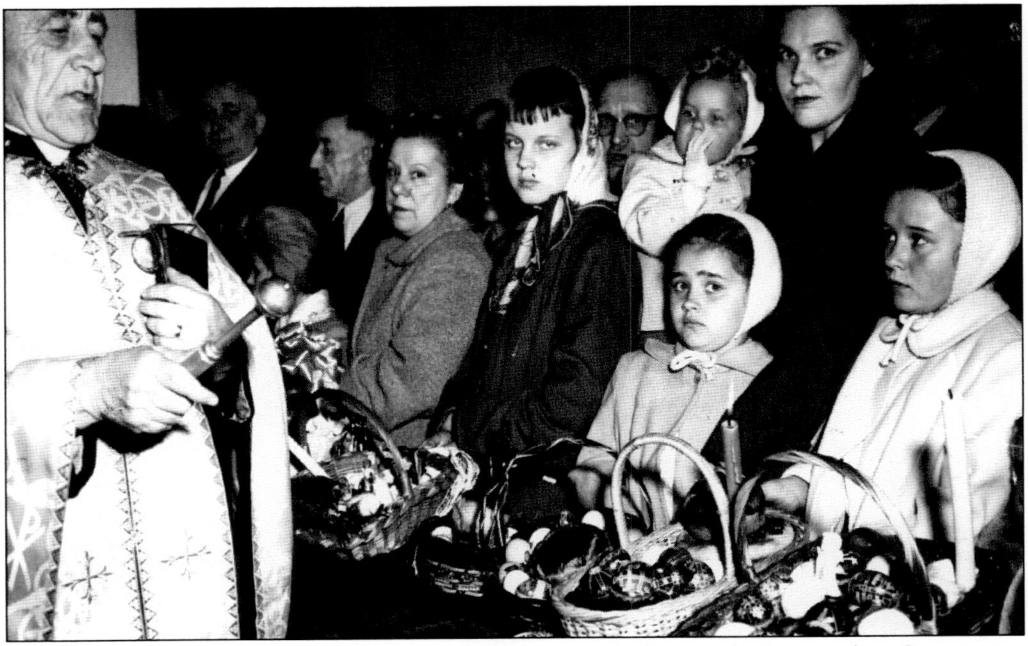

Reverend Andrew Tresznewsky blesses Ukrainian Easter baskets at the Immaculate Conception Ukrainian Catholic Church in 1953. On the day before Easter Sunday, the tradition is to fill a basket with pysanky (Ukrainian Easter eggs), paska (traditional Easter bread), and other assorted foods. The items are then covered with a hand-embroidered cloth (vyshyvka), taken to the church, and blessed by the priest. (Ukrainian Museum.)

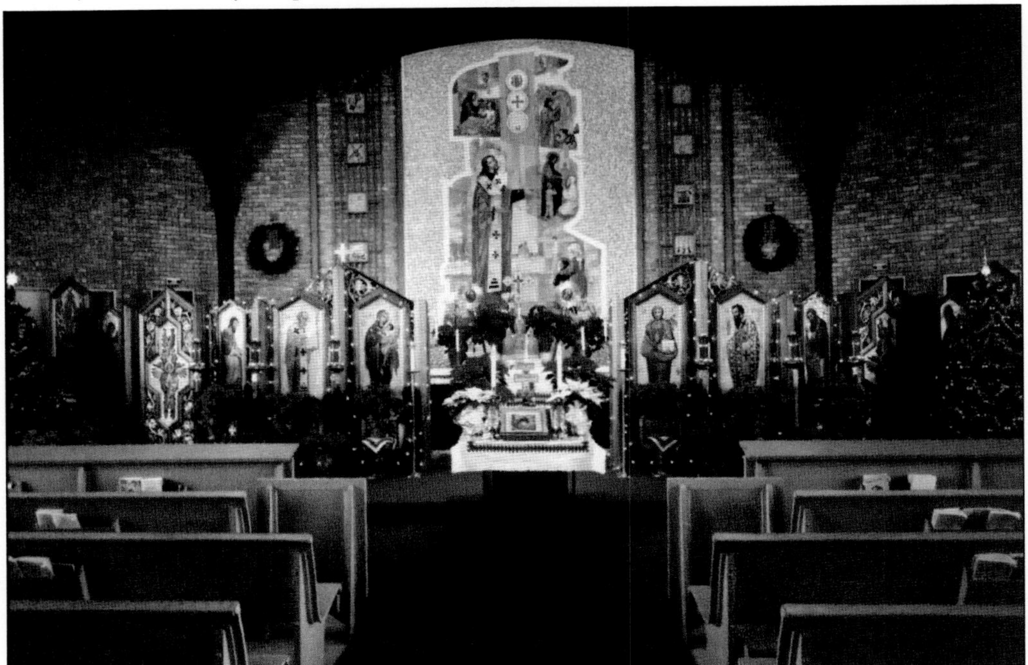

St. Josaphat Ukrainian Catholic Church, located in Warren, was constructed in the 1960s to meet the needs of parishioners who were moving to the east side suburbs from Hamtramck and Detroit. Artist and parishioner George Kozak painted the Byzantine icons. (Marie Zarycky.)

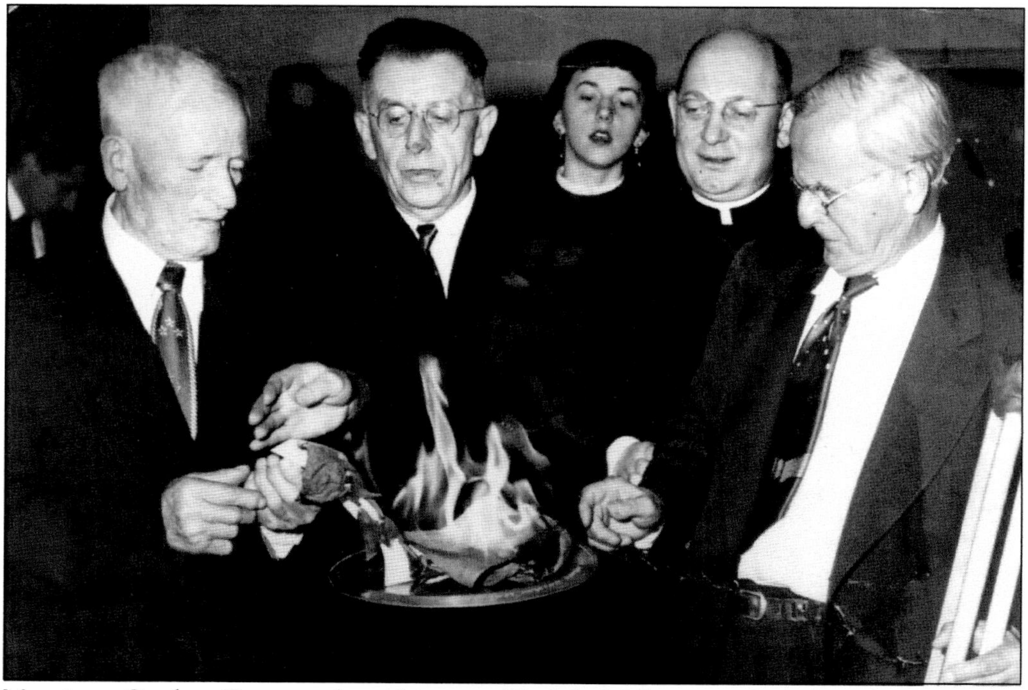

Monsignor Stephen Knapp and parishioners of St. John's Ukrainian Catholic School celebrate paying off the school by burning the mortgage. (Joseph Szafranski.)

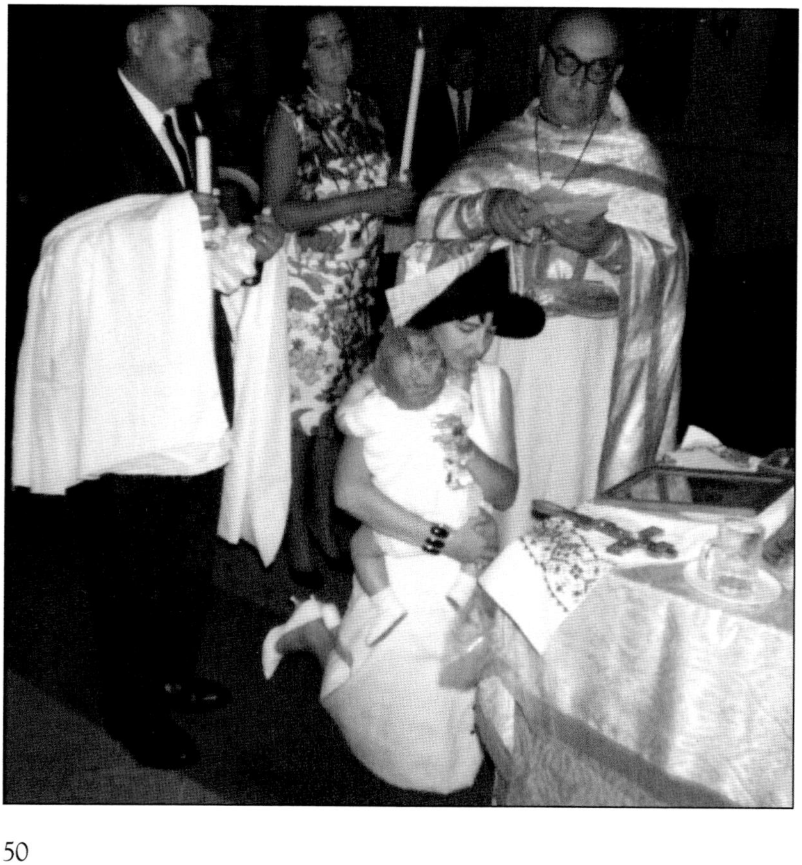

Father Alexander Novitsky baptizes David Sepell in 1963 at the original site of St. Mary's Ukrainian Orthodox Church in Detroit. David's parents, Ray and Nadya Sepell, participate in the ceremony. (Nadya Sepell.)

The Immaculate Conception Ukrainian Catholic Church clergy are, in front, Monsignor Stephen Knapp and Father Maxim Kobasiuk. In back are Bishop Michael Wiwchar and Monsignor Stephen Chepta. (Roman Maziak.)

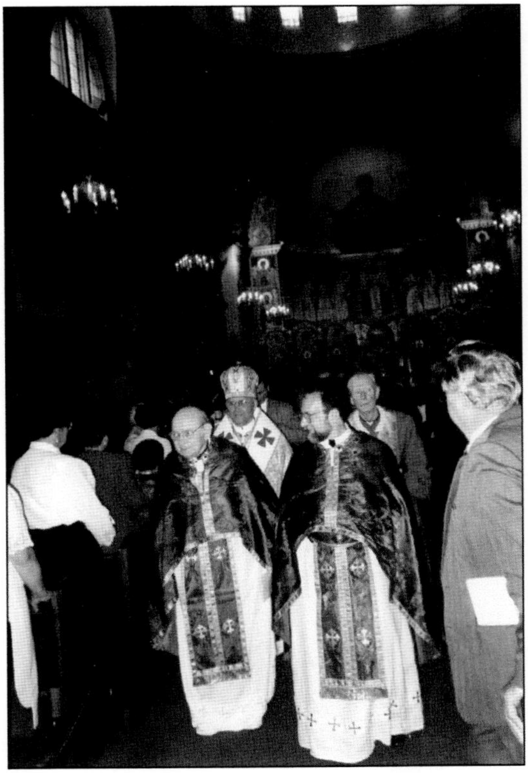

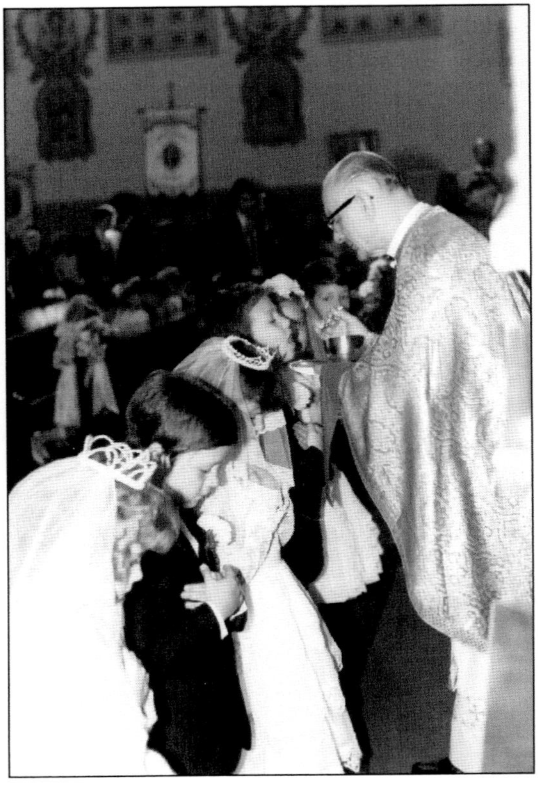

In 1984, Father Sabol celebrates the first holy communion with young parishioners. (Roman Maziak.)

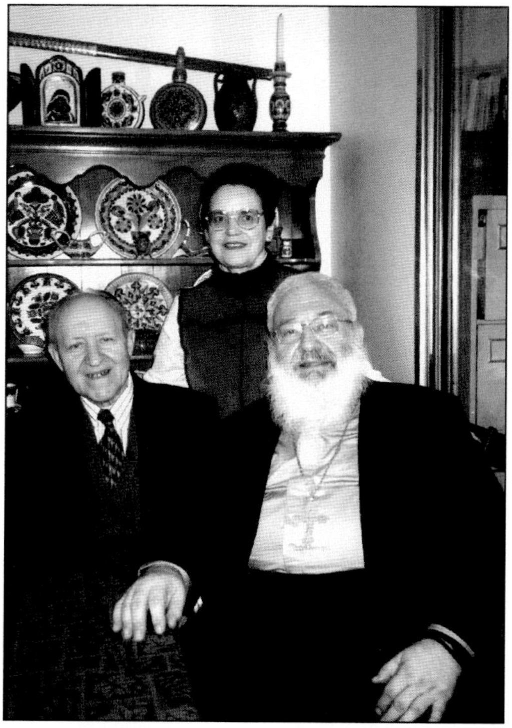

Formerly from Detroit, the Cardinal and Patriarch of the Ukrainian Catholic Church in Kyiv visits with brother-in-law Zenon Wasylkewych and his wife, Nina Wasylkewych, in 2003. (Zenon Wasylkewych.)

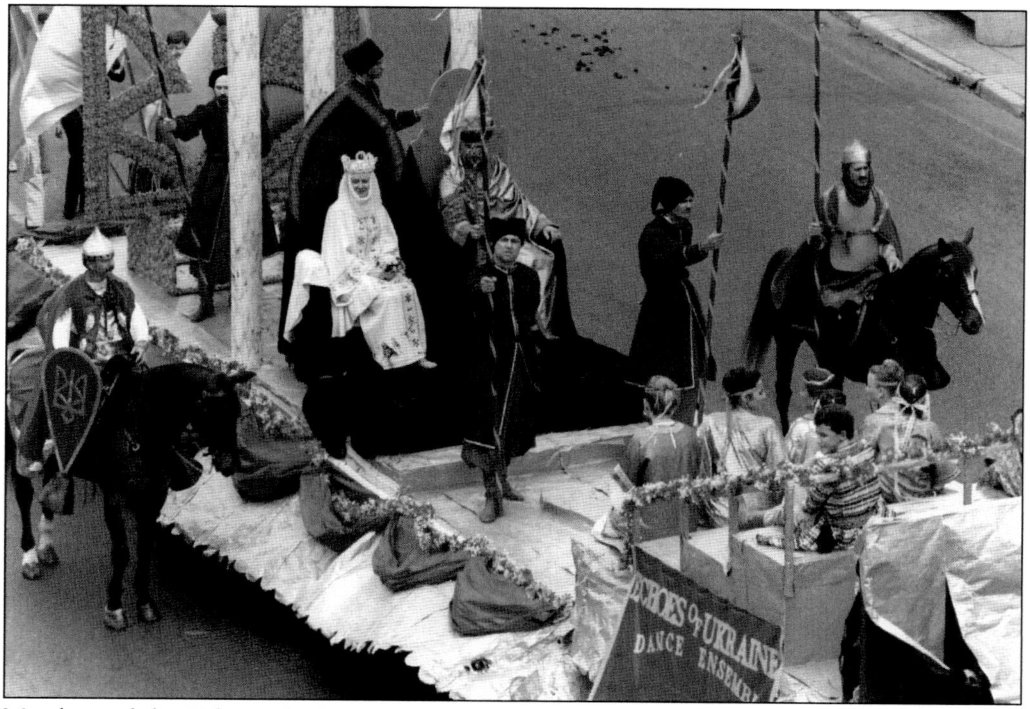

Members of the *Echoes of Ukraine* Dance Ensemble created this float for the Millennium of Christianity parade celebrated in Hamtramck, in 1988. The float is a historic depiction of the court of Vladimir the Great with Grand Princess Olga, his grandmother, who brought Christianity to Ukraine. (Ukrainian Museum.)

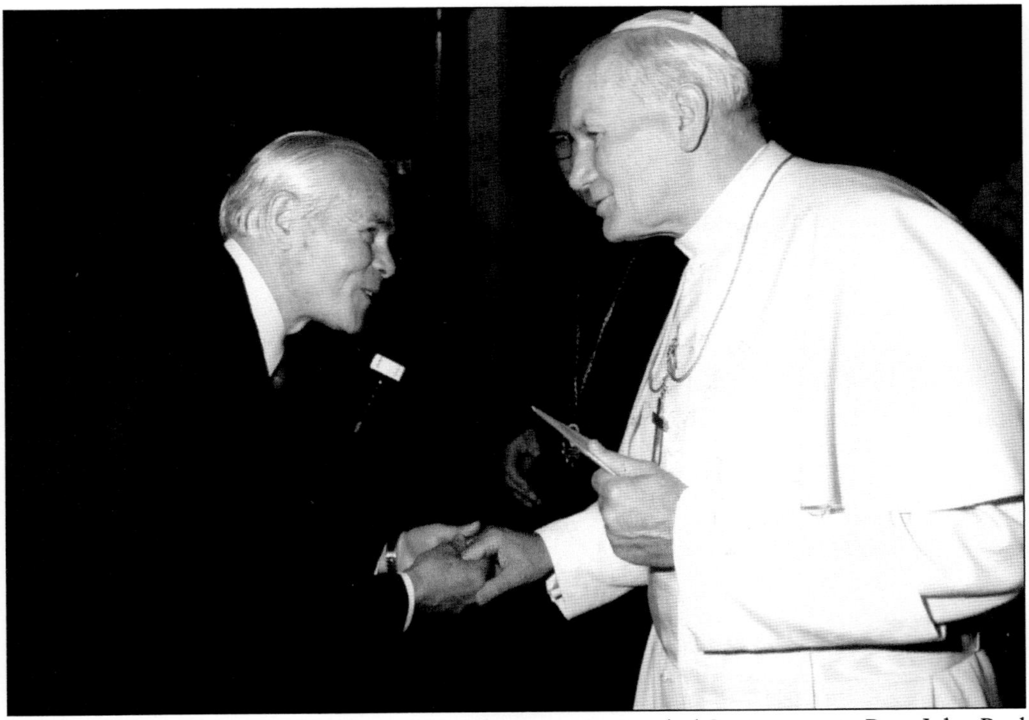

In 1987, Wasyl Kolodchin, president of the Ukrainian Patriarchal Society, greets Pope John Paul II in Rome. The goal of the meeting was to garner support for Cardinal Josyf Slipyj to become Patriarch of the Ukrainian Catholic Church. (Lydia Kolodchin.)

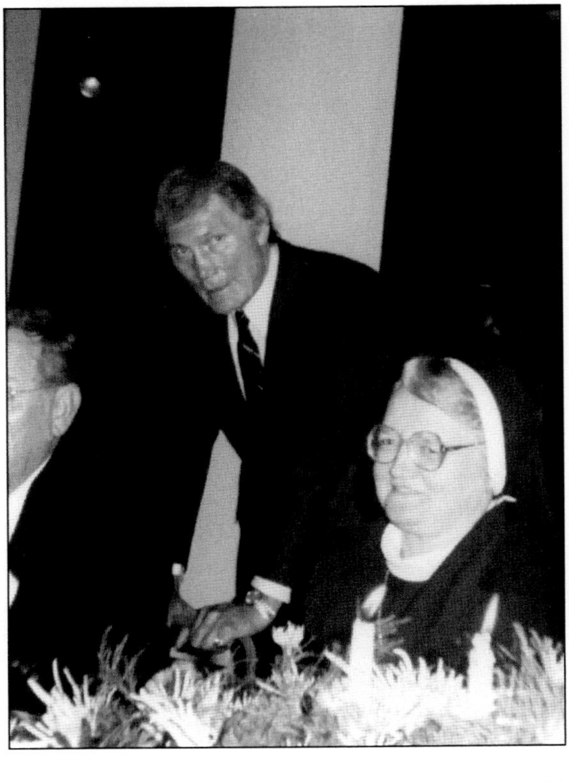

Jack Palance, famous Hollywood Ukrainian actor, attends a banquet to help raise funds for the Immaculate Conception Ukrainian Schools. Pictured with Palance is Sister Chrysostom. This image is from the late 1970s. (Roman Maziak.)

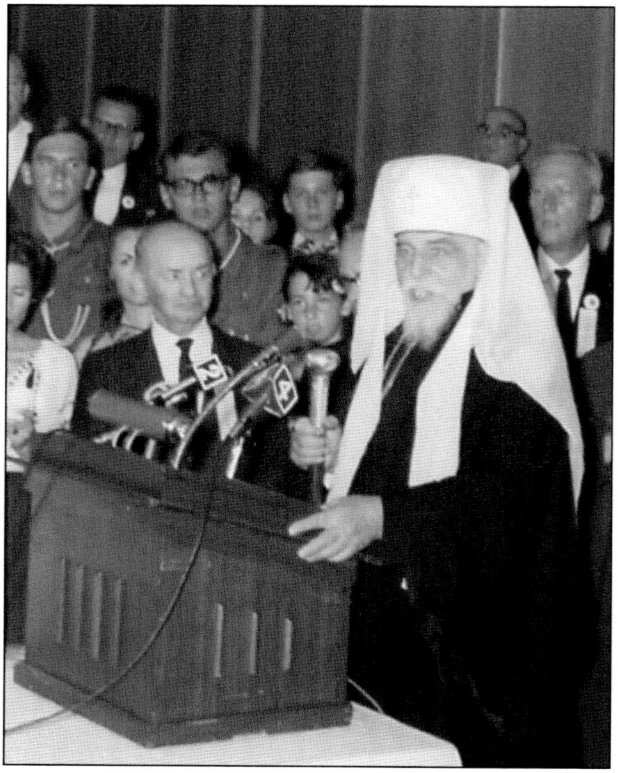

In 1968, Ukrainian Catholic Patriarch Cardinal Josyf Slipyj visited North American Ukrainians, including those in Detroit. Mychaylo Duzji, left, listens attentively to the cardinal's message. (Andrey Duzyj.)

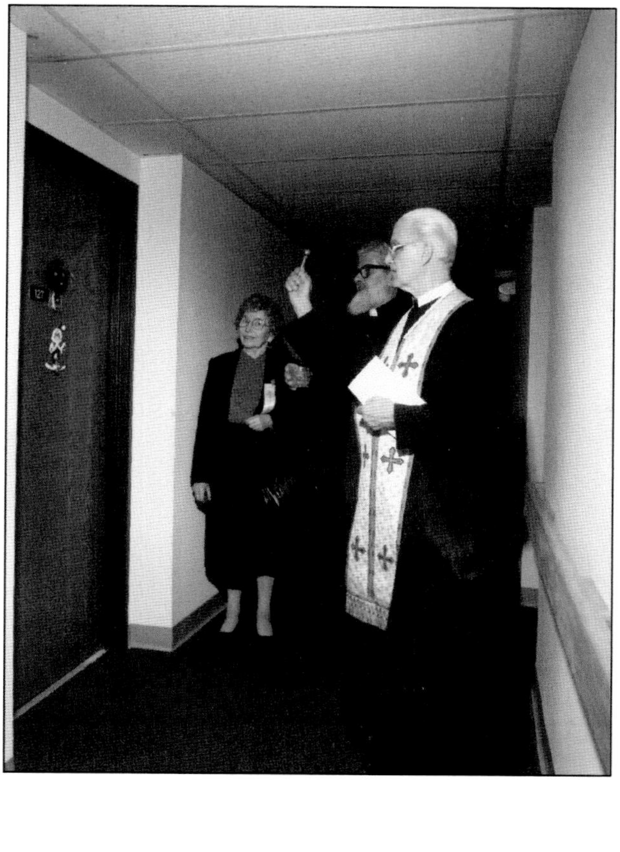

Reverend Constantine Wysochansky of St. Josaphat Ukrainian Catholic Church blesses the apartment of one of the occupants of the Ukrainian Village, a residency for seniors. This image is from 1991.

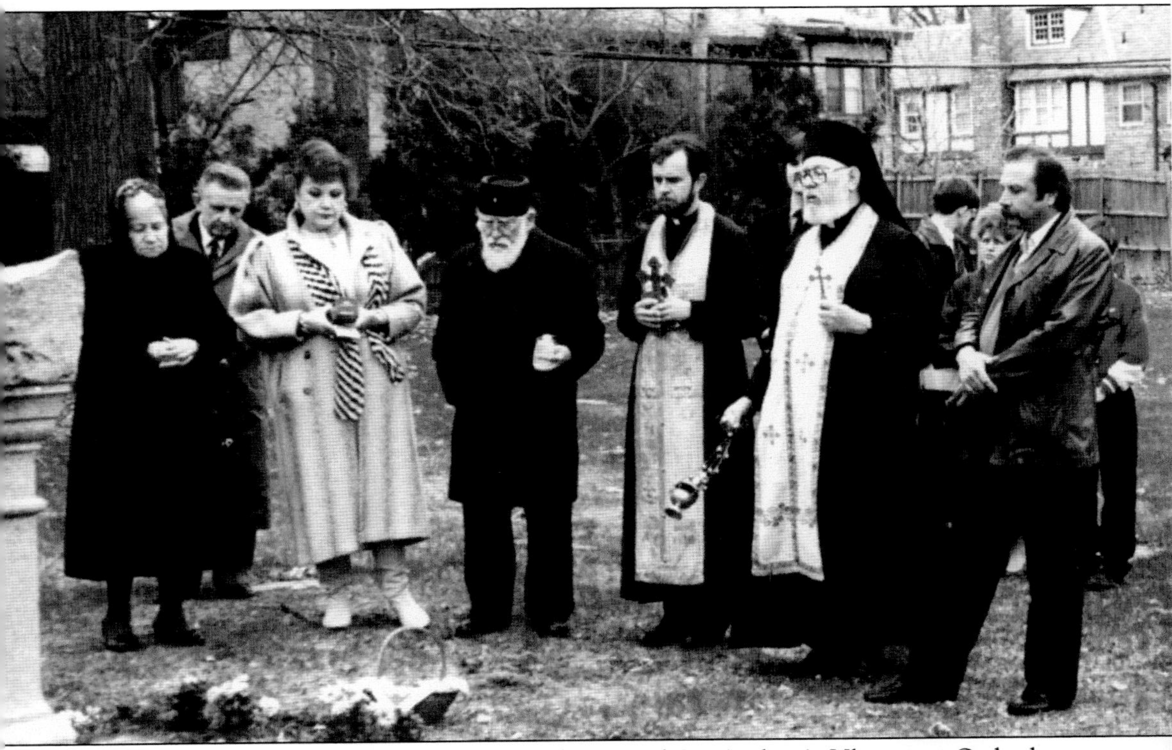

At Evergreen Cemetery, Bishop Alexander Bykowetz of St. Andrew's Ukrainian Orthodox Church in Detroit says a panachyda (religious prayer) at the graveside of one of his parishioners. There were many Ukrainians laid to rest at this cemetery. (Bohdan Nehaniv.)

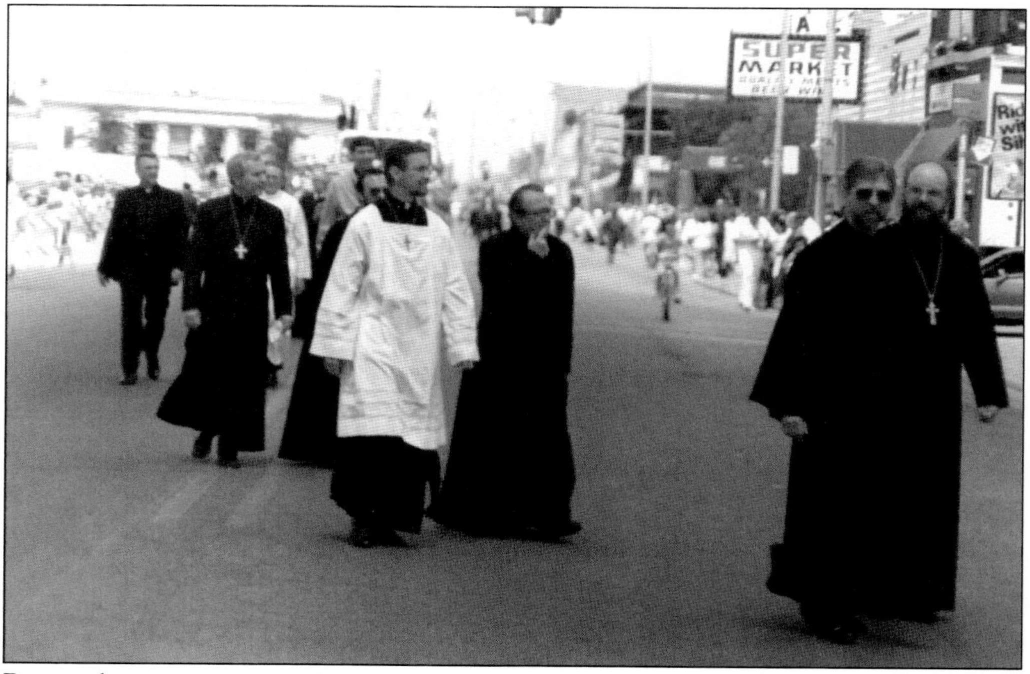

Detroit clergy participate in the Millennium March on Joseph Campau in Hamtramck in 1988. (Roman Maziak.)

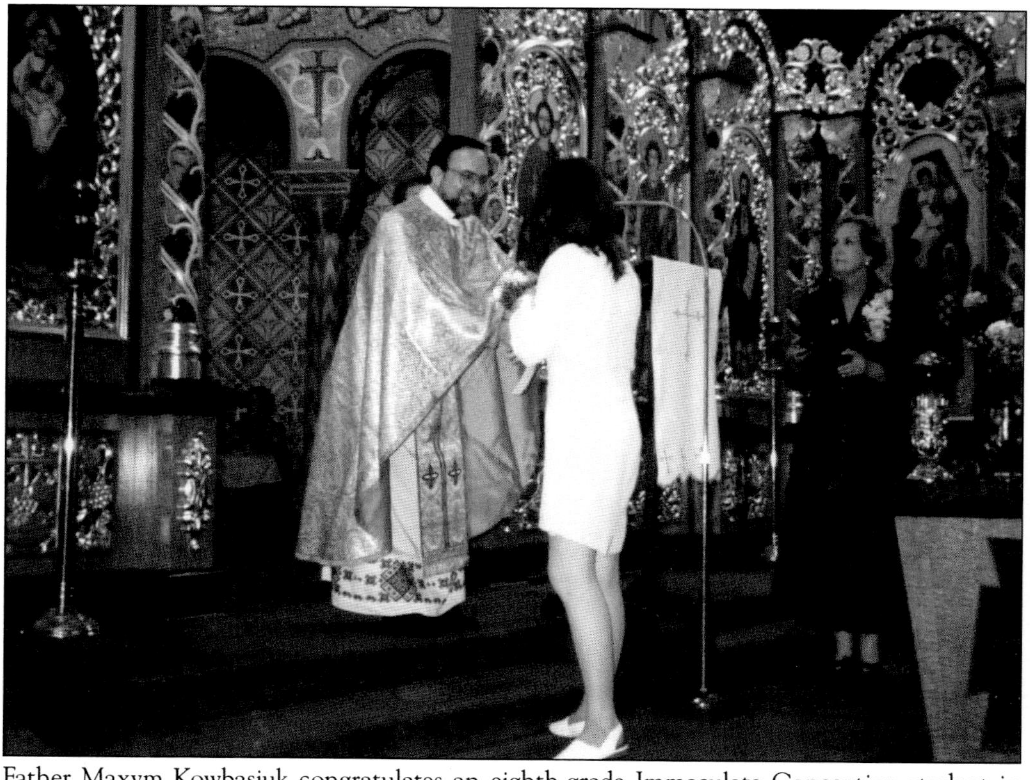
Father Maxym Kowbasiuk congratulates an eighth-grade Immaculate Conception student in 1996 while teacher Mrs. McPherson looks on. (Roman Maziak.)

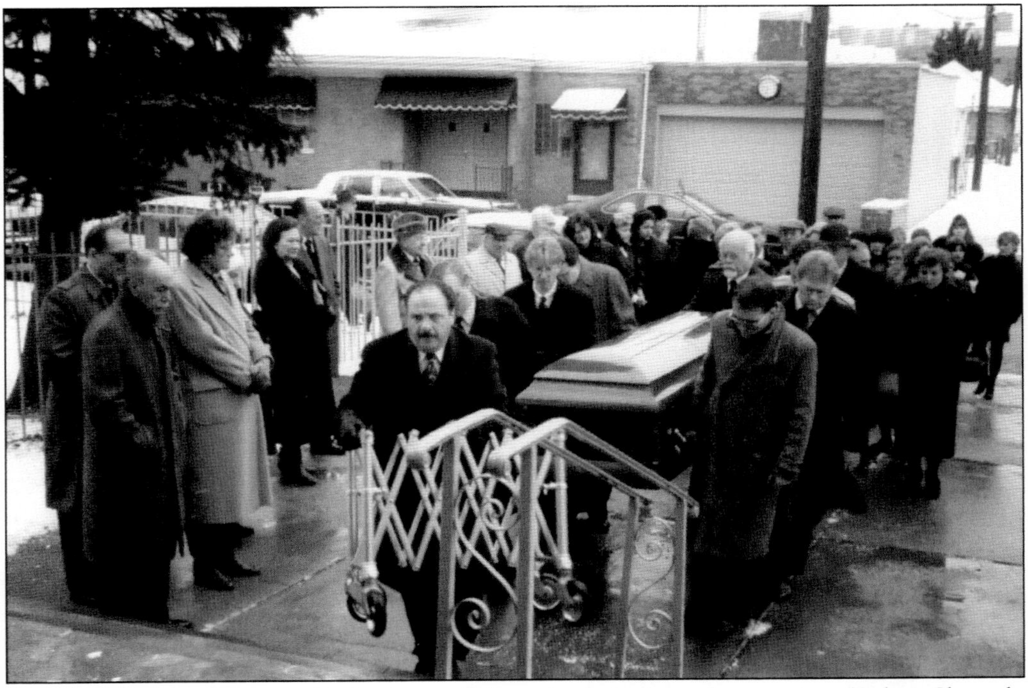

Christopher Buhay, director of Buhay Funeral Home, leads the funeral procession of Sohpia Shumylo into the Immaculate Conception Ukrainian Catholic Church in 1995. (Roman Maziak.)

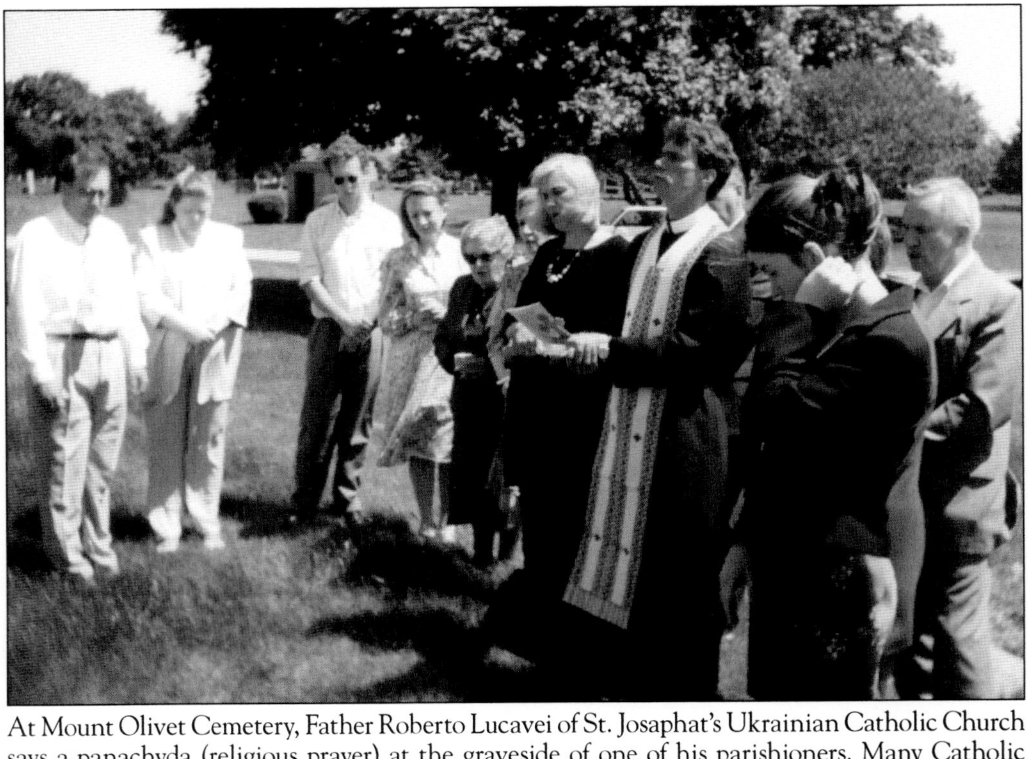

At Mount Olivet Cemetery, Father Roberto Lucavei of St. Josaphat's Ukrainian Catholic Church says a panachyda (religious prayer) at the graveside of one of his parishioners. Many Catholic Ukrainians have been laid to rest at this location. (Roman Maziak.)

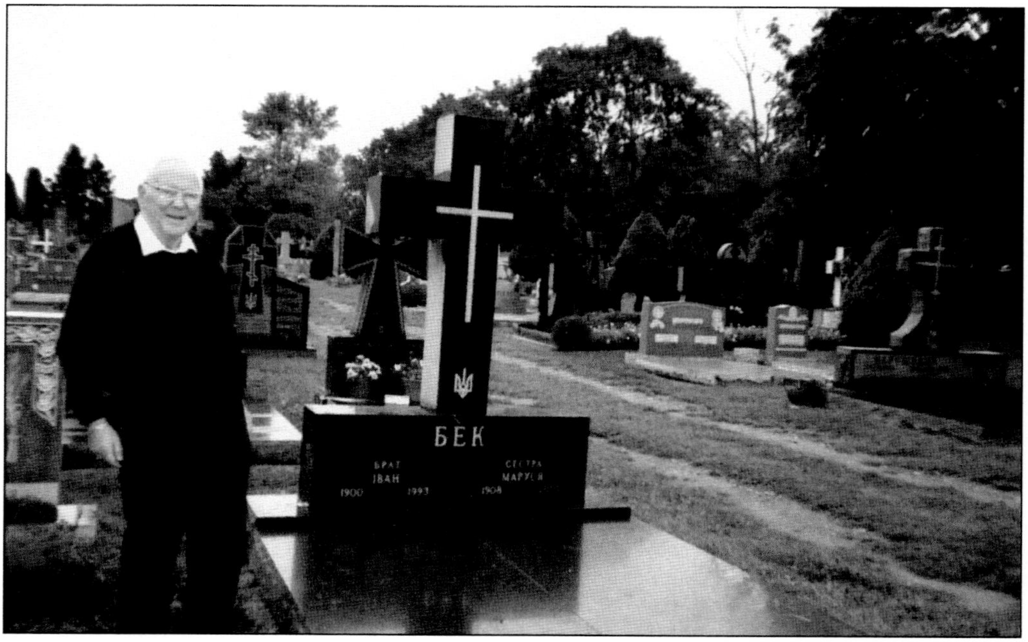

Oleh Cieply visits the gravesite of Dr. Mary Beck and her brother John Beck in Bound Brook, New Jersey, in 2008. Mary Beck was the first woman president of the Detroit City Council. She and her brother John were extremely active in the Ukrainian community. (Alberta Cieply.)

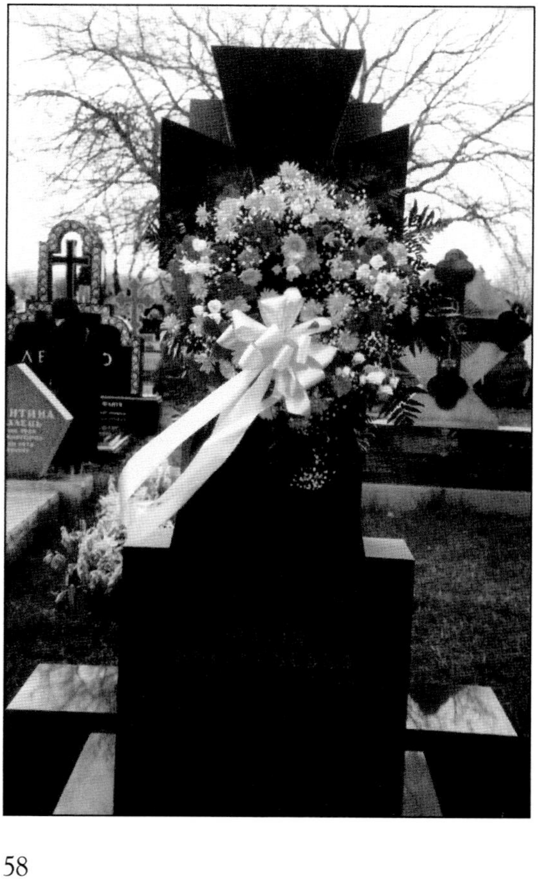

The Ukrainian American community mourns activist Dr. Denys Kwitkowsky and Maria Kwitkowsky, who were leaders in the cause of Ukrainian independence for many years. (Marta Kwitkowsky.)

Three

ARTISTRY

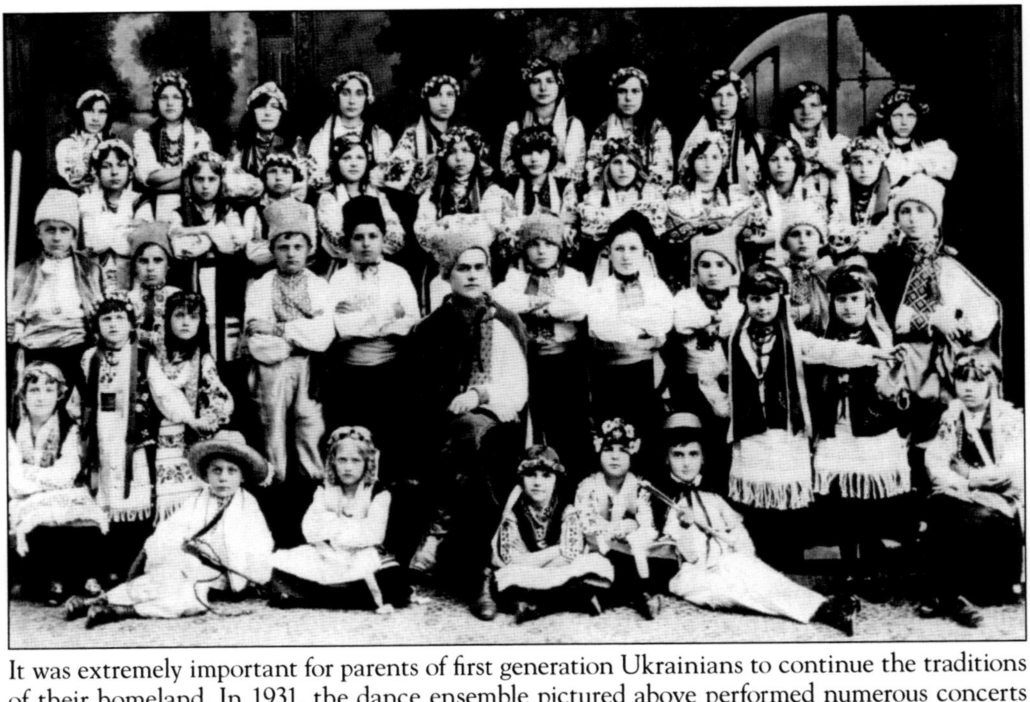

It was extremely important for parents of first generation Ukrainians to continue the traditions of their homeland. In 1931, the dance ensemble pictured above performed numerous concerts of traditional dances wearing hand-stitched costumes made by women in the community. Their teacher was Fred Matidiuk.

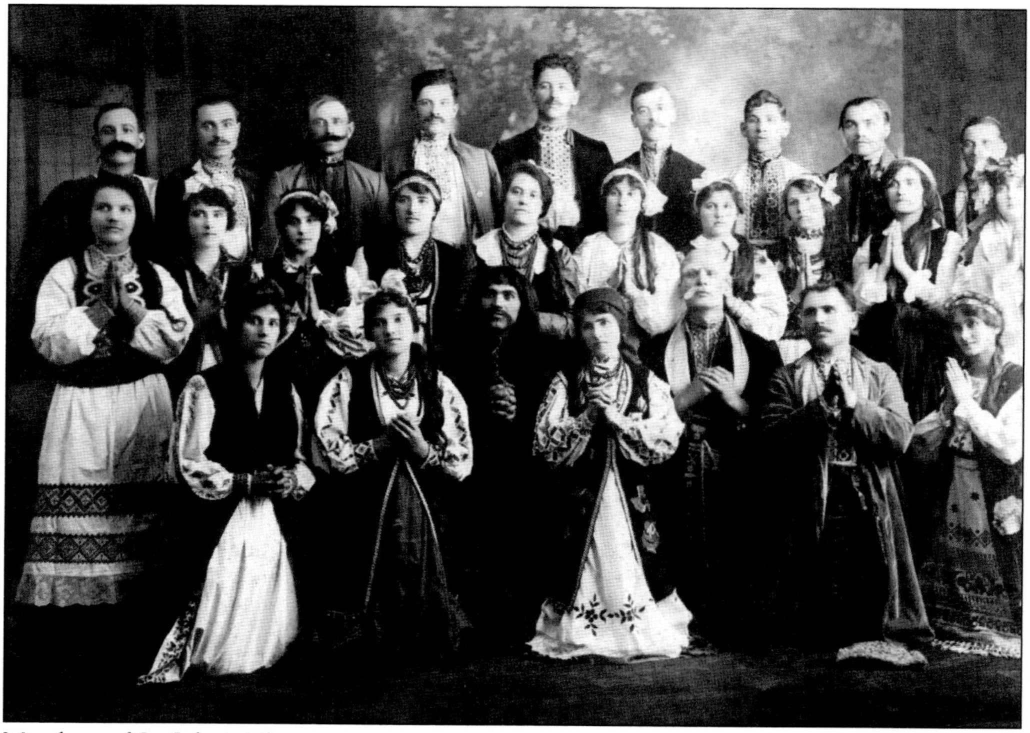

Members of St. John's Ukrainian Catholic Church perform the play *Cossak Beyond the Danube* in 1913. (Ukrainian Museum.)

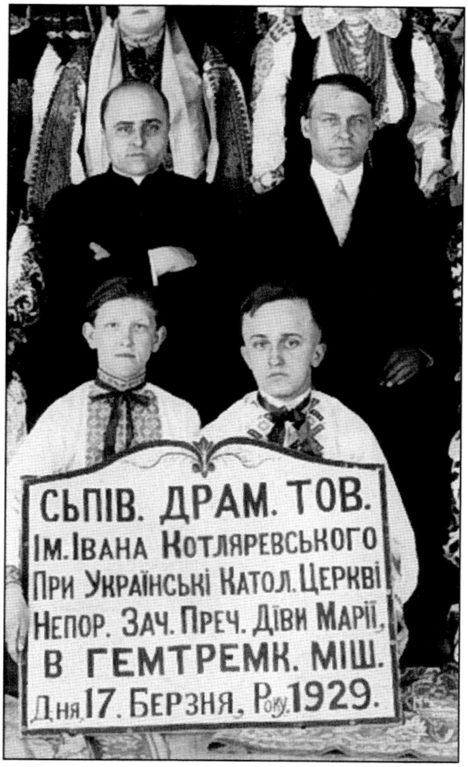

Young Ukrainian men display the poster for a musical dramatic group named after Ivan Kotlyarewsky at the Ukrainian Catholic Church of Immaculate Conception of the Blessed Mother, Hamtramck, Michigan, in 1929.

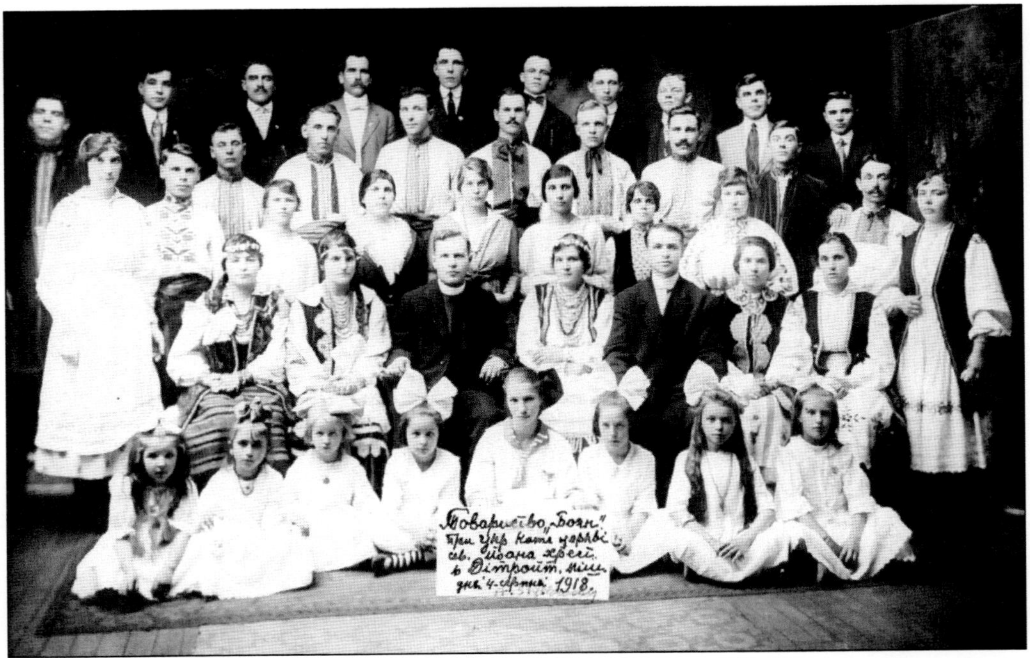

Director Andrew Styslowsky poses with his theatrical company in 1918. He is seated second row, fifth from the left.

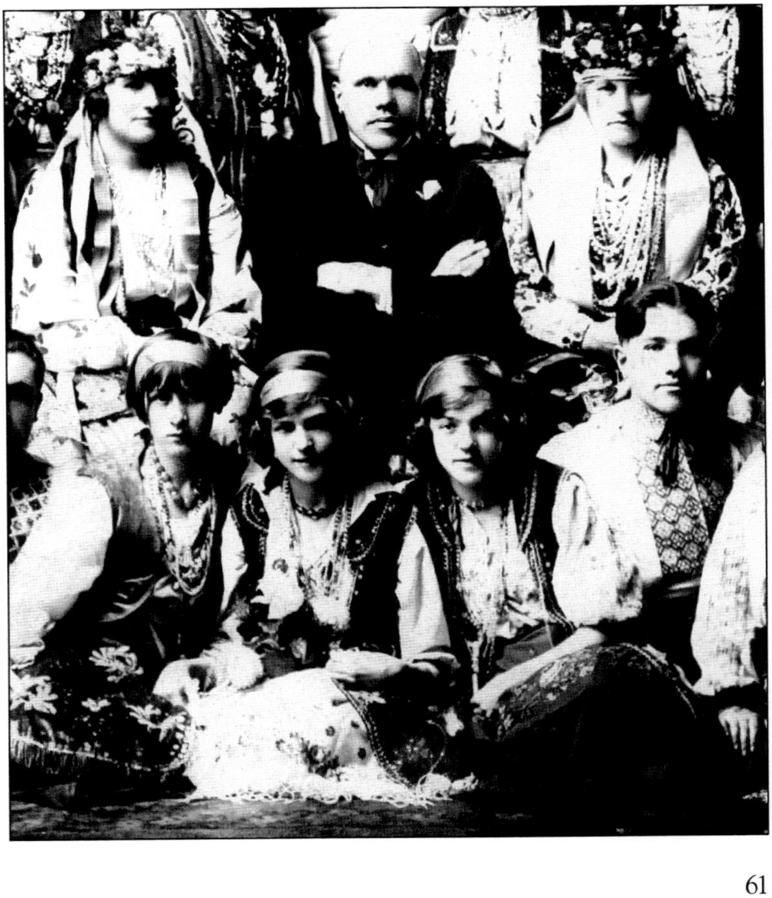

Members of the Detroit Ukrainian Theatrical Group pose with Director S. Korsky in the mid-1920s.

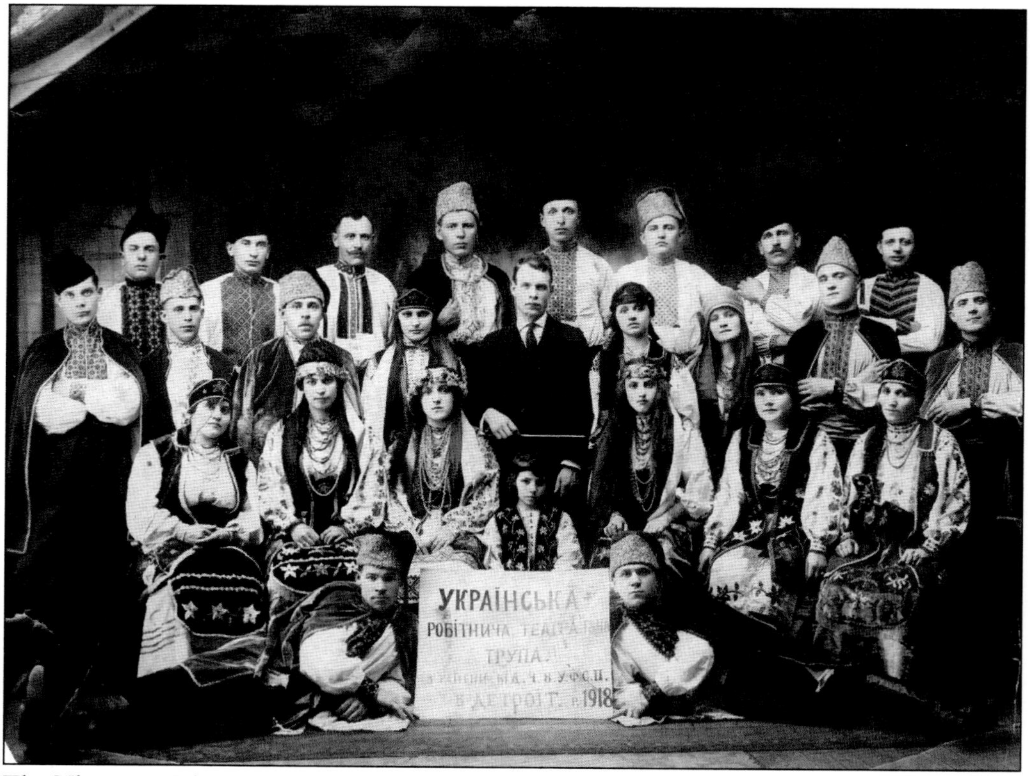

The Ukrainian Theatrical Group is pictured after a performance in 1918.

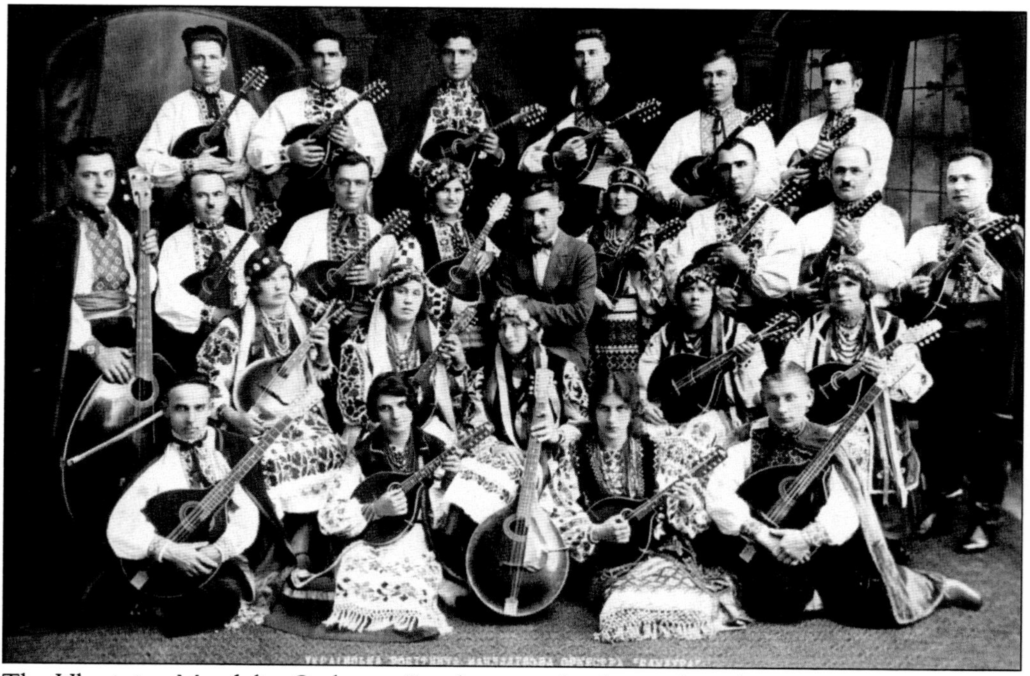

The Ukrainian Mandolin Orchestra Bandura was the first such orchestra in the Detroit area. This image is from 1915.

Hryhory Nazarenko received much of his musical training while still in Ukraine. After immigrating to America, he performed as a soloist in the Ukrainian community. He had many students in the Detroit area, some of whom were of American descent. He established the Prolisky Quartet in Detroit that performed on a professional level throughout the United States. (Maria Nazerenko.)

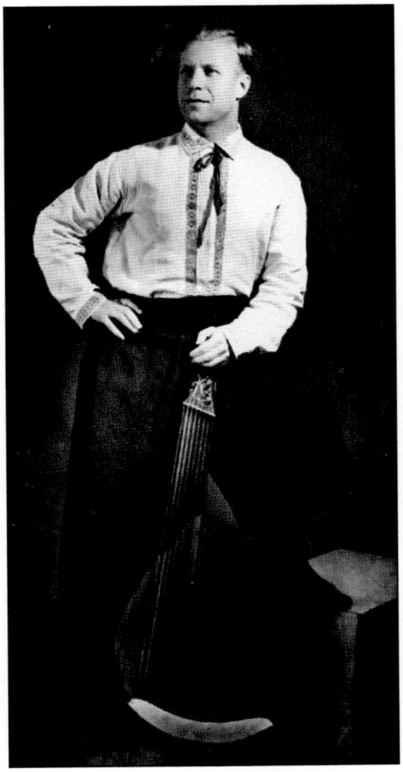

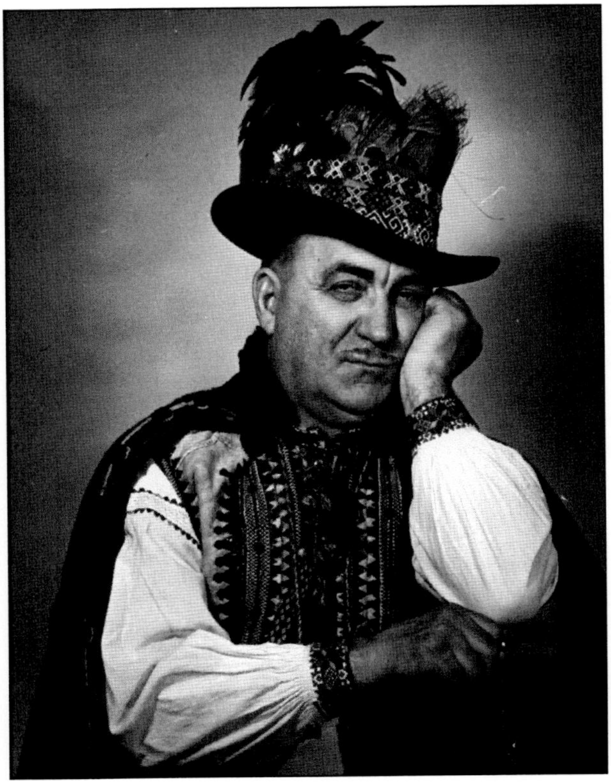

Eugene Draginda performed his repertoire of magic for many Ukrainian audiences in the area. (Ukrainian Museum.)

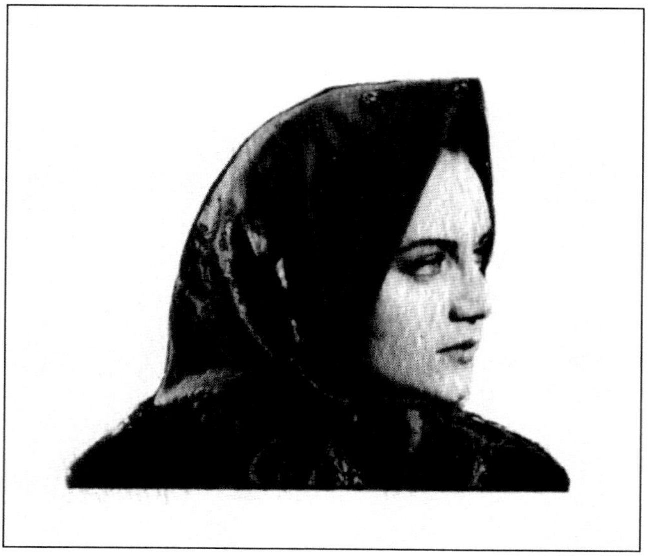

Donia Stephania Werbowetzka-Demray, an accomplished vocalist, costarred in the full-length feature film *Marusia* playing the role of Daryna. This musical was performed in Ukrainian, with English subtitles, in 1936. (Zinovia Ogrodnik.)

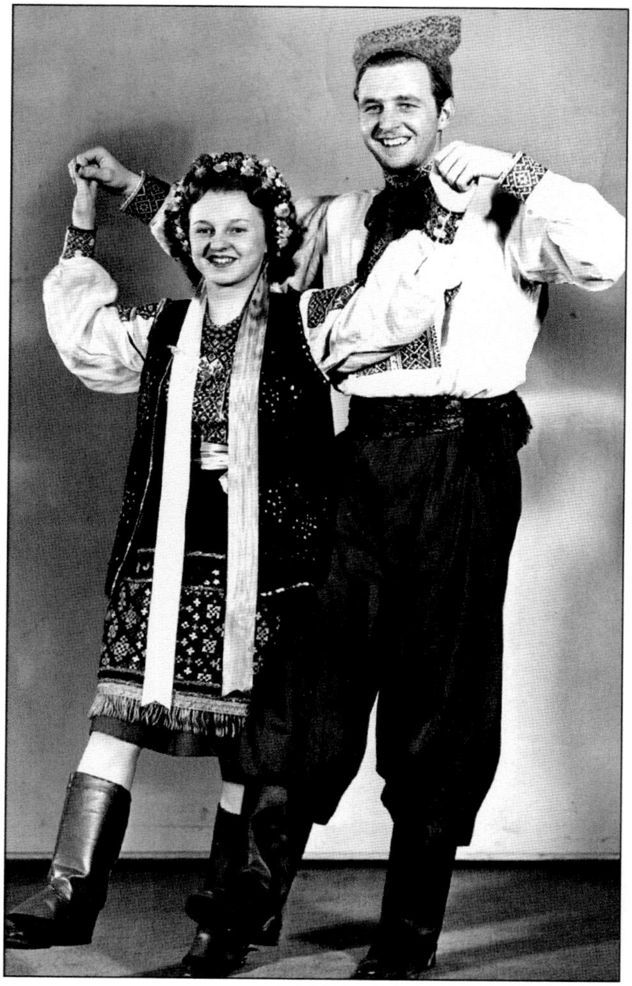

Club Boyan Ukrainian dancers Janette Smulka and Edward Holowchak perform in 1936. (Zinovia Ogrodnik.)

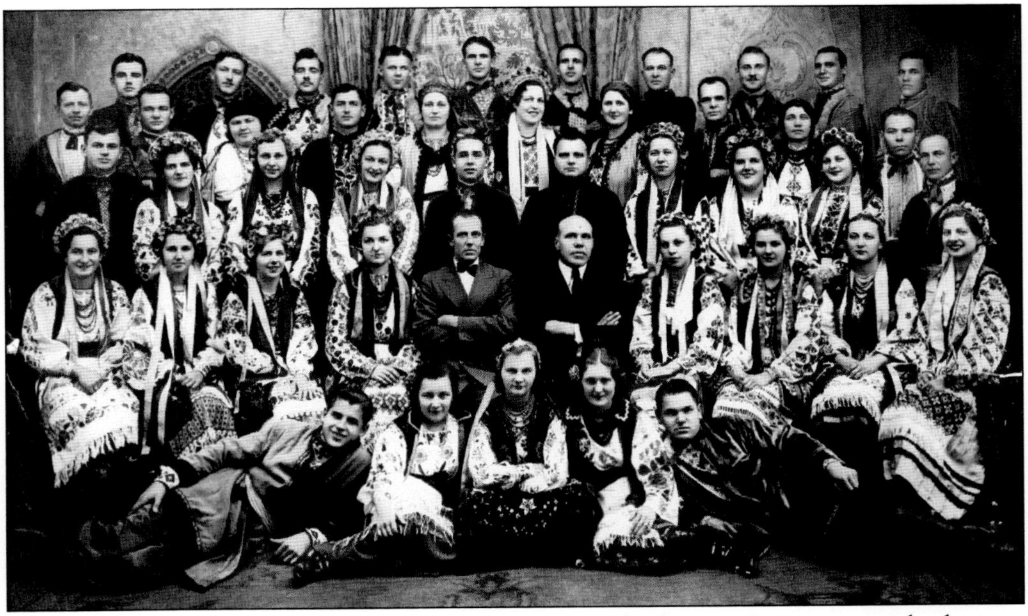

Club Boyan enjoyed an eventful and sometimes spectacular history. Its origin goes back many years to the summer of 1935 when five Ukrainian men met and began this organization. It was required of all prospective members to be of Ukrainian extraction and to possess a marked talent in dancing, singing, or playing a musical instrument. Their concerts became popular events in the Ukrainian community.

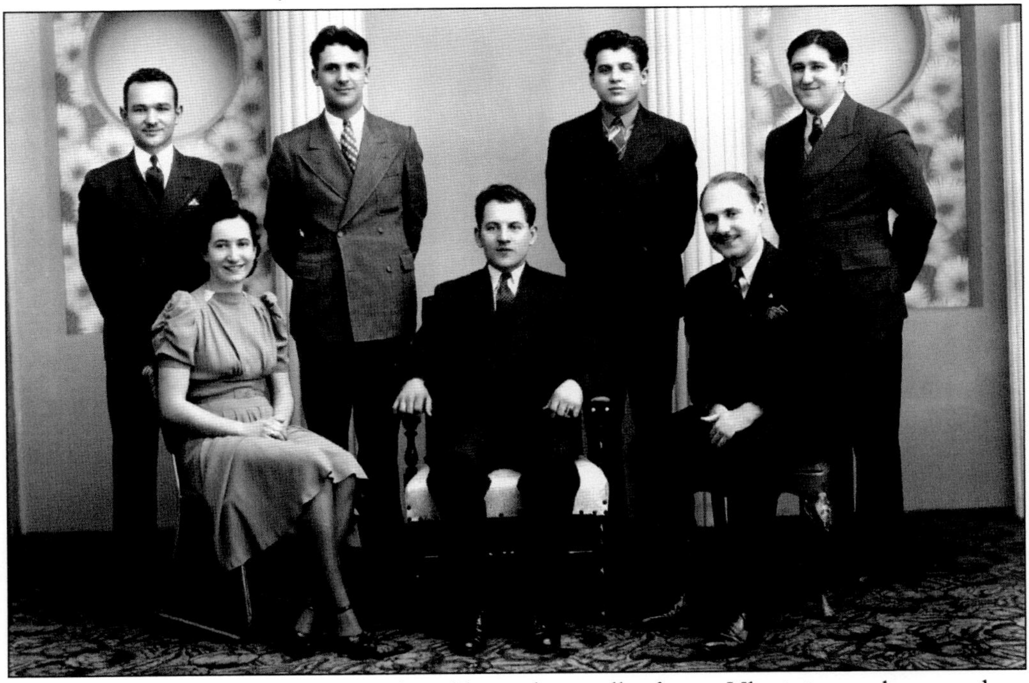

Club Boyan's mission was to undeniably and proudly foster Ukrainian culture and to unquestionably uphold democratic principles. The seated club officers are Nellie Gavriluk, Jack Warrick, and Rudy Rudicoff. Standing are Jimmy Los, Wallace Konicky, Stephen Wichar, and Mike Ogrodnik. (Olga Seniw.)

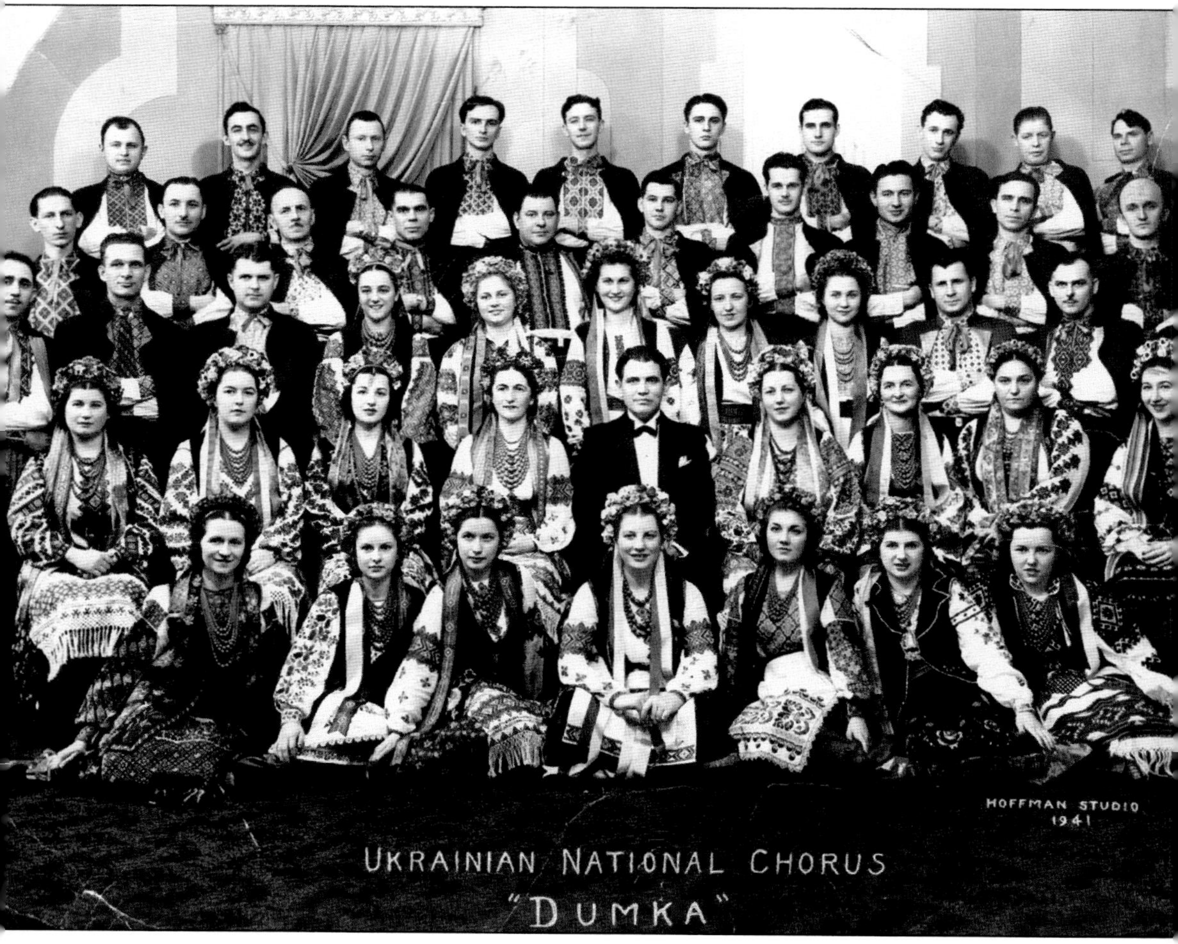

The Ukrainian National Chorus Dumka originated in 1926. Its first and only director, Ivan Atamanetz, did the major part of the work in organizing and training the chorus. His appreciation and love of the Ukrainian folk song has been sustained in his devoted work with the chorus. The members themselves could have no greater inspiration than the radiating enthusiasm of their director. Atamanetz's talented wife, Nadia, also contributed unsparingly of talent, time, and energy to make Dumka an outstanding choral ensemble. Though the chorus was not a professional unit, it appeared frequently with the Detroit Symphony and at the Belle-Isle Band Shell. While one successful engagement led to another, the Dumka singers added the Fox Theater, the Michigan Theater, Ford Symphony Hour, and several seasons of radio engagements to their laurels.

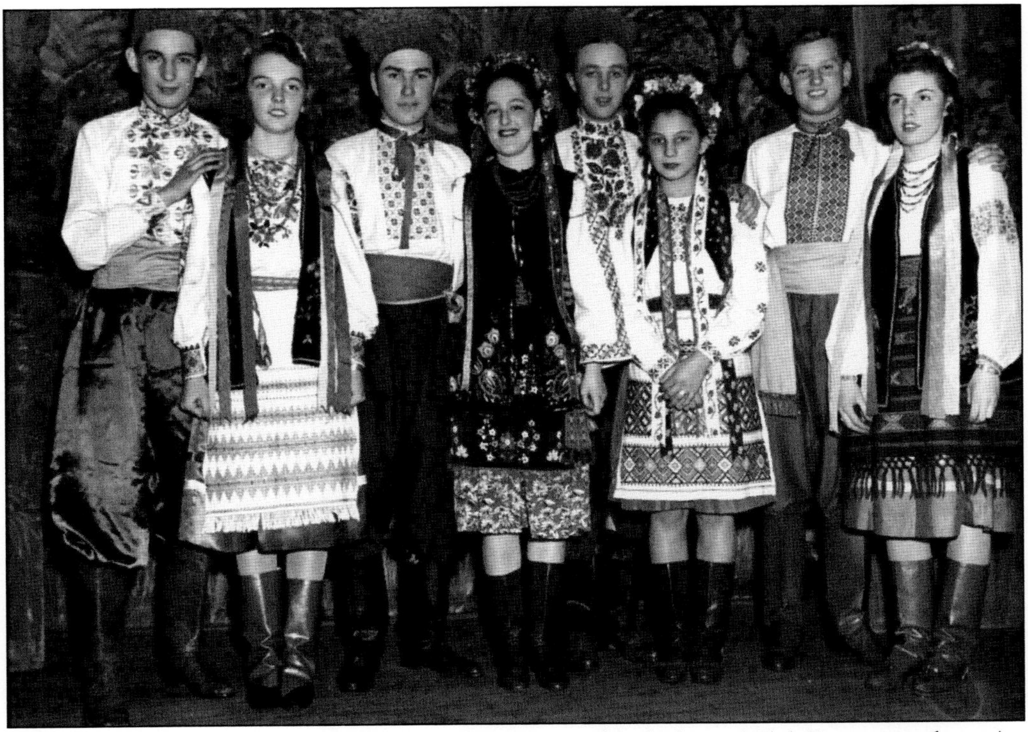

With the intervention of World War II came the inevitable decline of Club Boyan members. An appeal was made to the younger generation, still in their early teens, to carry on the activities of the club. They would come to be known as Club Boyan Juniors. The members are, from left to right, Walter Prowalny, Irene Maximiuk, Emil Onychkevich, Zinovia Marfey, Eddie Holowchak, Olga Tomiak, George Rusnak, and Ann Maximiuk. They are seen here in 1943. (Olga Seniw.)

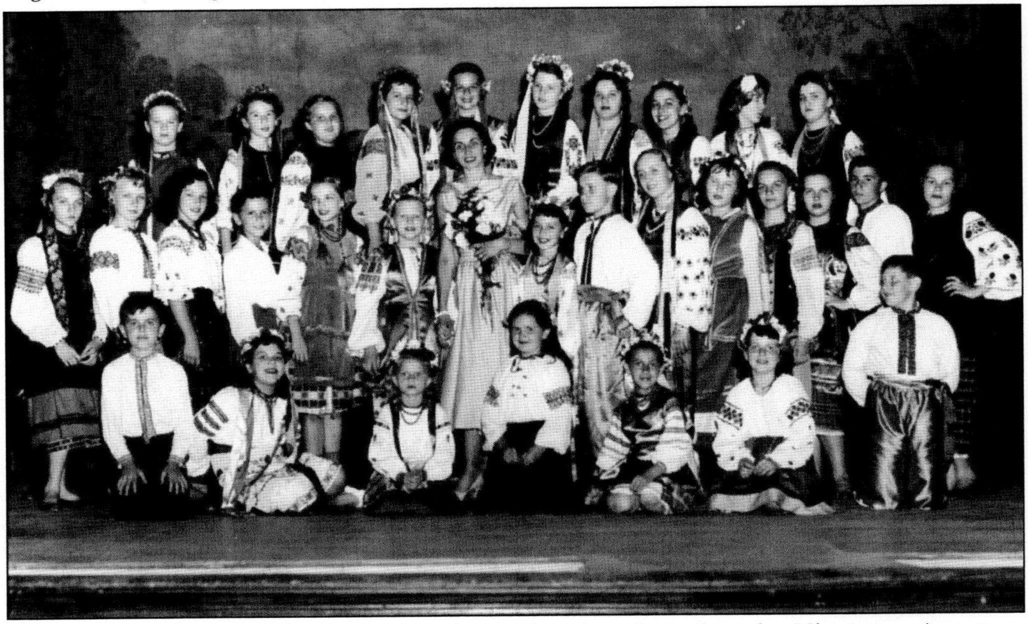

In 1957, the Ukrainian Dance Group rehearsed and performed at the Ukrainian American Center on Carpenter Street. (Marta Kwitkowsky.)

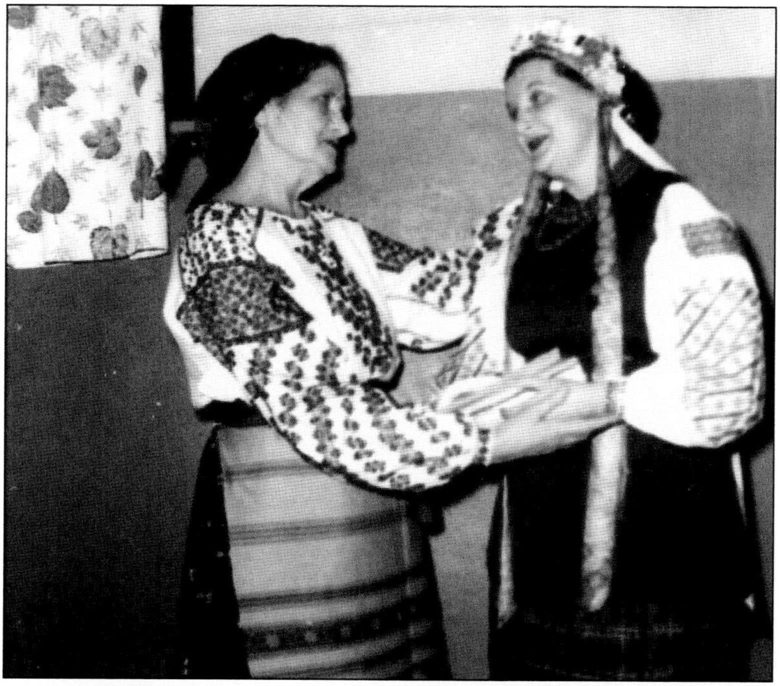

The Ukrainian American Center was home to many dramatic theatrical performances. An unidentified person and Nadia Wichar rehearse their roles for a play in 1958.

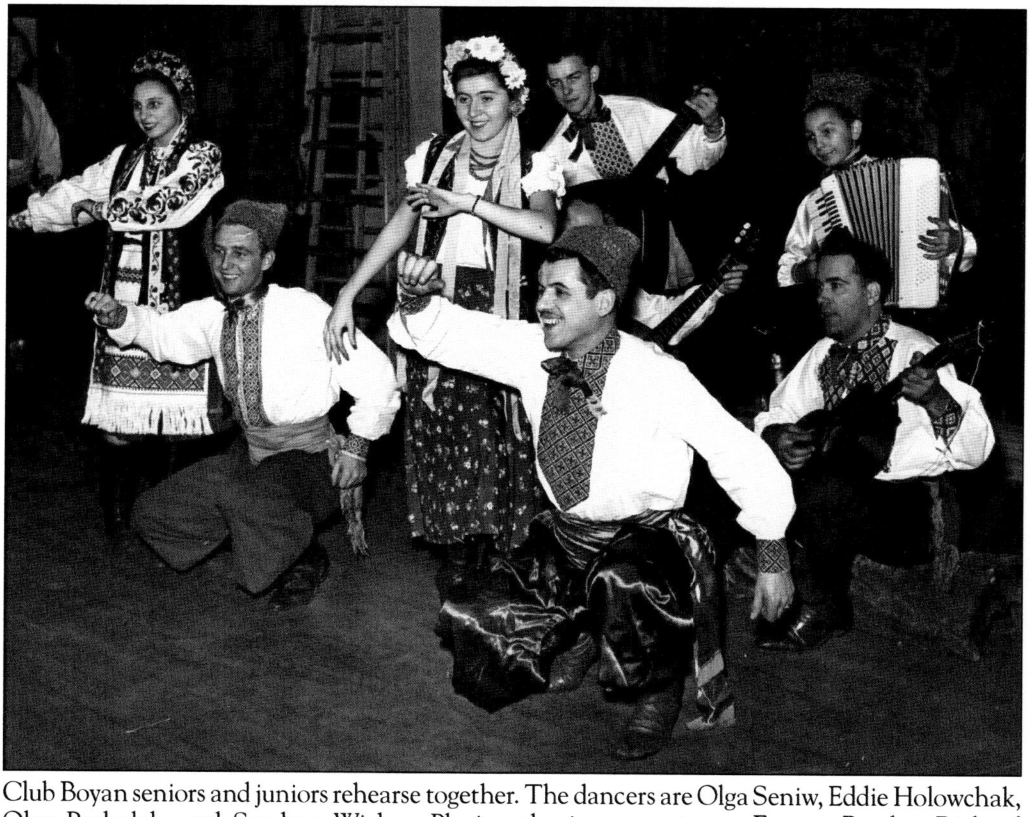

Club Boyan seniors and juniors rehearse together. The dancers are Olga Seniw, Eddie Holowchak, Olga Pacholak, and Stephen Wichar. Playing the instruments are Eugene Bartley, Richard Tomiak, and Sam Mills. (Leo Hulyk.)

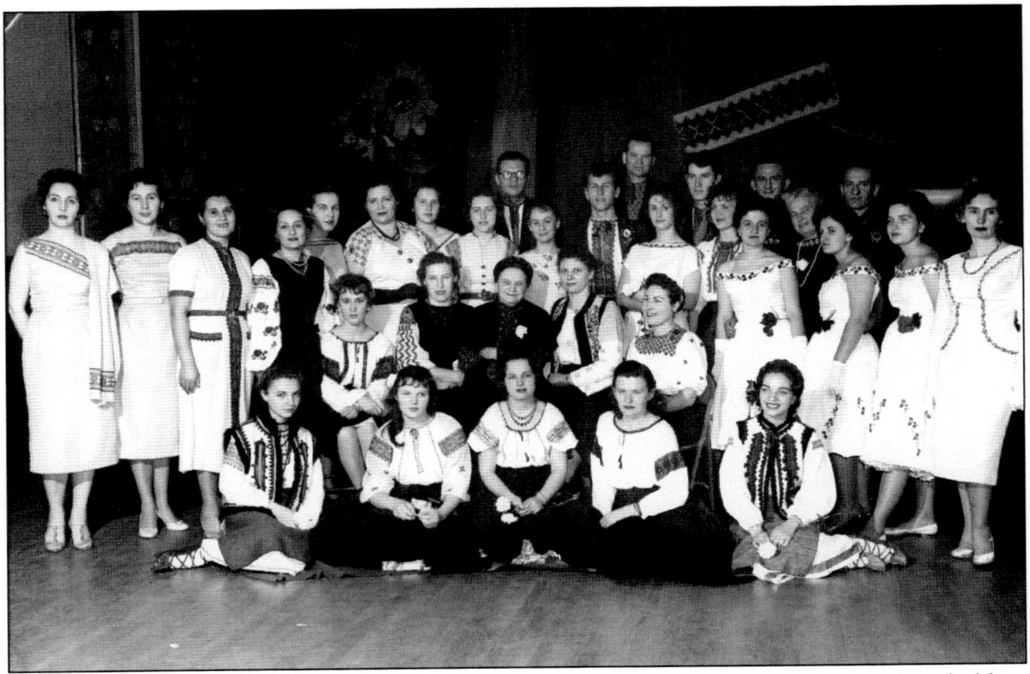

To preserve the art of embroidery, the Ukrainian National Women's League of America held an Embroidery Ball in 1962. Blouses, shirts, dresses, and men's ties were all in competition for the best-embroidered garment. (Roman Maziak.)

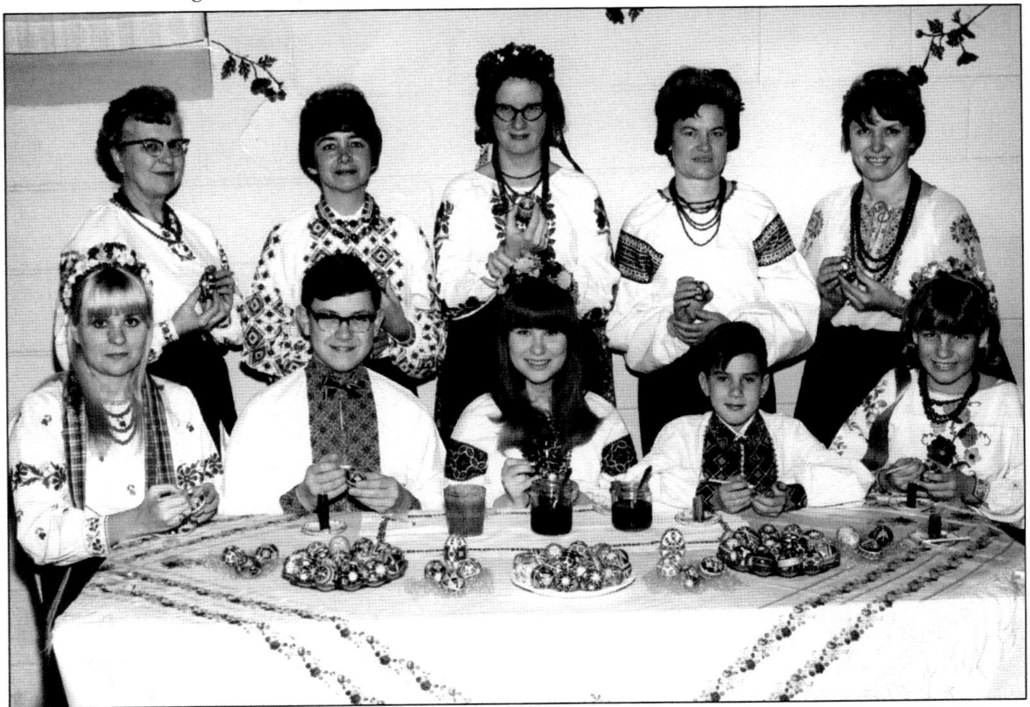

In 1958, Detroit women and children demonstrate the art of making pysanky (Ukrainian Easter eggs). The adults in the back row are, from left to right, Martha Wichorak, Irene Torrence, Nadia Stratelak, Nel Martyn, and Sonice Hulyk. (Leo Hulyk.)

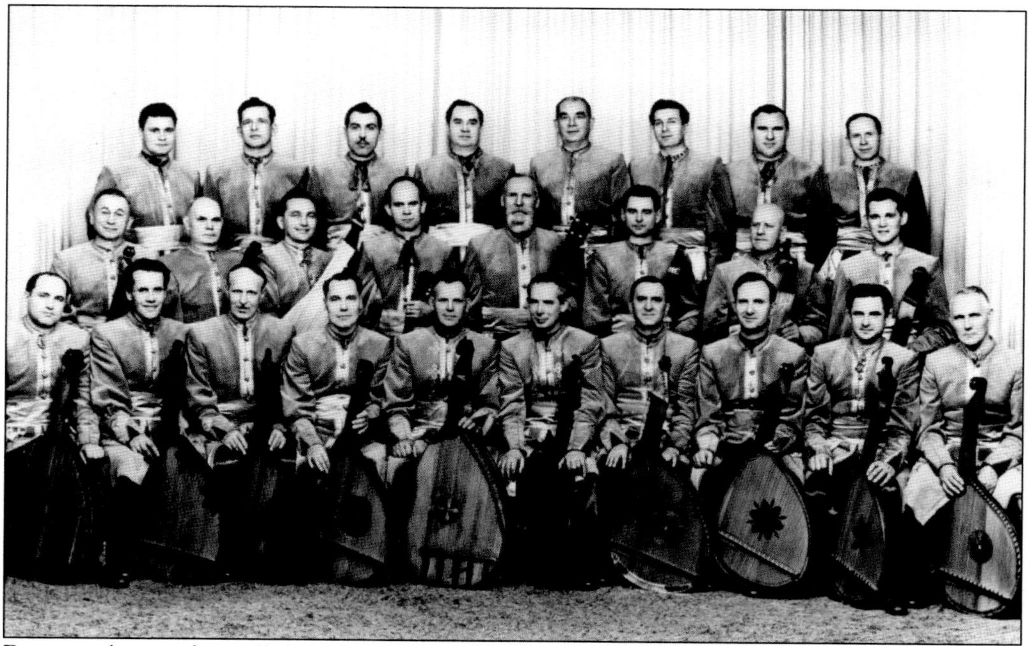

Detroit is honored to call the Ukrainian Bandurist Chorus its own since 1949. After persecution by the Soviets and the Nazis and with the assistance of allied forces, many members of the chorus immigrated to the United States, settling in Detroit. Reorganizing in their new homeland, the ensemble began to flourish worldwide. Their concert tours and numerous recordings were met with rave reviews throughout the world. This image is from around 1958. (Anatoli Murha.)

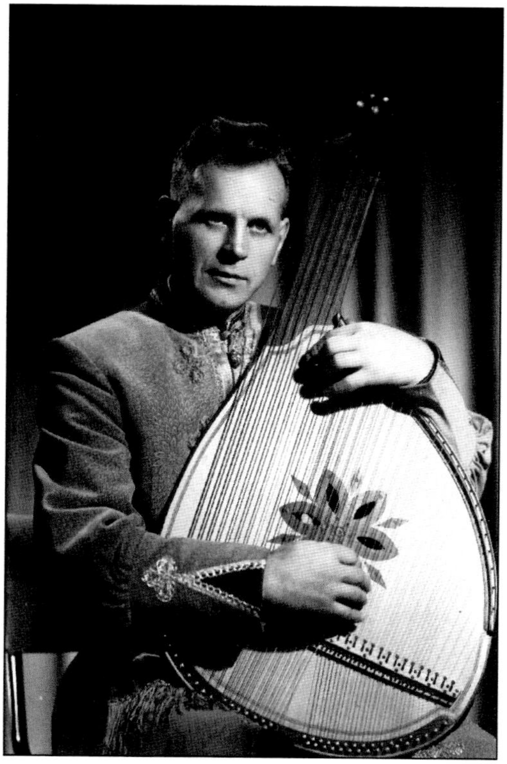

Of the many accomplished conductors of the Ukrainian Bandurist Chorus, Hryhory Kytasty is one of the most well known. As a composer and conductor, his leadership was inspirational to all who came in contact with him. He had a tremendous influence in promoting Ukrainian music and the art of the bandura (the national instrument of Ukraine). He continued his passion with the Ukrainian Bandurist Chorus until his death in 1984. He was laid to rest in Bound Brook, New Jersey, yet his memory continues to live on. (Anatoli Murha.)

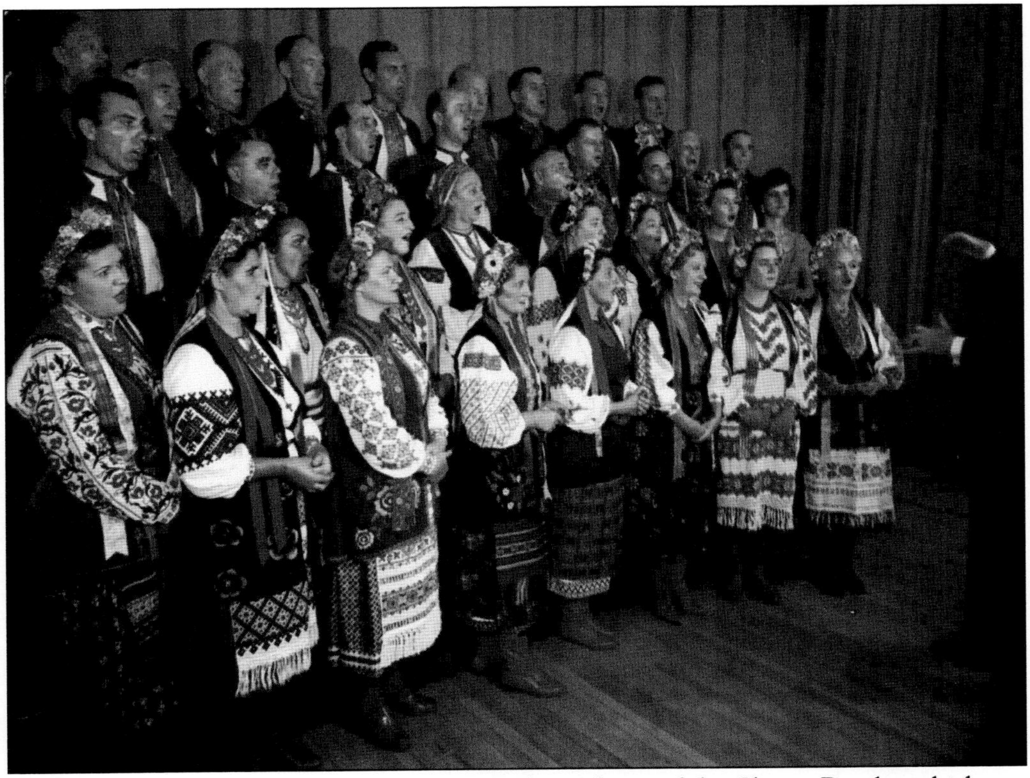

In 1961, a new generation of singers continues the tradition of the Chorus Dumka, which was established in 1926. Founder and director Ivan Atamanetz defined the purpose of the chorus saying, "Our aim is to foster Ukrainian folklore both as a cherished inheritance and as a contribution to American musical culture."

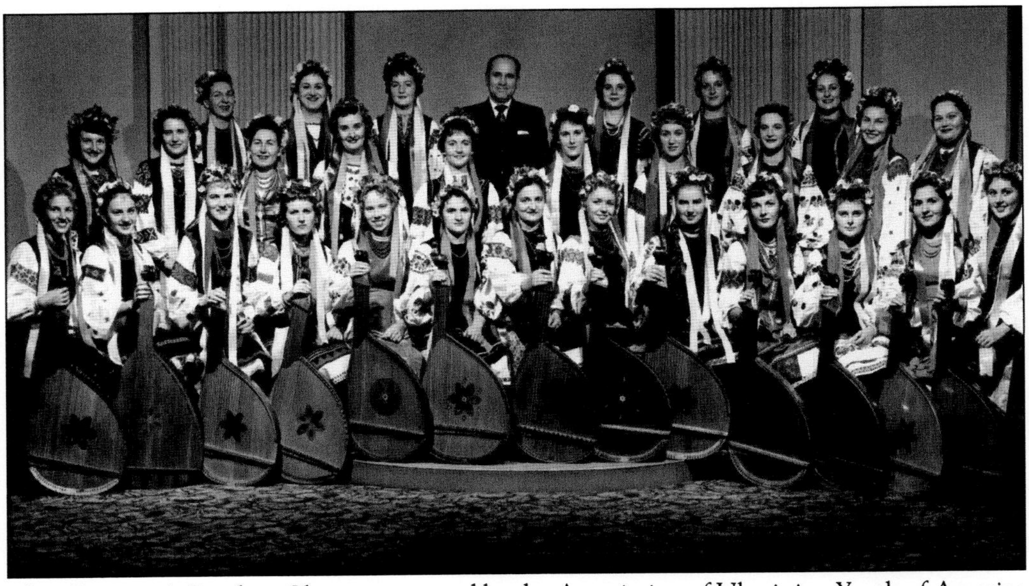

The all women's Bandura Chorus sponsored by the Association of Ukrainian Youth of America (SUMA) and under the direction of Petro Potapenko was an extremely talented ensemble based in Detroit. (Chrystyna Kozak.)

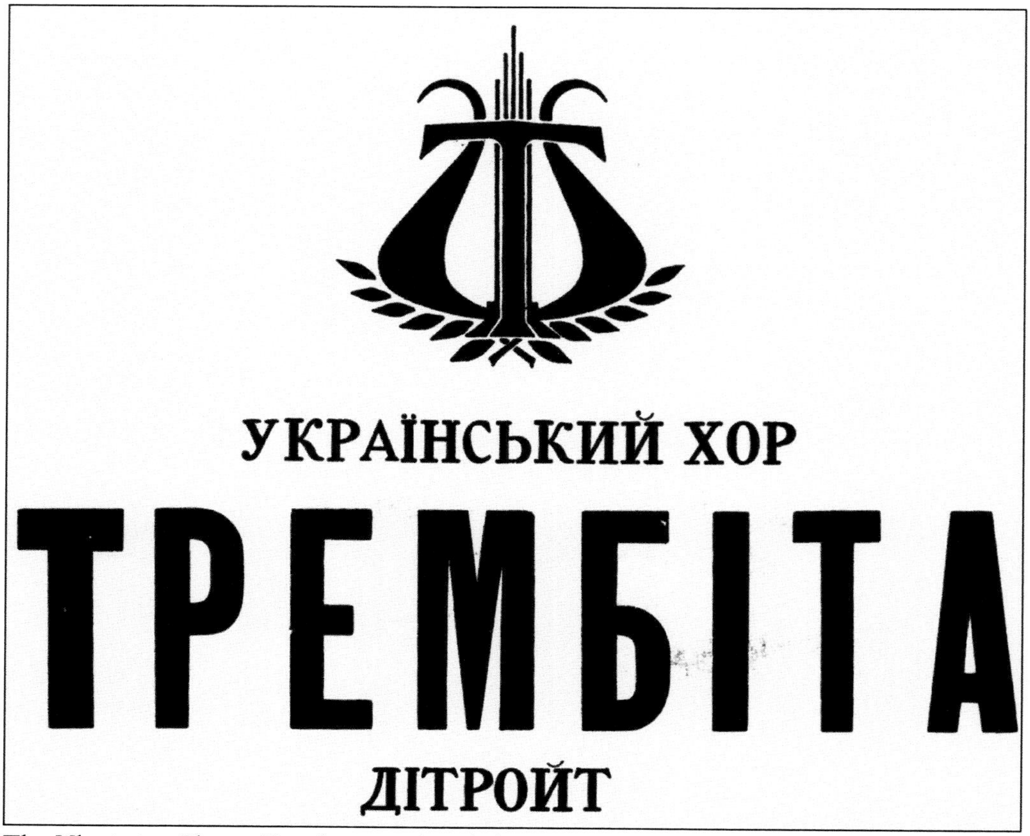

The Ukrainian Chorus Trembita was founded in 1957. Its initiator and head of the organizing committee was Wolodymyr Dyhdalo. In 1958, the mixed chorus was formulated, and in 1959, the female group was organized.

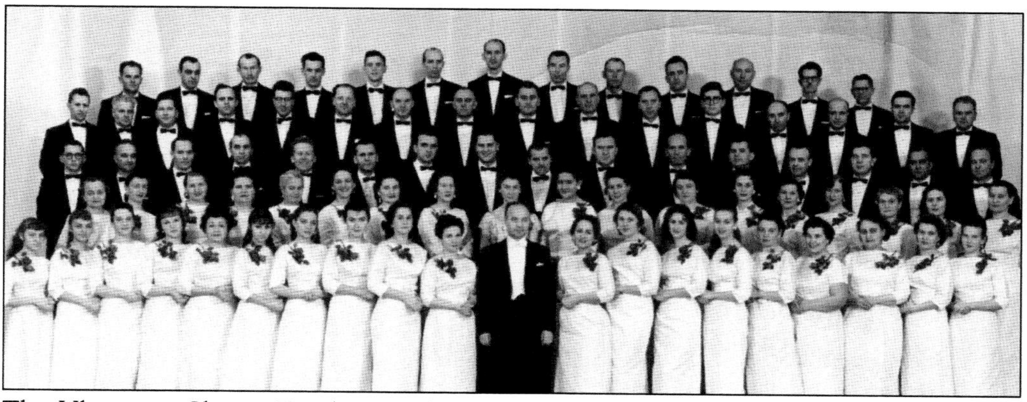

The Ukrainian Chorus Trembita, under the direction of Professor Kyrylo Cependa, had a membership of over 100 voices. During its first eight years of operation, the chorus had over 50 appearances in Detroit, Chicago, and Toronto. This image is from the 1960s.

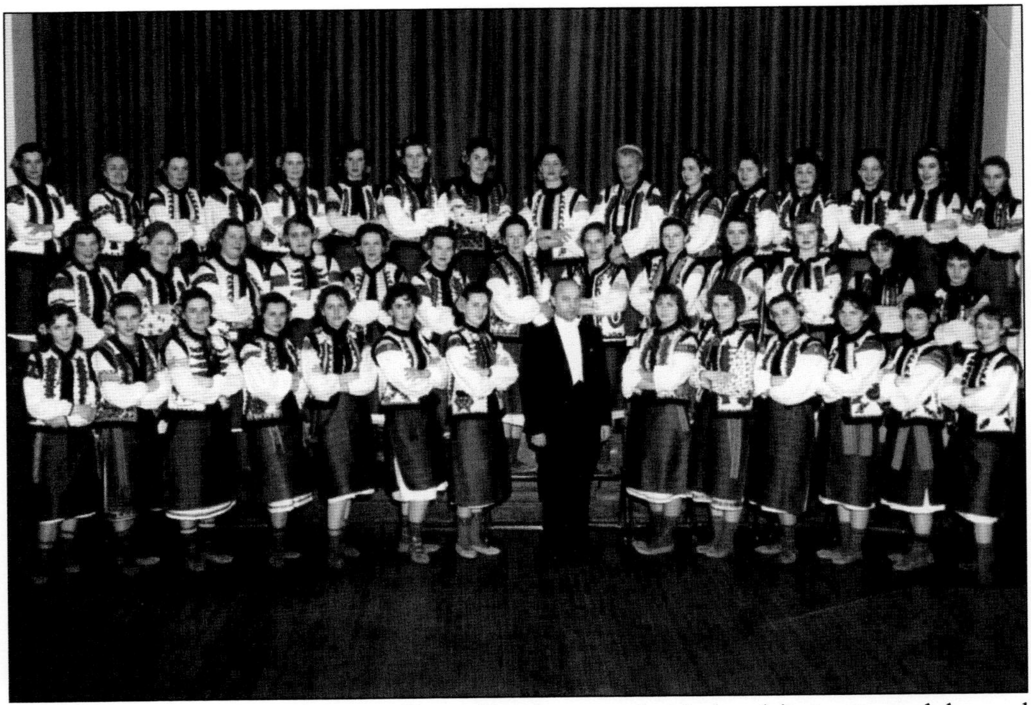

The female division of the Ukrainian Chorus Trembita served with choral distinction and charmed many audiences in their colorful, native Hutzul costumes. This image is from the 1960s.

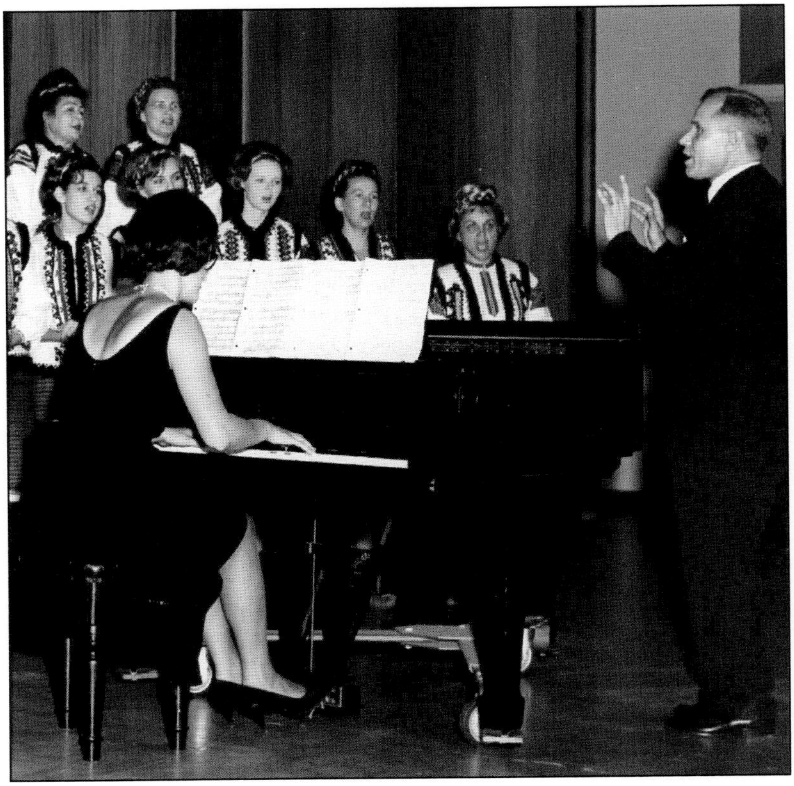

In later years, Dr. Bohdan Kushnir, an accomplished musicologist, directed the Trembita mixed chorus with accompaniment by Olgy Dubriwnyj-Solovey. Yaroslaw Fylypiw, who was previously a director of several choruses in Ukraine, conducted the male Trembita Chorus. This image is from 1965. (Olga Solovey.)

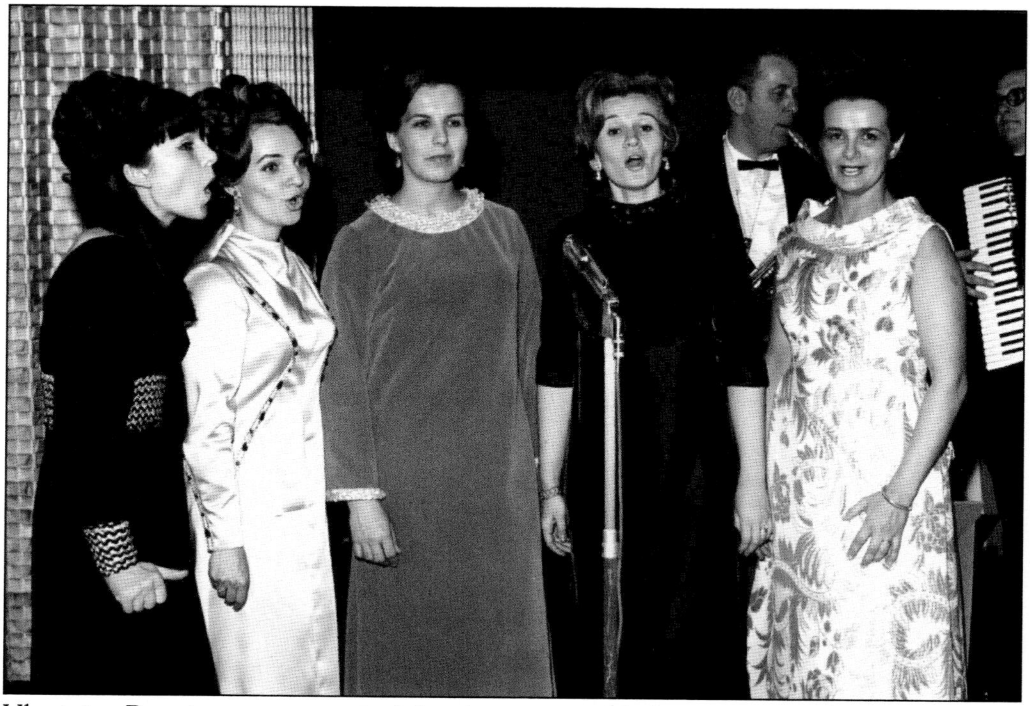

Ukrainian Detroit women organized the singing ensemble Luna in 1968. They are Christina Semeniuk-Lypeckyj, Myroslava Sawchuk-Stefaniuk, Myroslawa Makar-Mychalovych, Vera Laschyk-Andrushkiw, and Nadia Jurkiw Lawryn. (Vera Andrushkiw.)

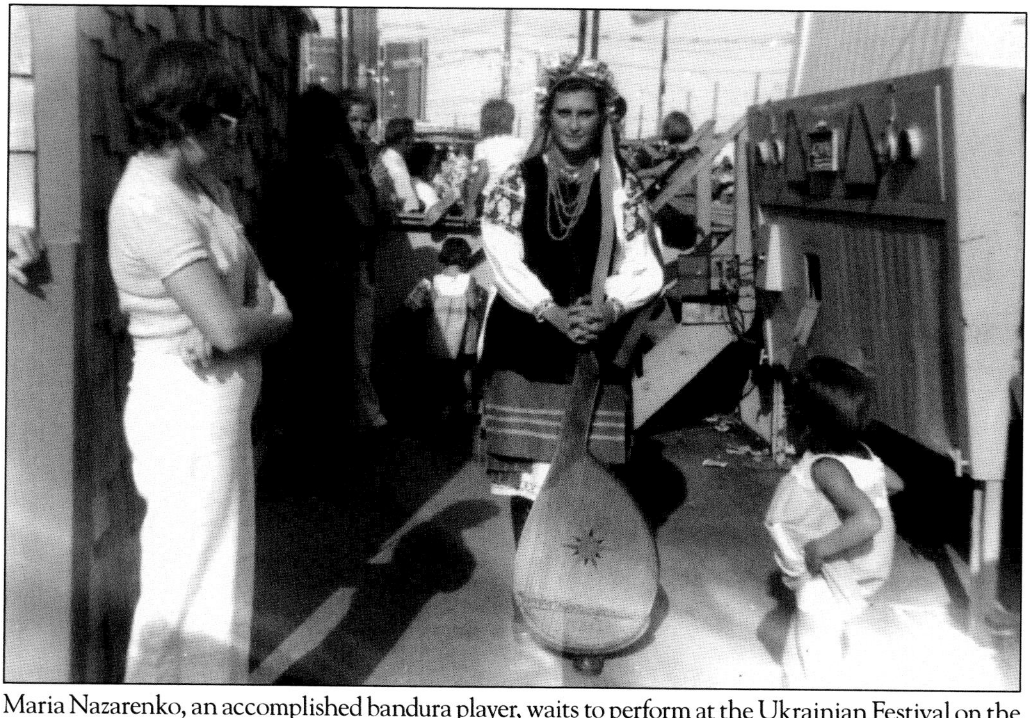

Maria Nazarenko, an accomplished bandura player, waits to perform at the Ukrainian Festival on the Detroit riverfront in 1979. The riverfront was home to many ethnic festivals. (Maria Nazarenko.)

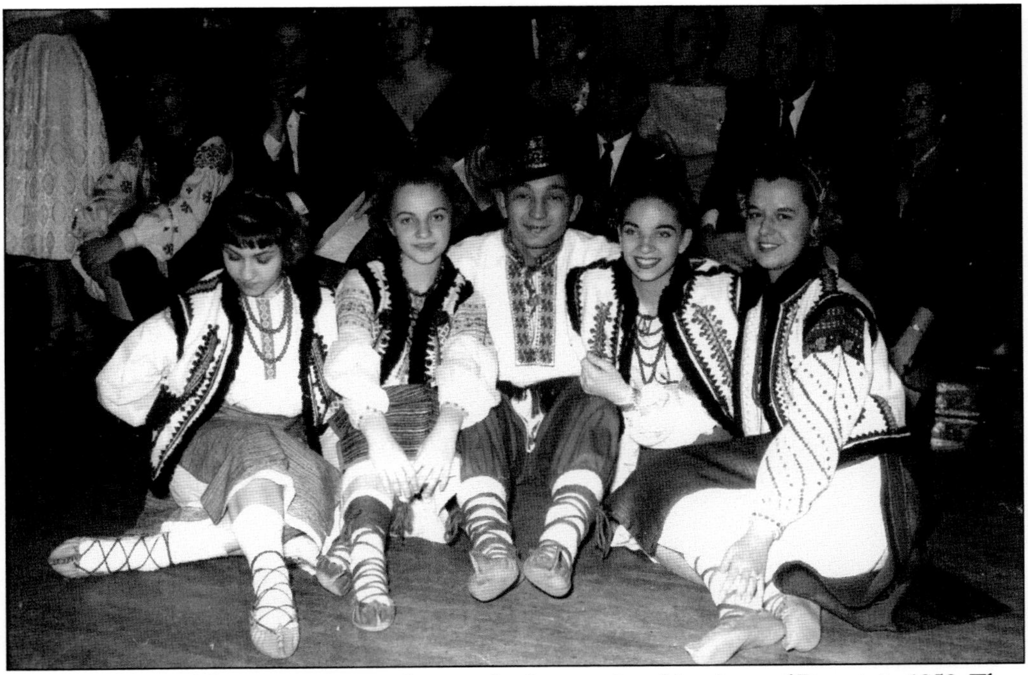

Ukrainian Hutzul dancers wait to perform at the International Institute of Detroit in 1958. They are Luba Sawchuk, Myroslava Sawchuk, Richard Tomiak, Christina Semeniuk, and Johanna von Draginda-Kulchesky. (Ukrainian Museum.)

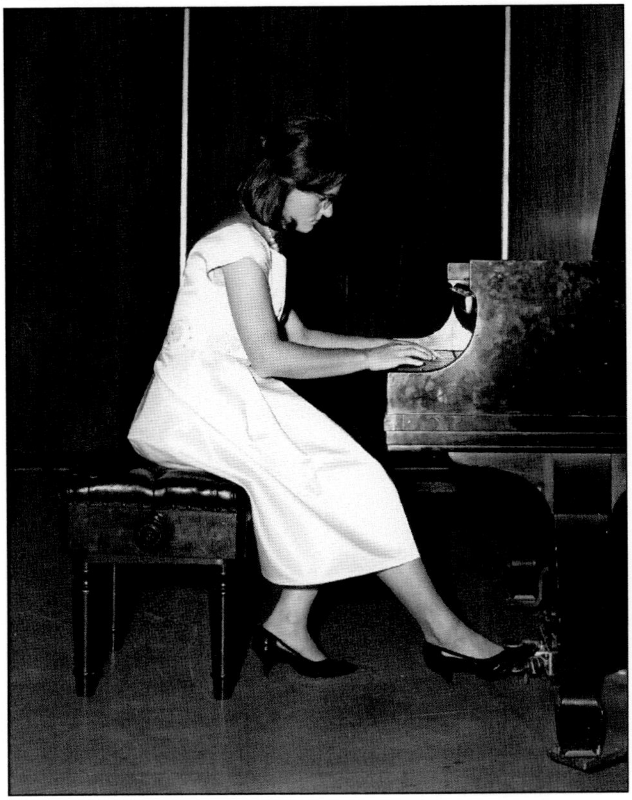

Maria Lonchyna-Lisowsky, Ukrainian Music Institute of America/Detroit, performs at the Day of Ukrainian Culture, Community Arts Auditorium, Wayne State University, in 1965. As an accomplished musician, she has made major contributions to Ukrainian culture in the Detroit area. (Maria Lonchyna-Lisowsky.)

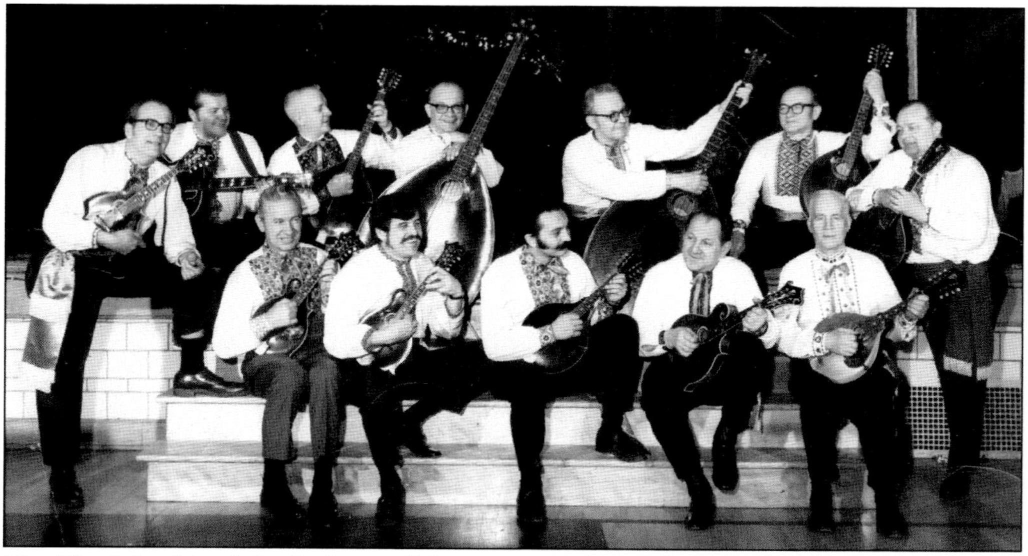

The Ukrainian Mandolin Orchestra Kobzar originated in 1958 for the purpose of perpetuating and achieving success in the field of Ukrainian music. Sam Mills, pictured on the far left, was the director of the group. The Kobzar Orchestra would go on to entertain the community at numerous concerts and functions. They also recorded two albums.

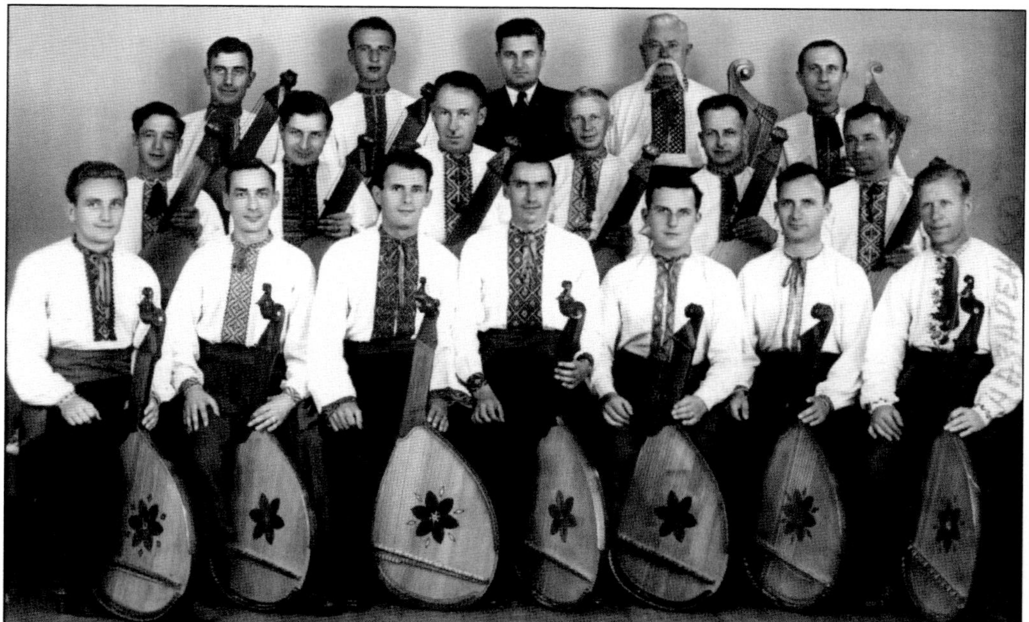

The Leontovych Bandurist Capella male choir was established in the displaced persons camp in Germany in 1946. Hryhory Nazarenko later directed the choir. Many members of this choir would later immigrate to the United States and become members of the Ukrainian Bandurist Chorus. (Maria Nazarenko.)

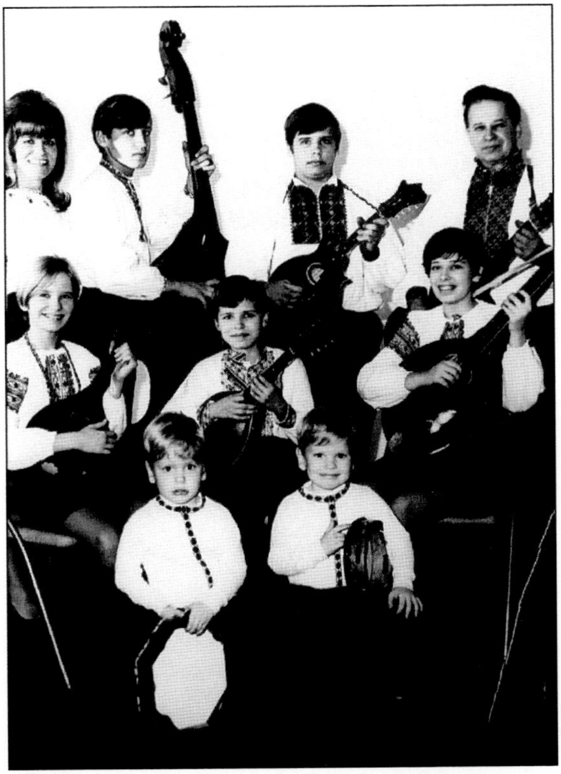

Jacob Ondusky organized his entire family to form Singing Strings, a musical ensemble that would entertain numerous audiences. The members are, from left to right, (first row) twins Tim and Terry; (second row) Lily, Jake, and Mary; (third row) Lily (mother), Ivan, Nick, and Jacob (father). (Lily Ondusky-Litynskyj.)

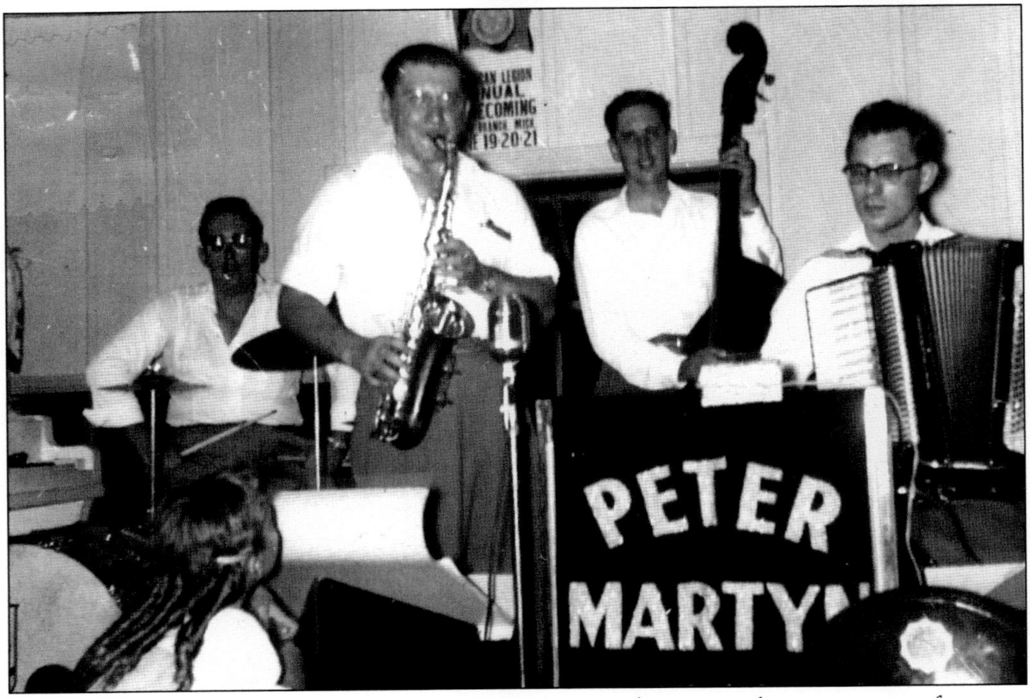

Peter Martyn and his Orchestra were responsible for providing musical entertainment for many Ukrainian events. Members of the Ukrainian community have fond memories of dancing to favorite Ukrainian melodies late into the evening. (Cathy Whitfield.)

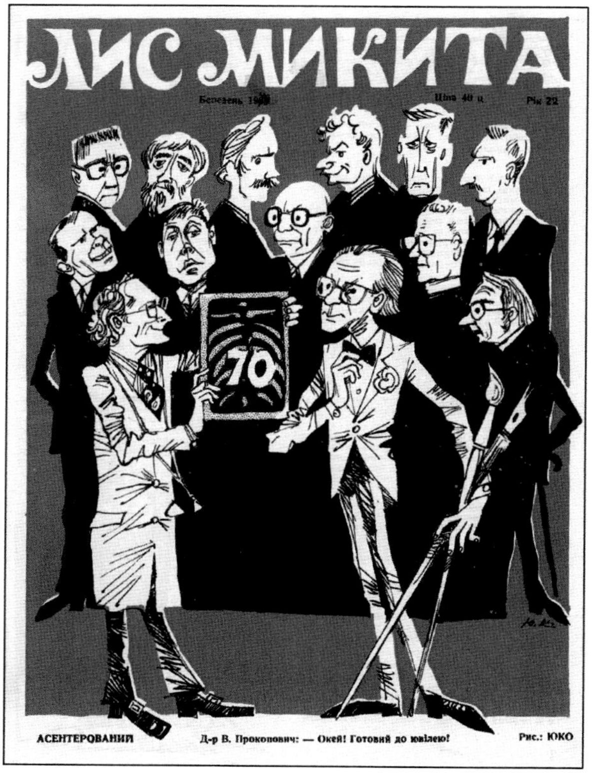

Edward Kozak was the editor and illustrator of the satirical periodical *Fox Mykyta*. The cover of the March 1969 issue depicts members of the Detroit Ukrainian community presenting Kozak with a humorous commemoration for his seventieth birthday. (Lydia Kolodchin.)

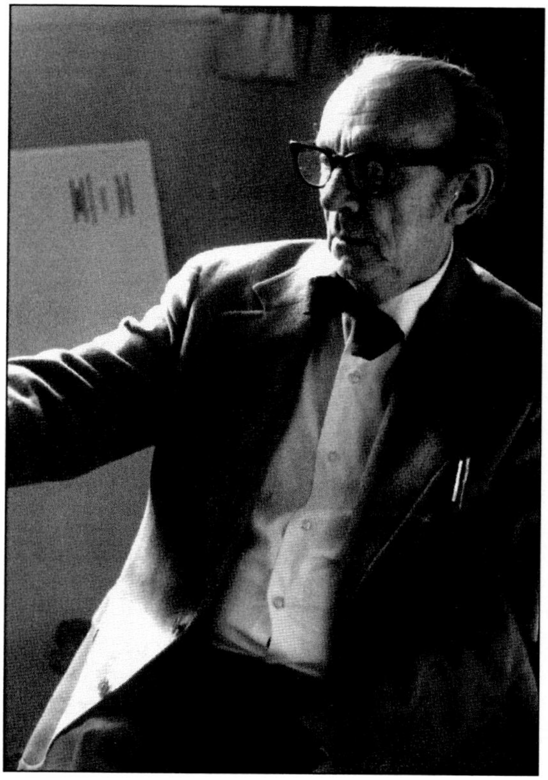

Edward Kozak, who went by the name "Eko," immigrated to the United States with his family after World War II and settled in the Detroit area. The remarkable talents he shared with the Detroit community were those of a painter, caricaturist, illustrator, humorist, editor, publisher, and author. He was also a film animator and an artist for children's television programs. His legacy will be appreciated for generations to come. (Lydia Kolodchin.)

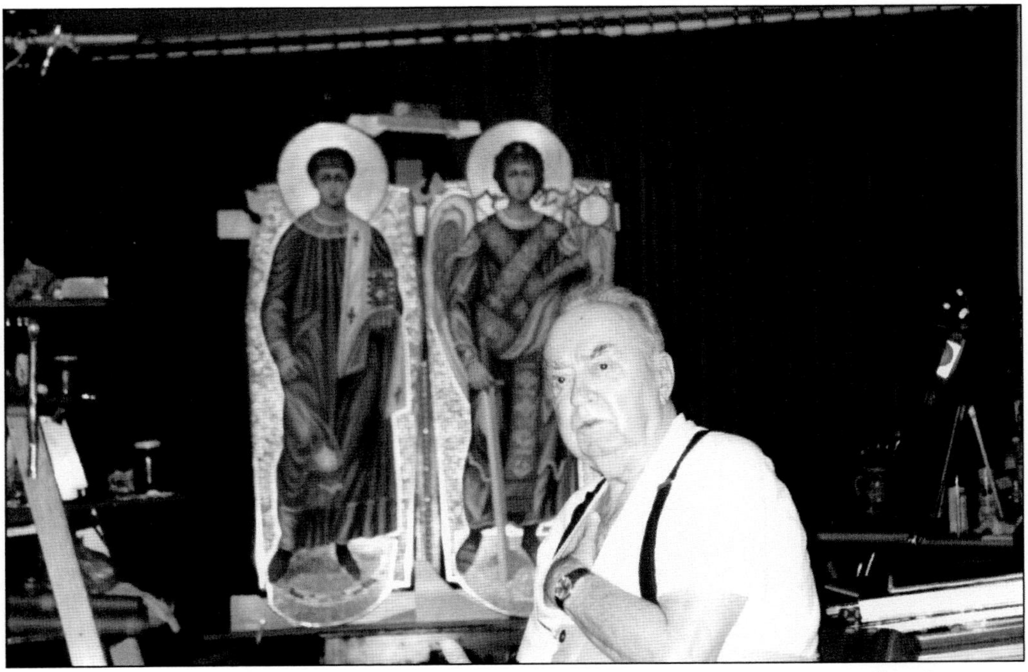

Renowned artist Mychajlo Dmytrenko is best known for his portraits, especially of women, graphic art, and illustrations, as well as icon and mural painting. He was distinguished for his design of mosaics and stained glass. Dmytrenko's iconography talents can be seen in many churches across the United States. Locally the Immaculate Conception Ukrainian Catholic Church in Hamtramck houses some of his best work. (Bohdan Nehaniv.)

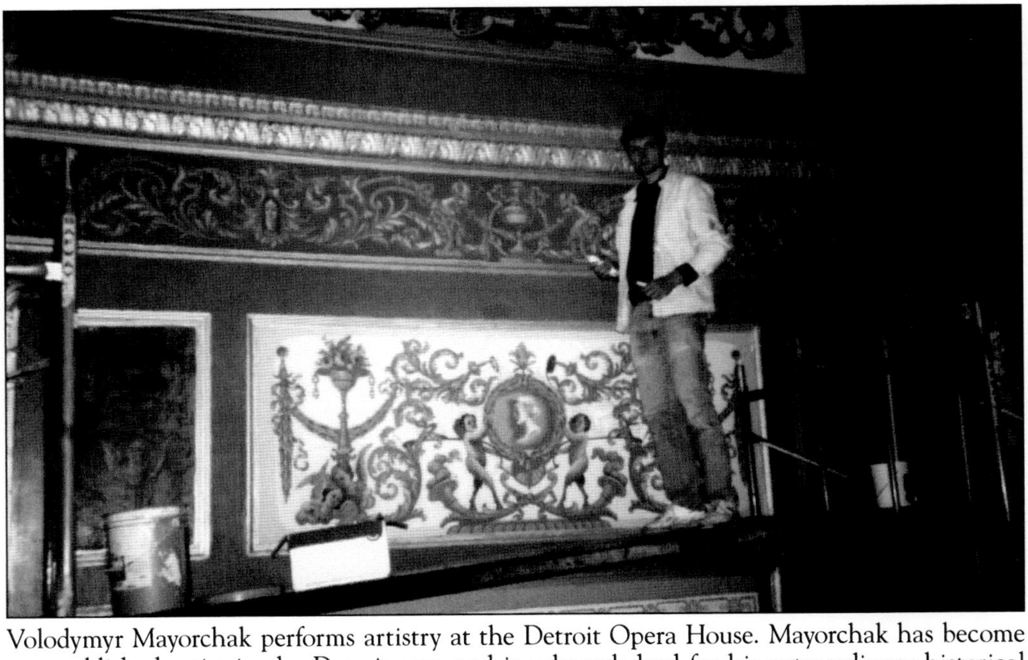

Volodymyr Mayorchak performs artistry at the Detroit Opera House. Mayorchak has become an established artist in the Detroit area and is acknowledged for his extraordinary historical Ukrainian mural, which appears on the back wall of the Ukrainian Heritage Room at Wayne State University. This image is from around 2001. (Olga Solovey.)

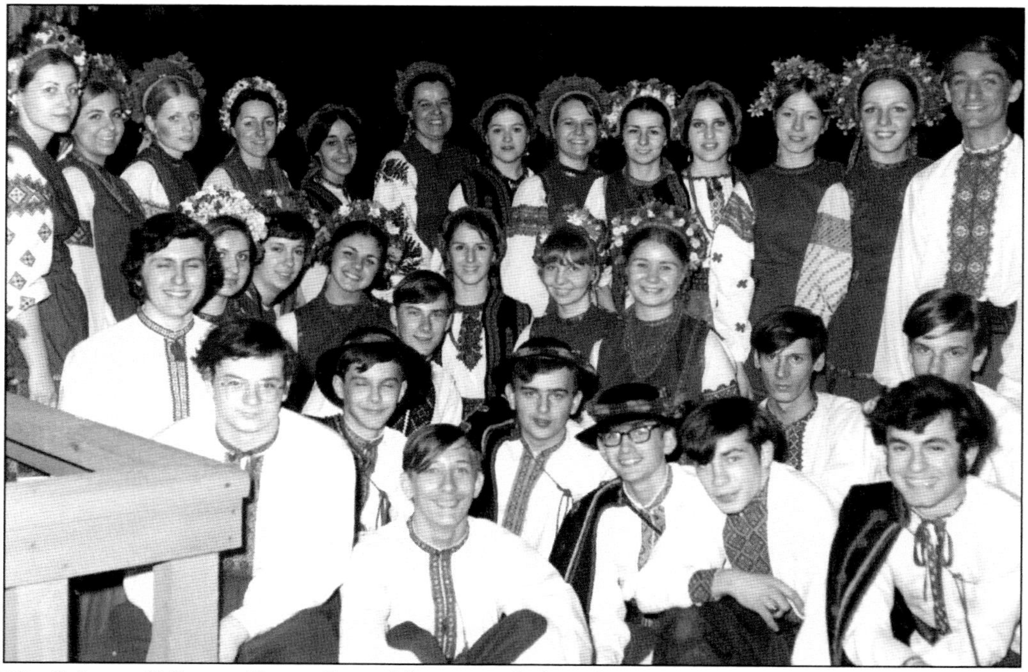

The Echoes of Ukraine Dance Ensemble pose with their director, Joanna von Draginda-Kulchesky. The dance group was well received by Detroit audiences as well as across the United States and Canada. This image is from the 1980s. (Joanna von Draginda-Kulchesky/Ukrainian Museum.)

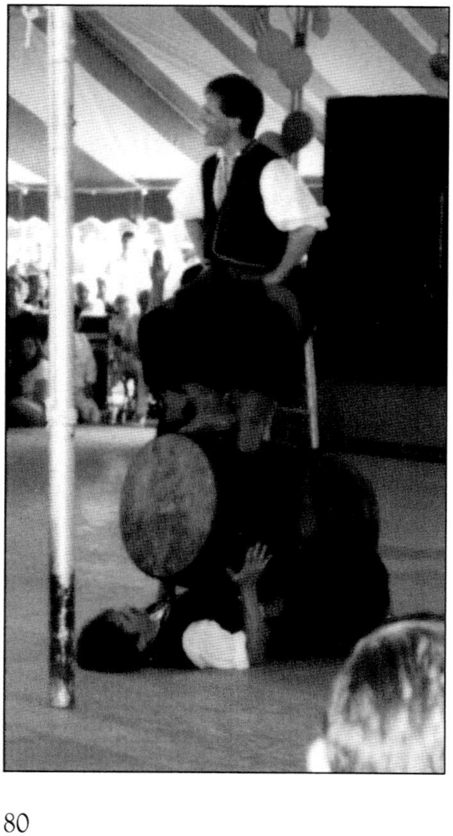

Echoes of Ukraine dancers perform the traditional barrel dance, showing off their athletic prowess in a humorous manner. They performed at the Ukrainian Sunflower Festivals on the grounds of St. Josaphat Ukrainian Catholic Church in Warren. (Marie Zarycky.)

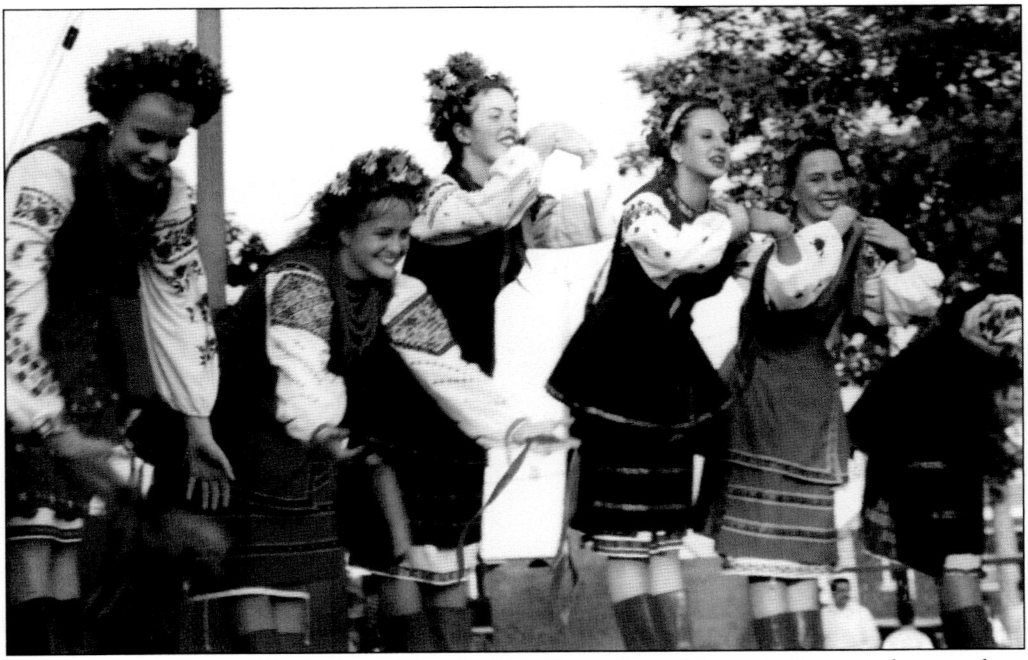

Marta Hnatiuk, Larisa Hotra, Anya Maziak, Lesia Baranyk, and Myrosia Stepnowska, members of the Echos of Ukraine Dance Ensemble, perform the traditional "pryvit" at the Sunflower Festival. This dance opens the program welcoming the audience. (Roman Maziak.)

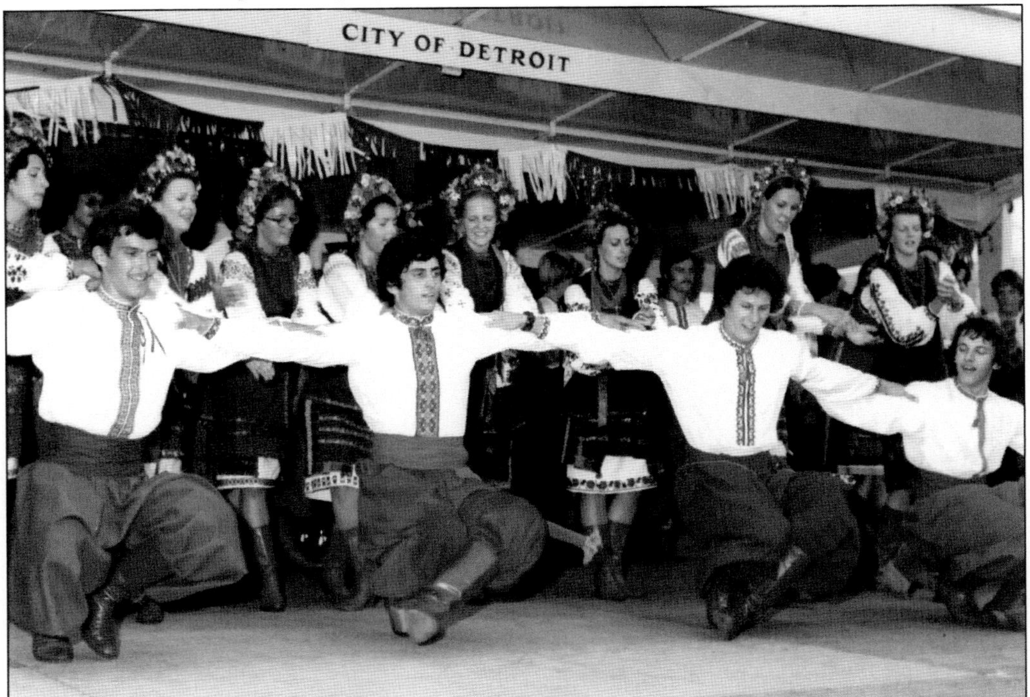

The Ukrainian Festival at Hart Plaza in Detroit features the Echoes of Ukraine dancers performing the grand finale selection, the Hopak. This image is from the 1970s. (Johanna von Draginda-Kulchesky.)

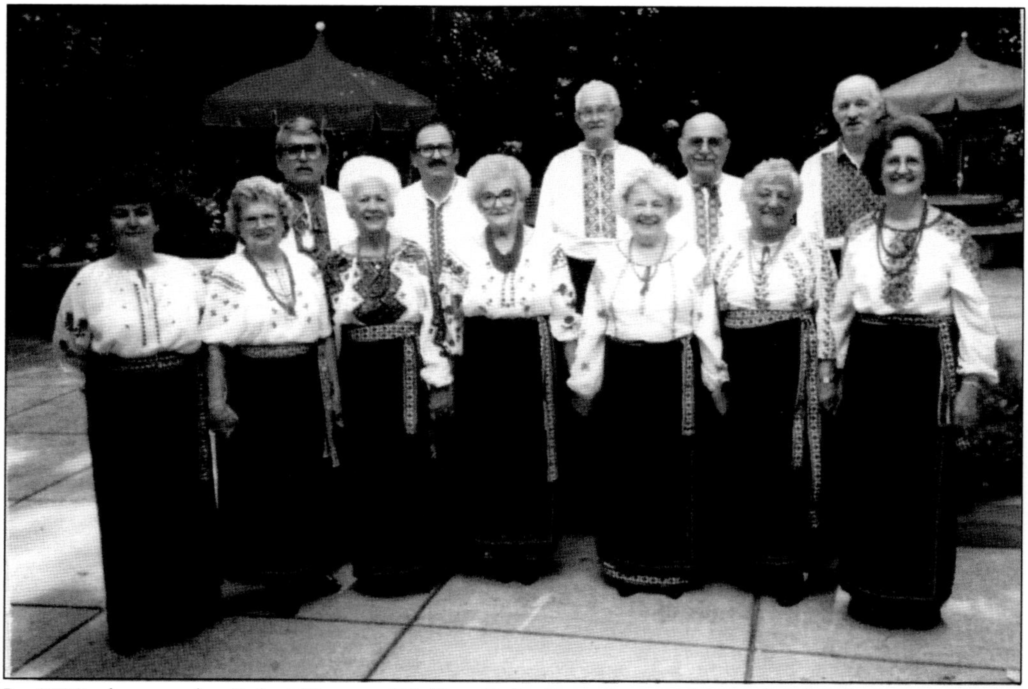

In 1980, the popular Zoloti Dzvony (Golden Bells Song Ensemble), under the direction of Olga Dubriwnyj-Solovey, was composed of seniors who entertained with an informal style of singing. The original singers in the front row are Christine Shumeyko, Donia Demray, Justine Nelligan, Nadia Wichar, Anne Strokon, Elsie Dodson, and Olga Dubriwnyj-Solovey, director. In the back row are Stephen M. Wichar, John Melnyk, John Strokon, John Dodson, and A. J. Nelligan.

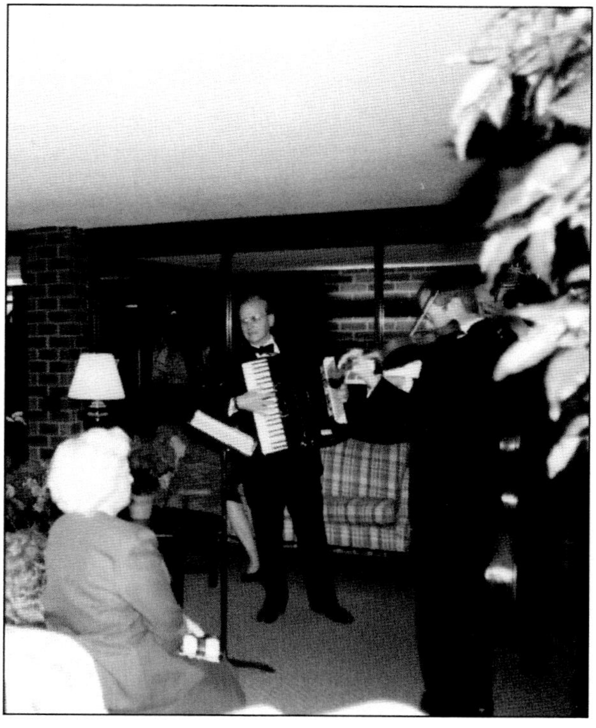

Ukrainian musician Stephen Koltyk entertains guests at the Ukrainian Village during an anniversary celebration. His masterful skills on the accordion have entertained area residents for decades. This image is from the 1990s.

Christina Romana Lypeckyj performed extensively as a mezzo-soprano in the United States, Canada, Italy, and Ukraine. Her engagements have been with various symphony orchestras and opera companies including the Michigan Opera Theater. She appeared as Carmen in *Carmen*, Azucena in *Il Trovatore*, Amneris in *Aida*, Dorabella in *Cosi Fan Tutte*, Charlotta in *Werther*, and others. This image is from around 1965. (Lubomyr Lypeckyj.)

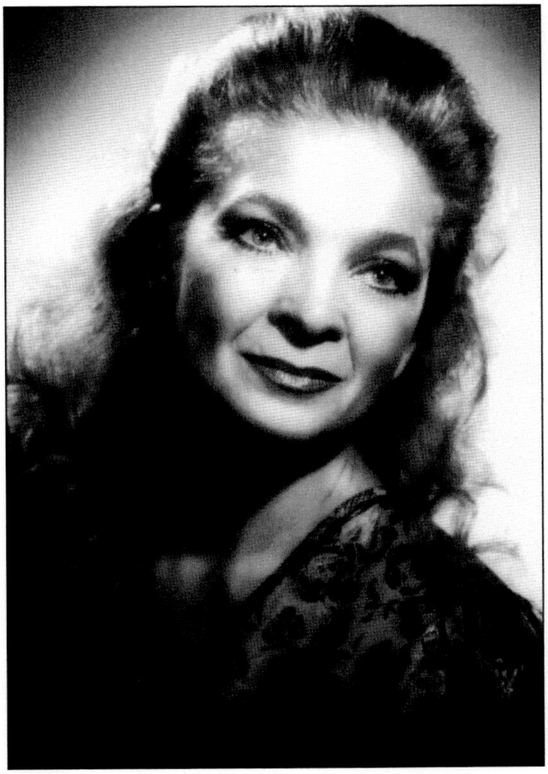

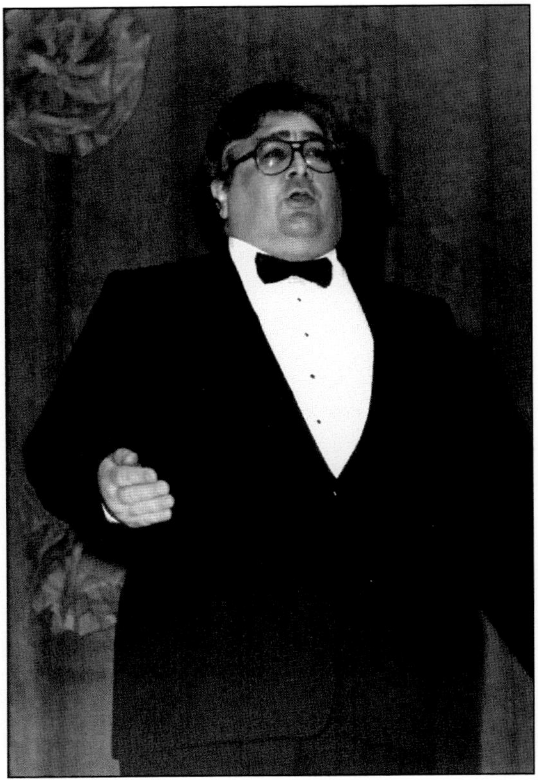

Jarema Cisaruk was born in Ukraine and immigrated to Detroit in 1949. He became a soloist for the Trembita Chorus of Detroit, and was also the leading baritone soloist for the Ukrainian Bandurist Chorus. Performing with the Michigan Opera Theater and the Detroit Symphony Orchestra increased his popularity in the Ukrainian community. Recordings of the Ukrainian Bandurist Chorus also featured Cisaruk. This image is from 1993. (Olga Solovey.)

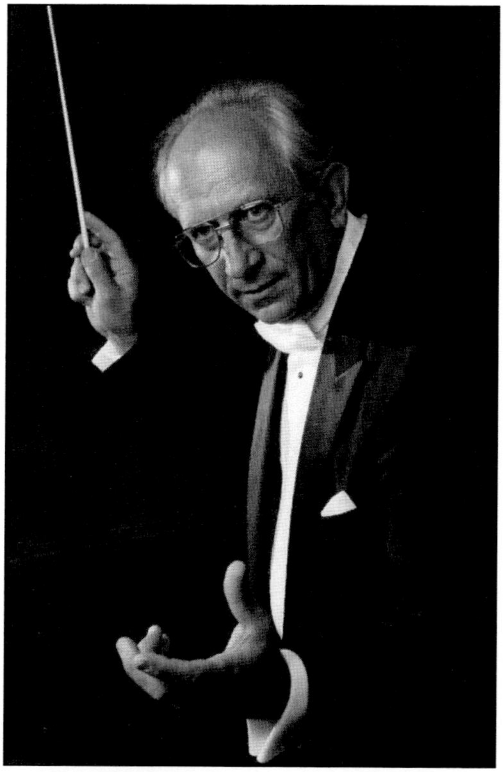

Volodymyr Shesiuk, world-famous Ukrainian conductor, received his training in Ukraine. He was the conductor of the Lviv National Opera and Ballet Theater of Ukraine and the Lviv Philharmonic Symphony Orchestra. Maestro Shesiuk has a wide reputation as a conductor of opera, ballet, and symphony. In Detroit, he is best known as the conductor of the Livonia Symphony Orchestra. This image is from 2008. (Olga Solovey.)

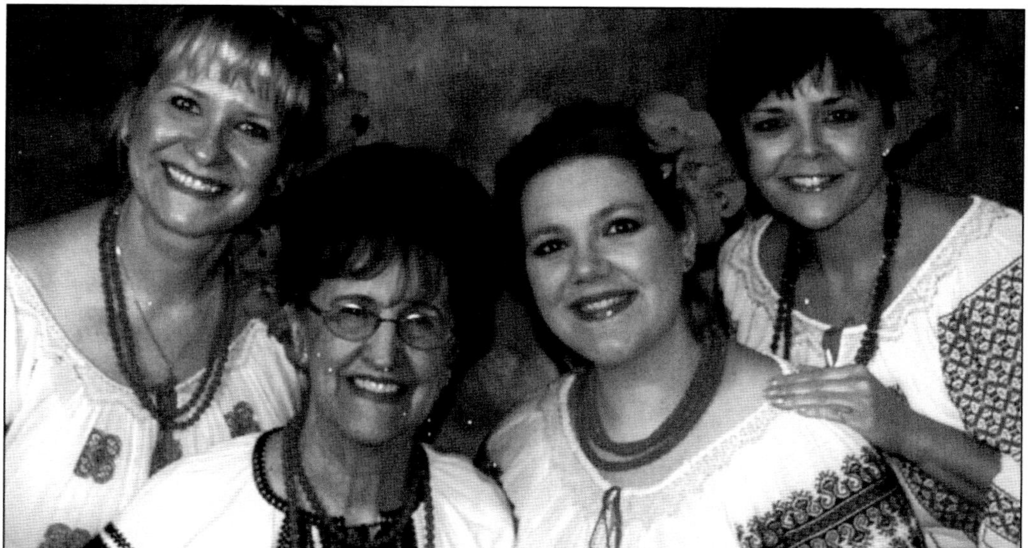

The Soloveyky (nightingales) are Lily Litynskyj, alto; Olga Dubriwnyj-Solovey, director; Kristie Olszewski, second soprano; and Natalka Maruszczak, first soprano. American born, these women embrace the spirit of Ukraine through song. Their wish is that all people experience the captivating essence of their culture. As musical director, Olga Solovey has played an integral part in the Ukrainian community for over 50 years. Not only is she an accomplished pianist, she also skillfully arranges musical compositions to suit the talents of her singers. This image is from 2008. (Lily Litynskyj.)

Four

TAKING A STAND

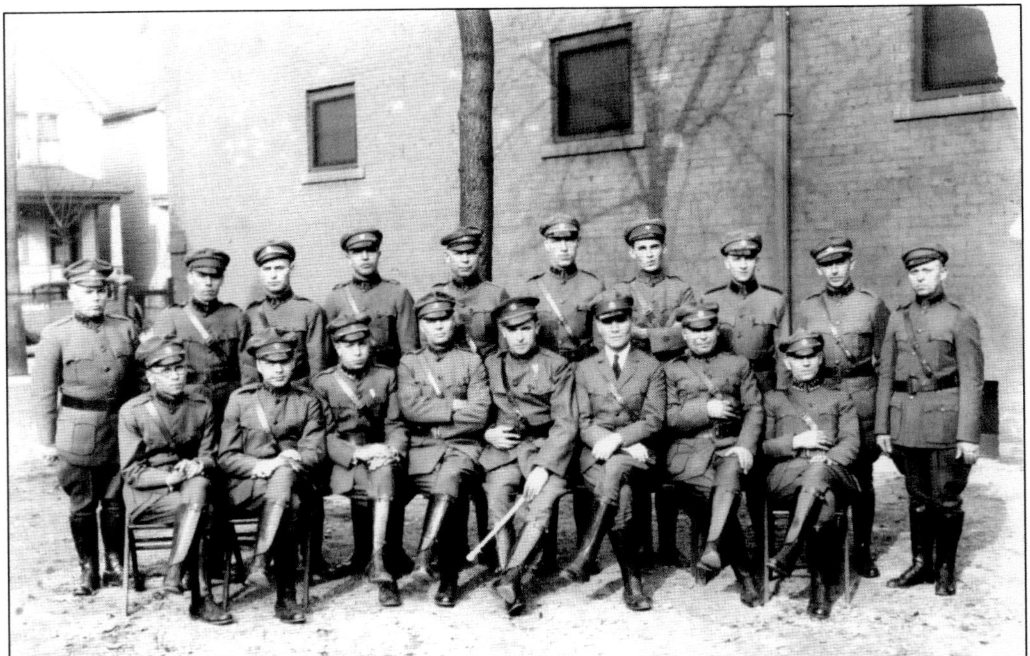

The members of the Fourth Hetman Division commemorate the event of the Ukrainian forces takeover of Lviv on November 1, 1918. This photograph was taken on Grayling Street in Hamtramck on November 3, 1929. The Hetman Organization of America evolved from the original United Hetman Organization comprised of immigrants, many of whom were former soldiers in Ukraine during World War I. They were patriotic people who desired the restoration of the Hetman state for Ukraine under Peter Skoropadsky. They stressed respect for God, country, the Hetman, work, and order. (Ukrainian Museum.)

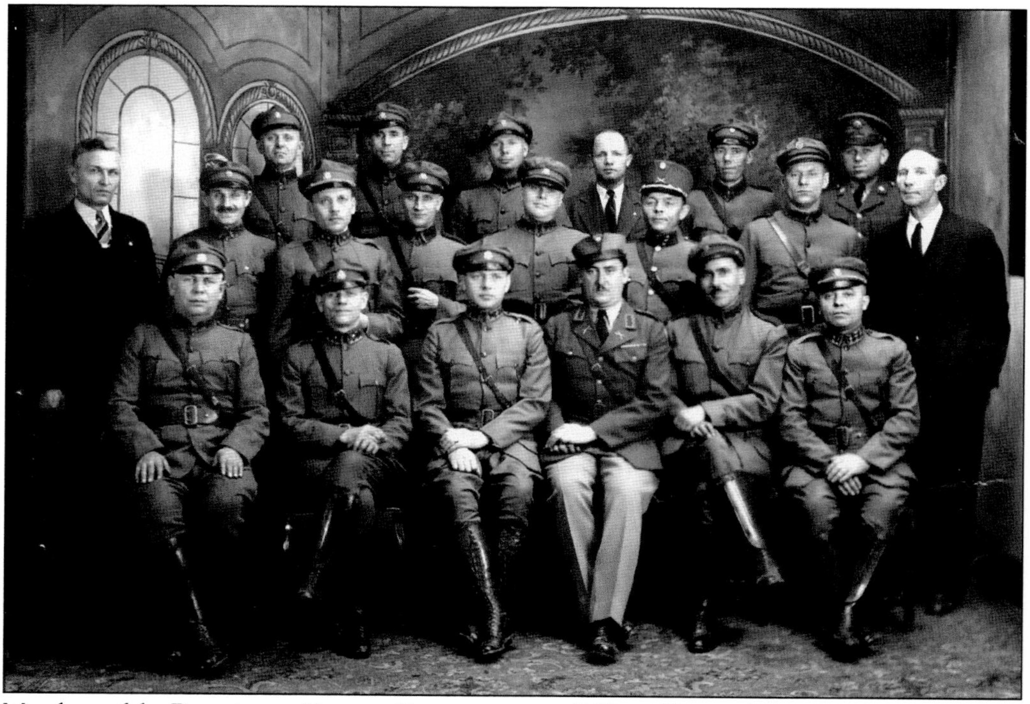

Members of the Detroit area Hetman Organization in 1937 are (first row) O. Dzawala, J. Prychitko, S. Gawa, E. Draginda, P. Zaporozhetz, and P. Demian; (second row) T. Bilyca, M. Cymbaluk, M. Nebozenko, B. Les, M. Kushner, I. Sheremeta, M. Bashko, and T. Poloway; (third row) P. Semkiw, J. Barlow, J. Yurkevich, B. Yavorsky, B. Dorosz, and A. Derkacz. (Mary LaDouceur.)

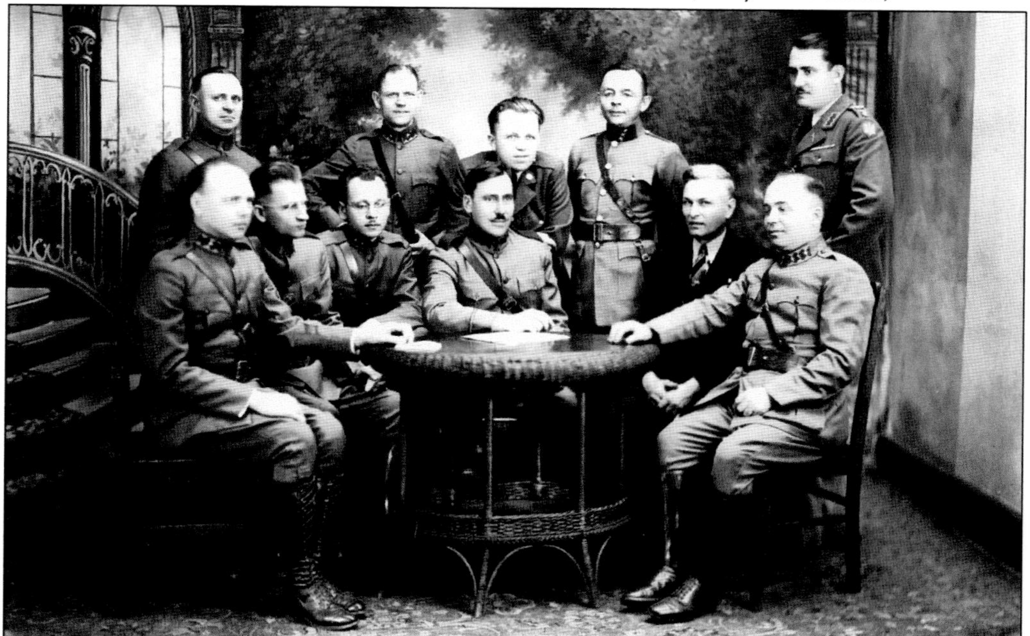

The Detroit area Hetman Organization officers in 1937 are (first row) S. Gawa, B. Les, M. Nebozenko, P. Zaporozhetz, T. Bilyca, and P. Demian; (second row) R. Semkiw, J. Prychitko, A.Derkacz, J. Sheremeta, and E. Draginda. (Mary LaDouceur.)

In 1917, Dmytro Dubrivnyj joined the United States Army during World War I. Many Ukrainian Americans demonstrated their patriotism by serving in the military in times of war and peace. (Cathy Koneya.)

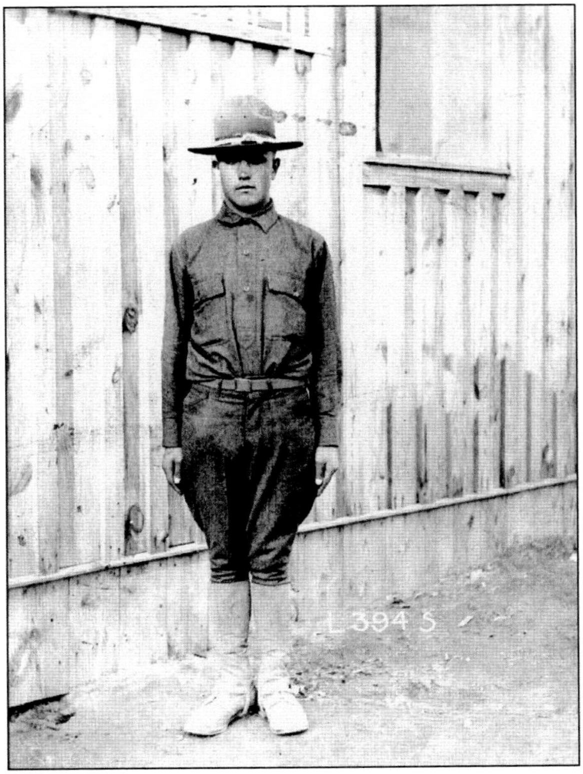

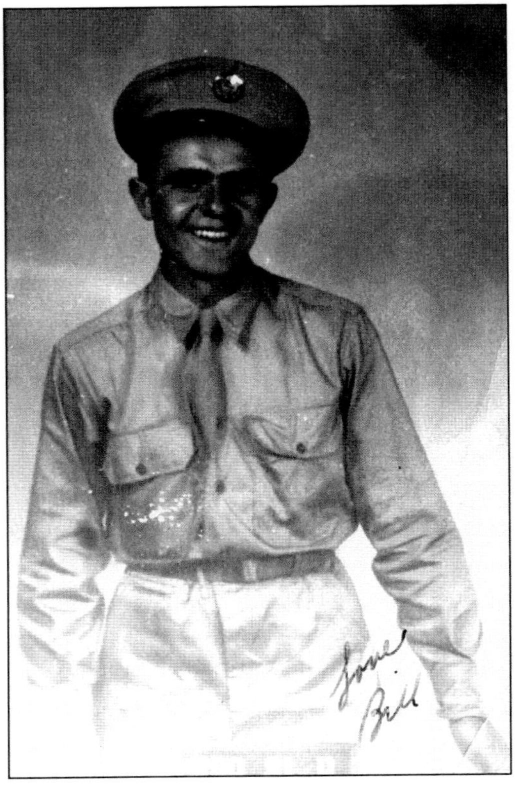

During World War II, William "Chick" Senyk sent this photograph home to Detroit. On the back he wrote, "Make more pictures and send them to Vera, Natalie, the neighbor, and Club Boyan."

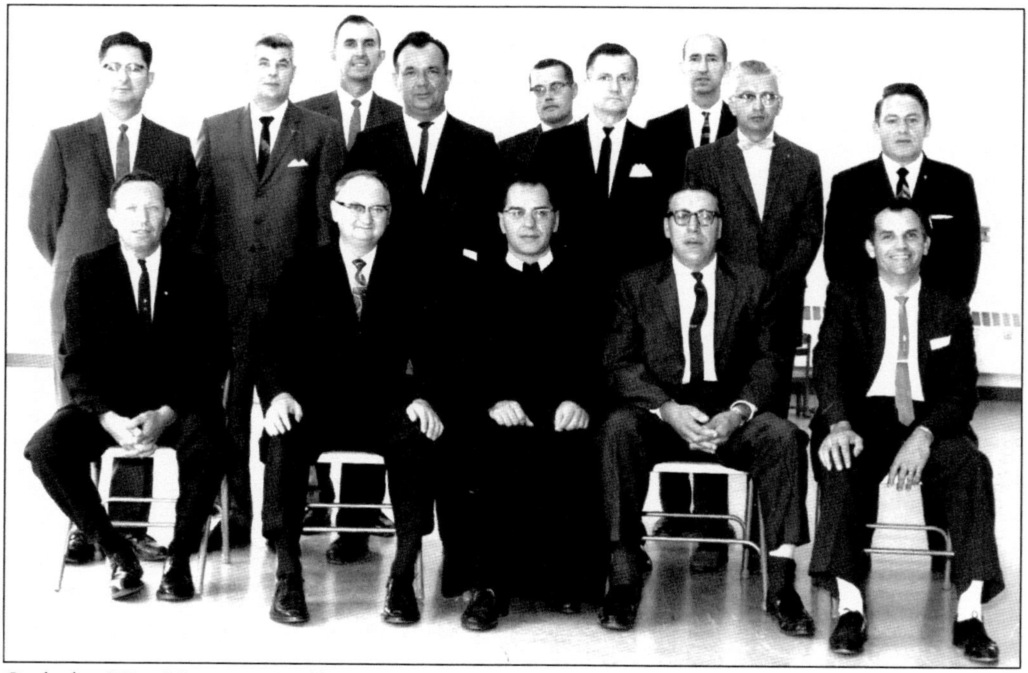

Catholic War Veterans, William Melnyk Post No. 645, was established in 1946. This post participates in many Ukrainian Catholic functions providing both the Honor Guard and Color Guard. They also provide ceremonies for the funerals of their deceased members. This image is from the 1950s. (Olga Seniw.)

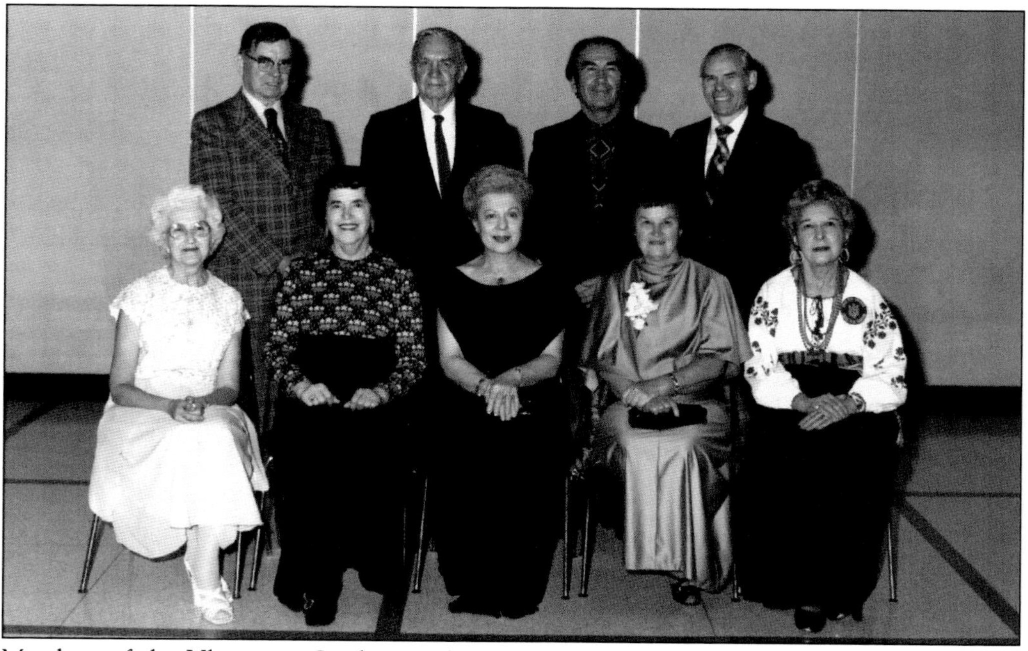

Members of the Ukrainian Graduates of Detroit and Windsor are (first row) Sally Hawrish, Dr. Mary Beck, Judge Valerie Kasurak, P. Yuzyk, and Emily Zaporozhetz; (second row) Michael Wichorek, Dr. John Panchuk, Senator Paul Yuzyk, and Vasyl Kolodchin. This image is from 1979. (Ukrainian Museum.)

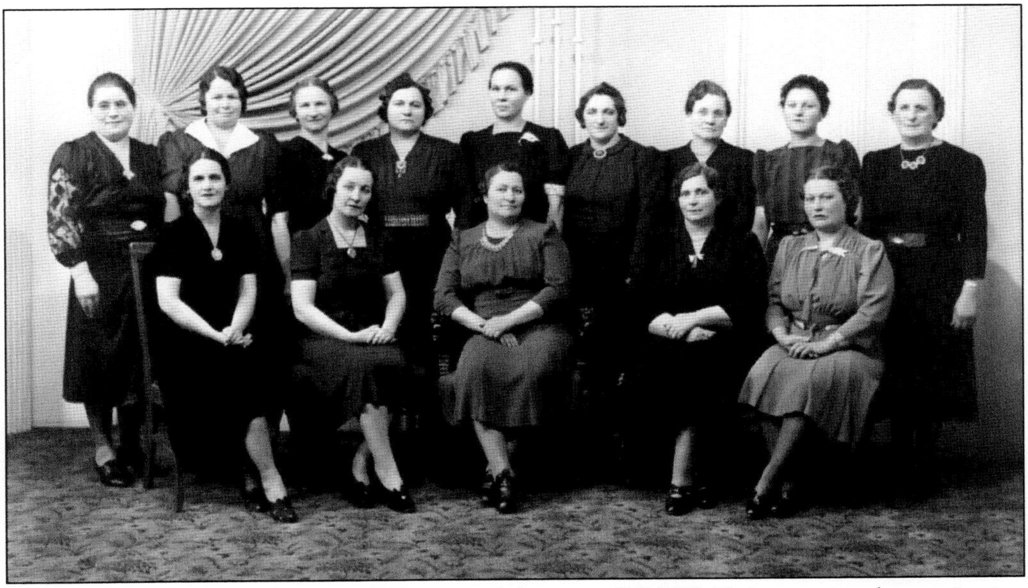

The Ukrainian National Women's League of America (UNWLA) is a national organization established in 1925 with the goal of uniting American women of Ukrainian descent to preserve their ethnic identity and cultural heritage within a framework of volunteer and humanitarian endeavors. There are 12 branches of the UNWLA in the Detroit area. This image is from around 1942. (Ukrainian Museum.)

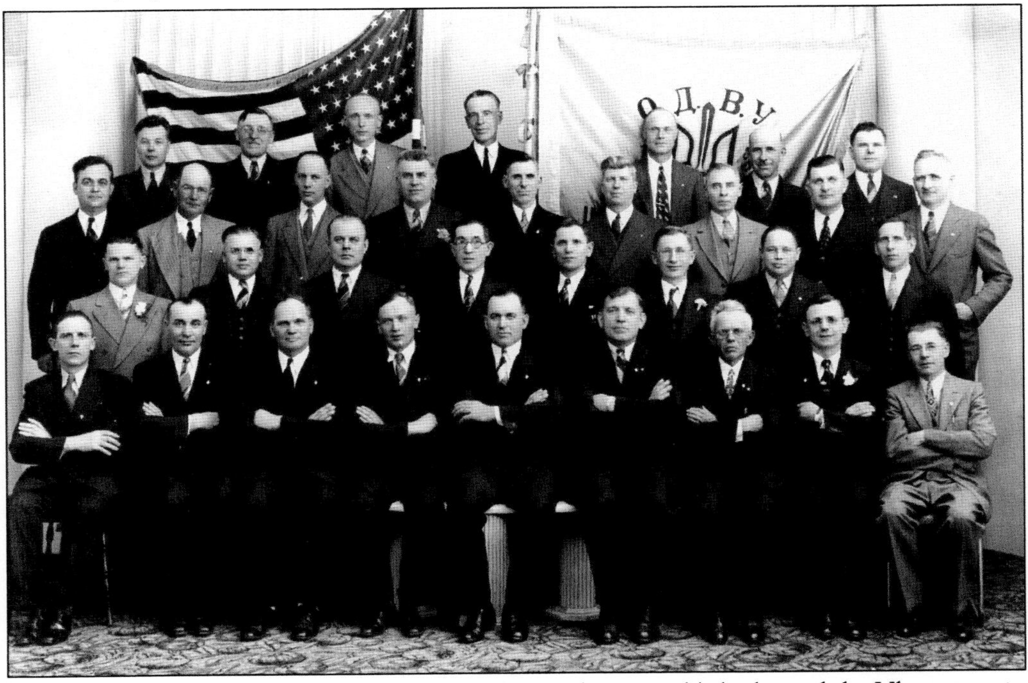

The Organization of the Rebirth of Ukraine (ODWU) was established to aid the Ukrainians in Ukraine in all possible ways and to assist them in gaining their sovereignty. The organization received a great deal of support from the Ukrainian community as members joined the ranks of the organization, particularly the former officers and soldiers of the Ukrainian army who had immigrated to the United States after World War I. (Ukrainian Museum.)

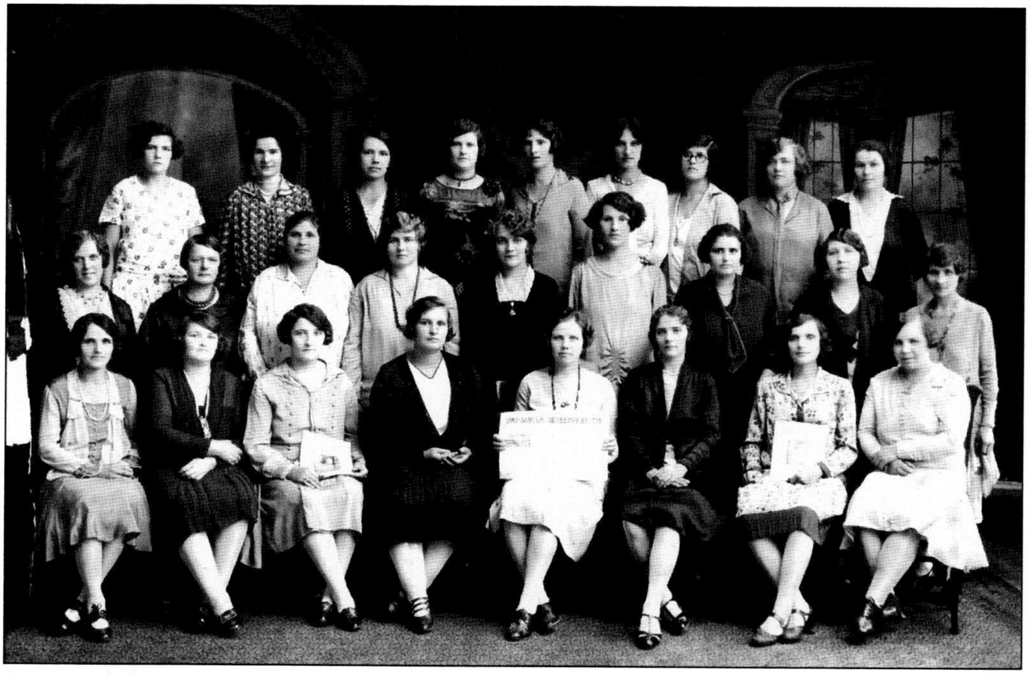

Prosvita (Ukrainian Women's Educational Society) was organized by M. Ukrainec and M. Vovchuk in 1921 and was the first independent Ukrainian women's organization in the Detroit area. Founders of the organization are pictured above in 1928.

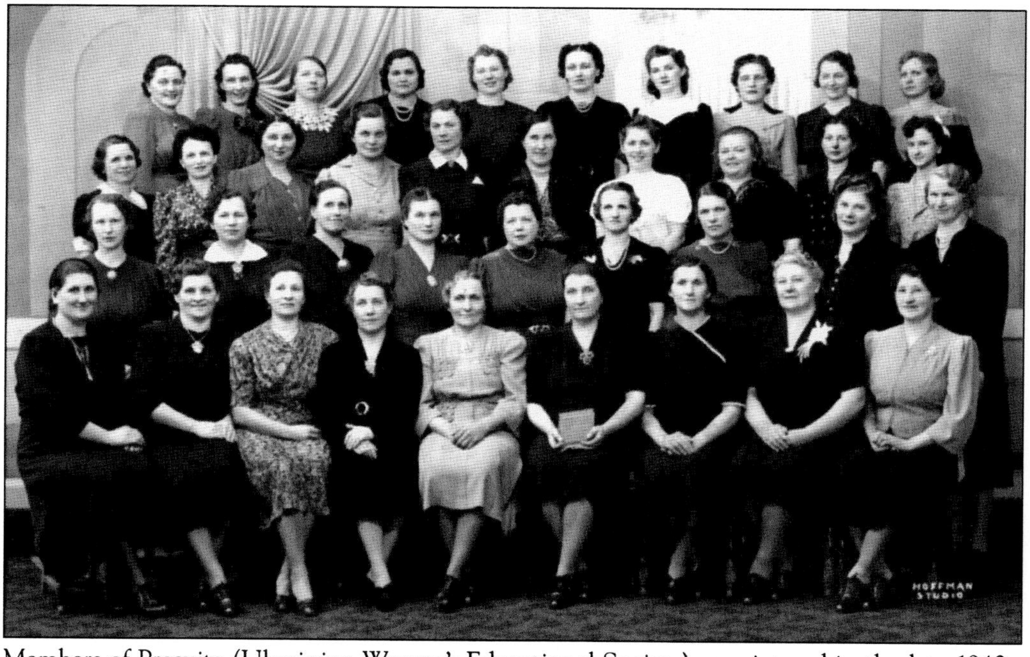

Members of Prosvita (Ukrainian Women's Educational Society) are pictured in the late 1940s. Their weekly meetings featured speakers who focused on critical issues of the day. Prosvita was closely aligned with the members of the Ukrainian American Center. They supported political candidates who were sympathetic toward Ukrainian causes, especially Dr. Mary V. Beck, the first female president of the Detroit City Council.

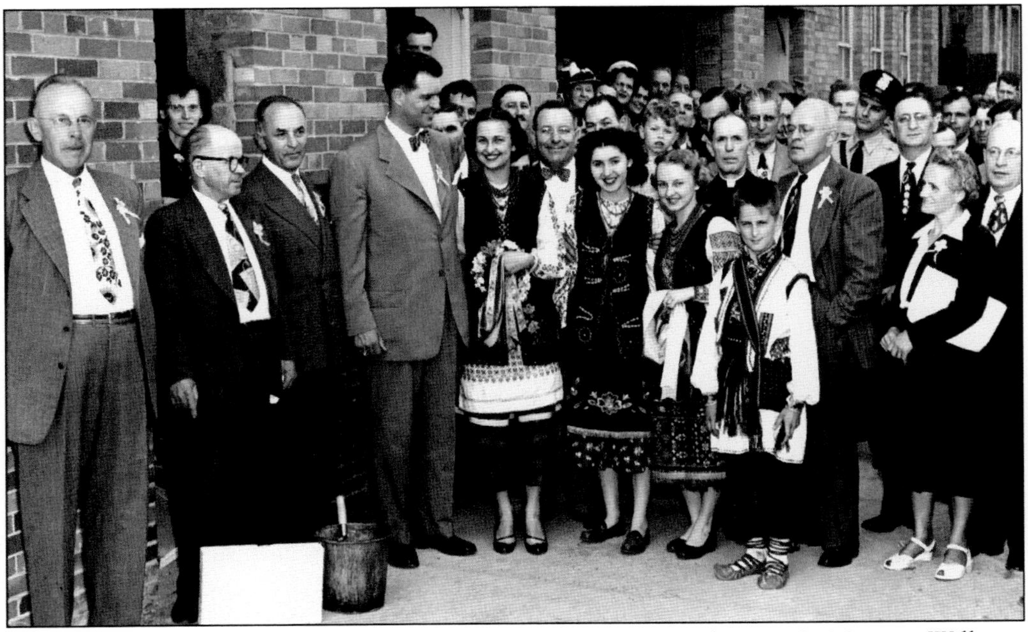

In 1950, the Ukrainian American Center membership meets with Gov. G. Mennen Williams to lay the cornerstone for the new addition to their building. The Ukrainian community often sought support from political officials. (Leo Hulyk.)

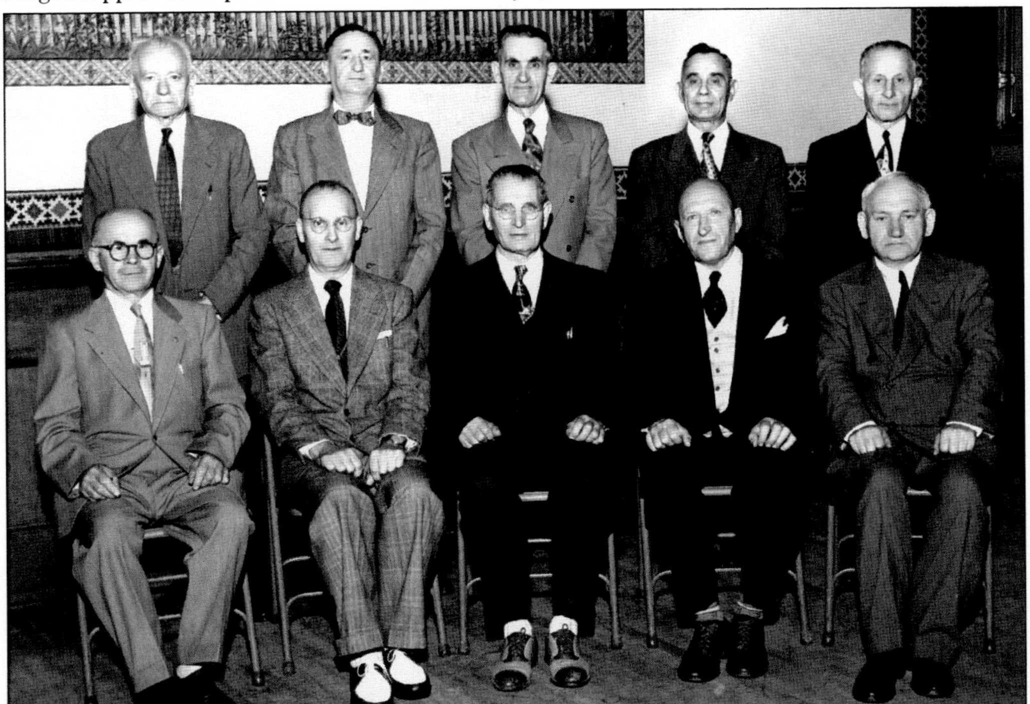

Officers of the Ukrainian American Center are pictured in this photograph from the 1950s. The center was utilized by many Ukrainian organizations including the Ukrainian Banduist Chorus, Ukrainian Chorus Trembita, and Ridna Shkola.

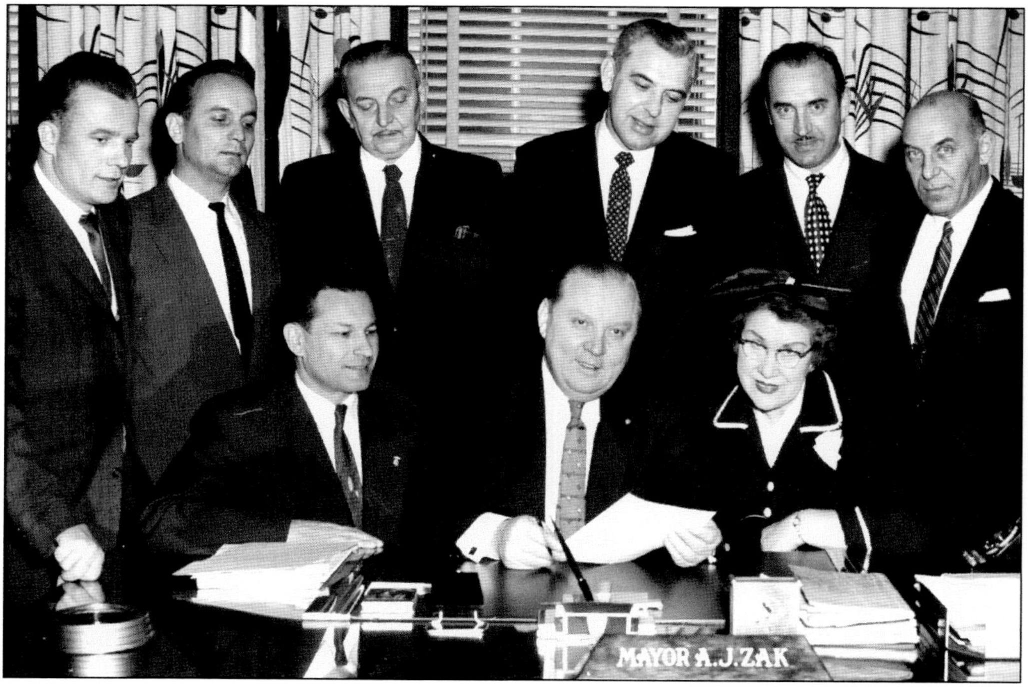

In 1956, Mayor Zak of Hamtramck signs a proclamation commemorating the anniversary of Ukraine's independence, which occurred on January 22, 1918. In the front row, seated on each side of the mayor are Ukrainian Congress Committee of America president Wolodymyr Tustaniwsky and treasurer Leontyna Halazenko. Standing UCCA members are M. Wytiahlowsky, Dr. Z. Horak, Dr. A. Maritchak, unidentified, J. Panchak, and J. Wirstiuk. (Ukrainian Museum.)

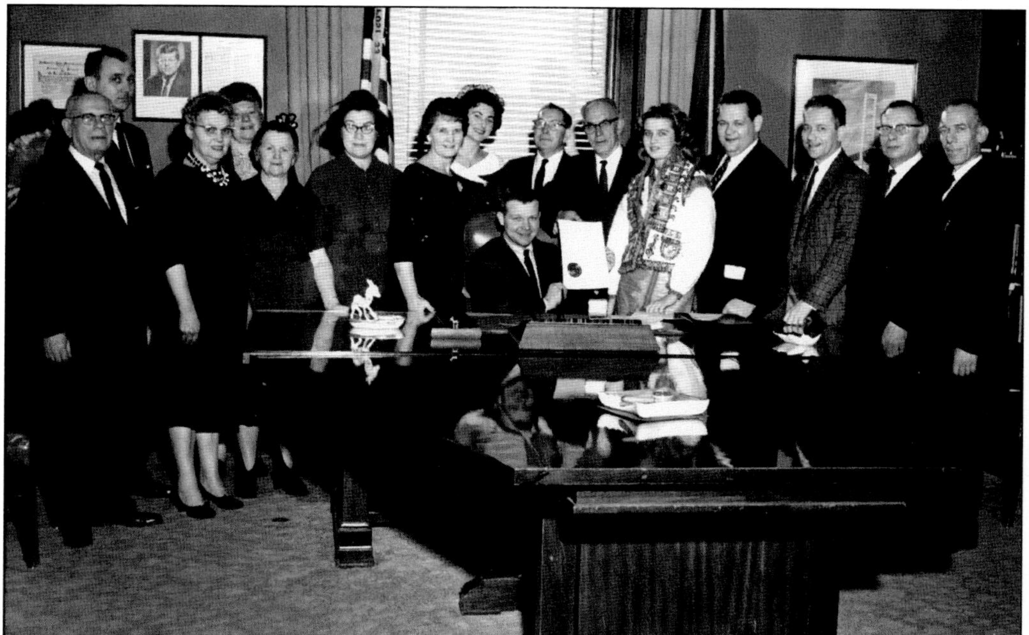

Ukrainian leaders meet with Gov. John Swainson in 1962 to commemorate Ukraine's 1918 independence. (Ukrainian Museum.)

General Mychajlo Krat's wife proudly places a medal of honor on her husband, a member of the Ukrainian Army in World War II. Ukrainian activist William Dowhan participates in the 1960 ceremony. (William Dowhan.)

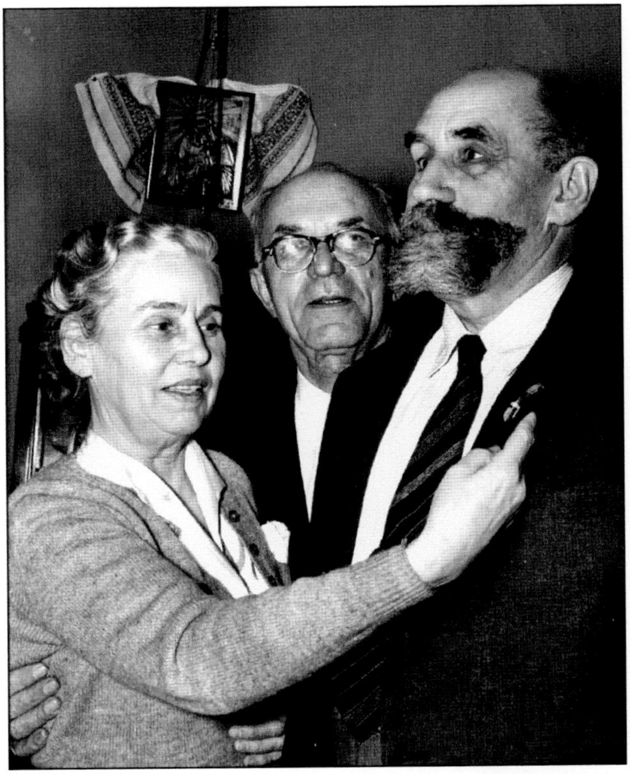

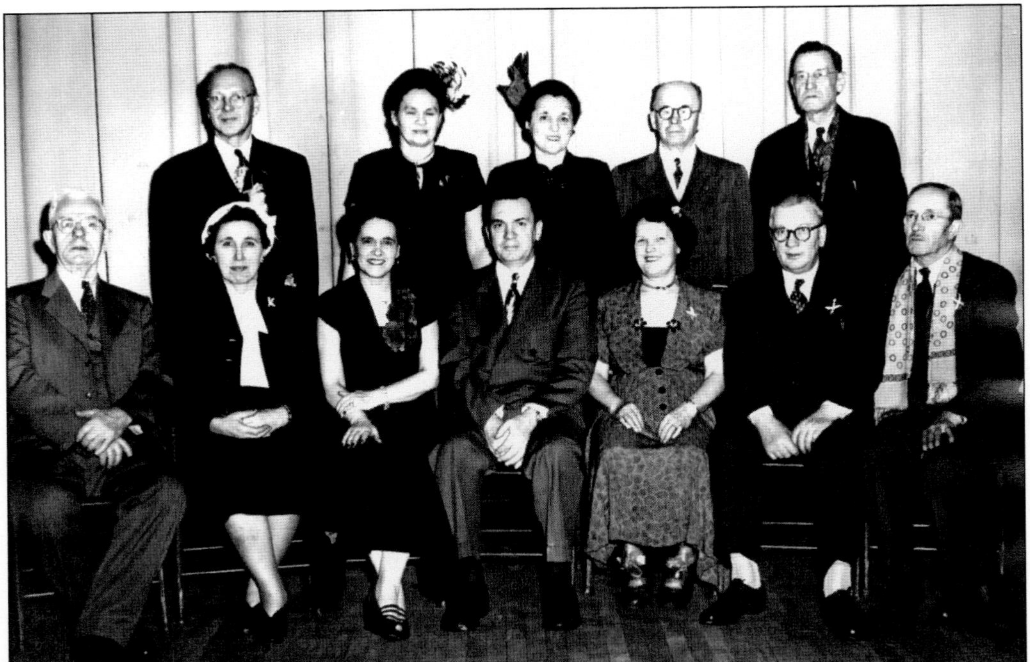

The Ukrainian-American Federation of Michigan, under the direction of John Panchuk (first row center), concentrated its efforts on Ukrainian displaced persons in Europe and how to best serve their interests. This image is from 1952. (Ukrainian Museum.)

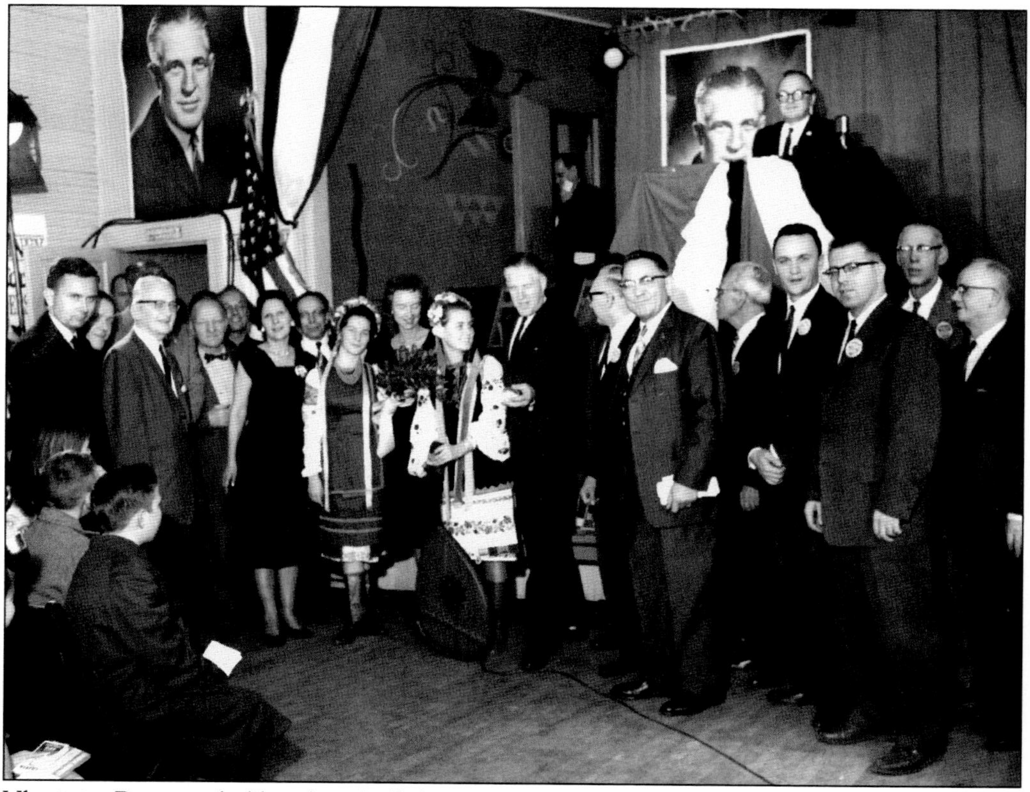

Ukrainian Detroiters hold a political rally for George Romney's campaign for governor at the Ukrainian American Political Club on Cicotte Street, Detroit, in the early 1960s. (Mary LaDouceur.)

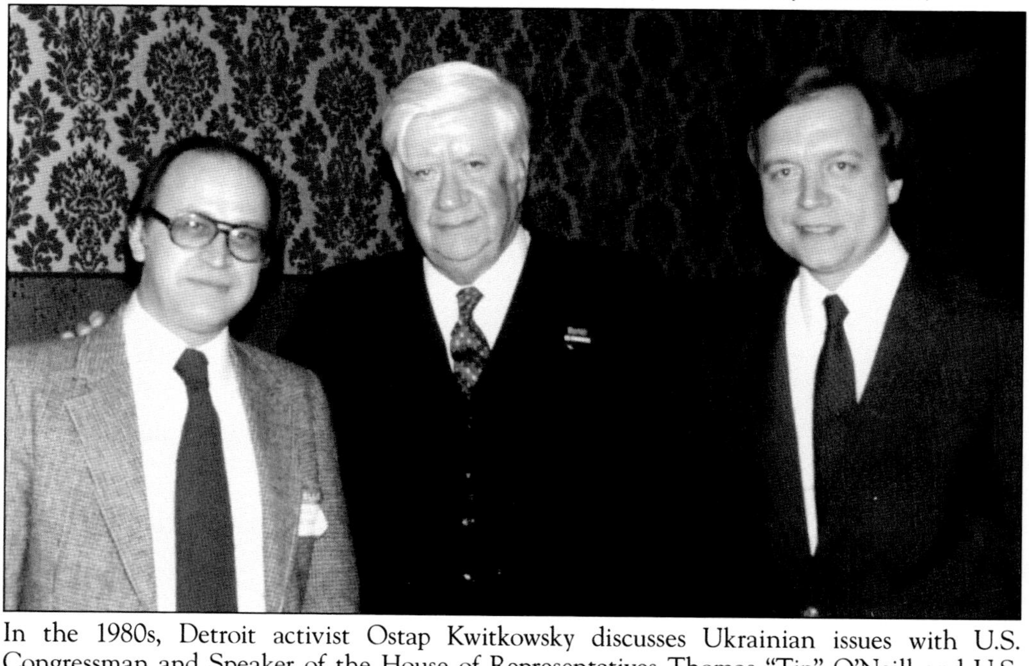

In the 1980s, Detroit activist Ostap Kwitkowsky discusses Ukrainian issues with U.S. Congressman and Speaker of the House of Representatives Thomas "Tip" O'Neill and U.S. Congressman Dennis Hertel.

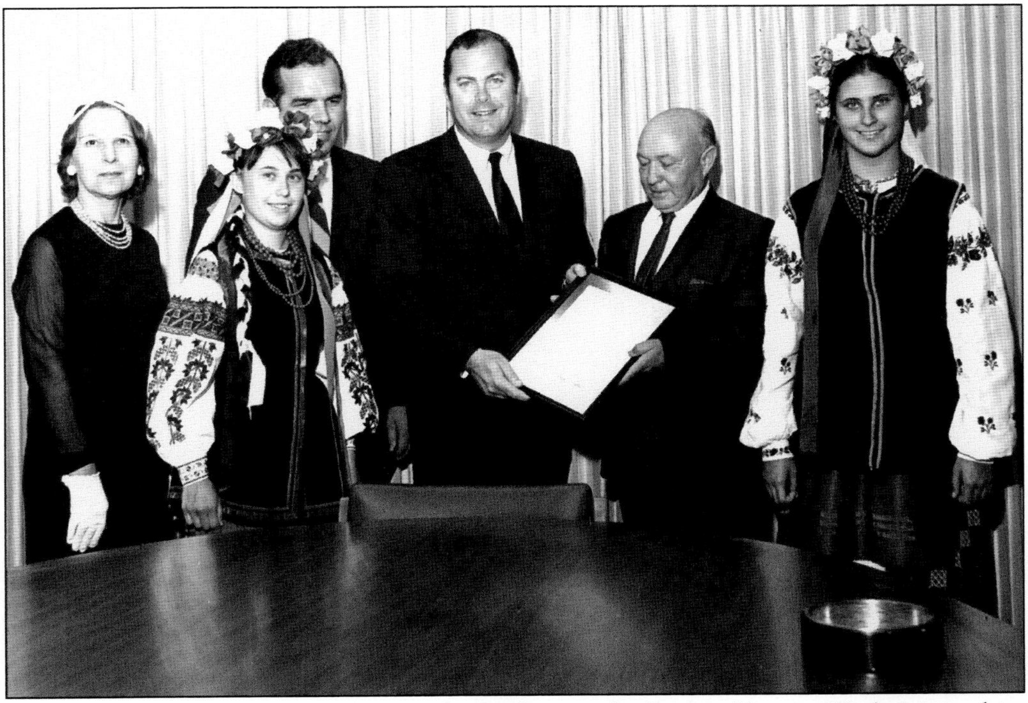

Detroit Mayor Cavanaugh, center, signs the Declaration for Captive Nations Week. Joining him are Ukrainians Emily Zaporozetz, Mariana Liskiwsky, Bohdan Fedorak, Michajco Bazanski, and Maria Nazarenko. This image is from around 1960. (Maria Nazarenko.)

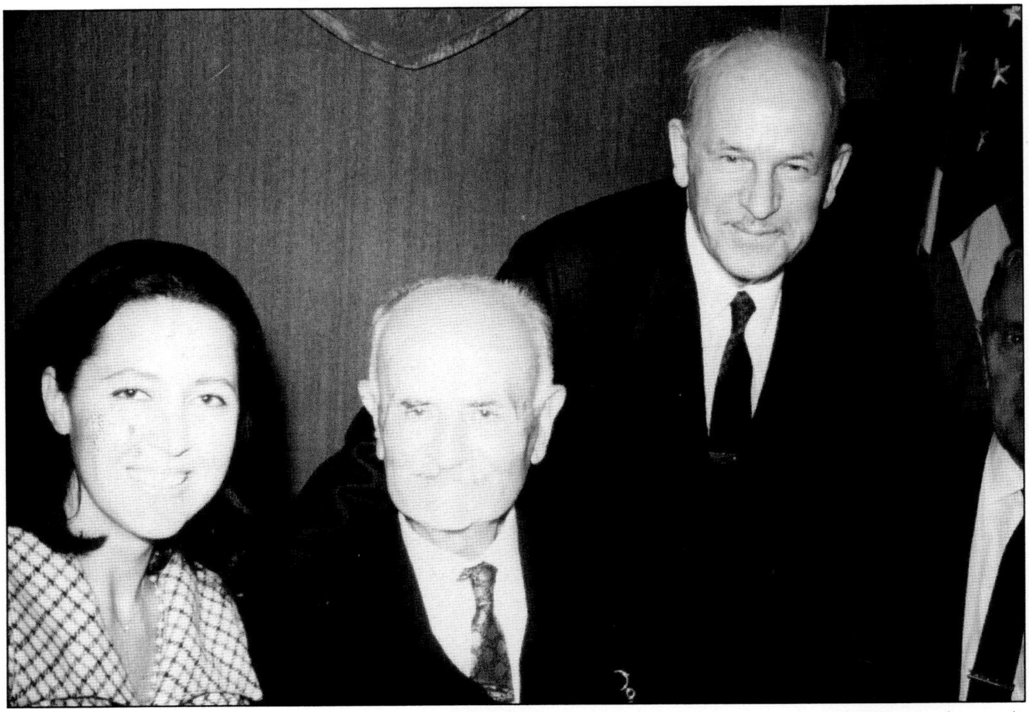

In November 1967, a press conference was held with Borys Martys, prime minister of Ukraine (center). Detroit Ukrainians Nadya Sepell (left) and Denys Kwitkowsy (right) were present. (Nadya Sepell.)

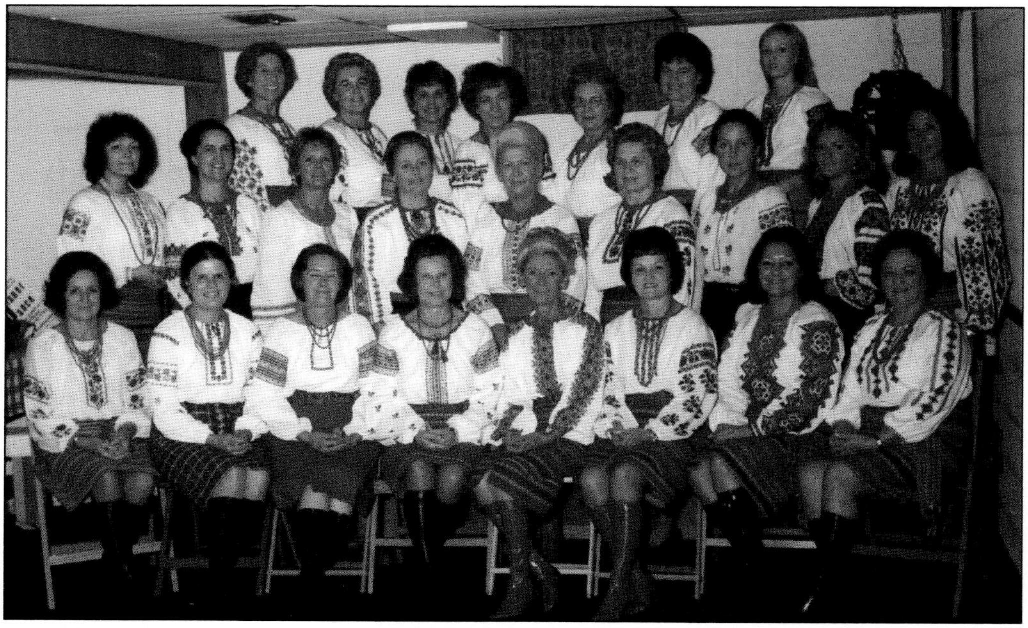

The Ukrainian National Women's League, Olehna Teliha, Branch No. 58, celebrates its 50th anniversary in 1975. Among dozens of accomplishments throughout the years, this group was instrumental in raising funds for the construction of the Ukrainian Village. Seen here are (first row) Ann Sedorak, Helen Lampi, Olga Kinnes, Helen Sedorak, Sonya Hayes, Helen Paluha, Olga Hubchik, and Rose Slupecki; (second row) Sandra Feneck, Olga Solovey, Evelyn Godzak, Ann Makar, Justine Nelligan Sonia Hazen, Nadya Sepell , Oresta Karalash, and Jean Fitzsimons; (third row) Anastasia Sosnowsky, Mary Lee Prowalny, Jenny Materyn, Mary Kowalczyk, Anne Zablocky, Nell Martyn, and Chris Coulter. (Olga Solovey.)

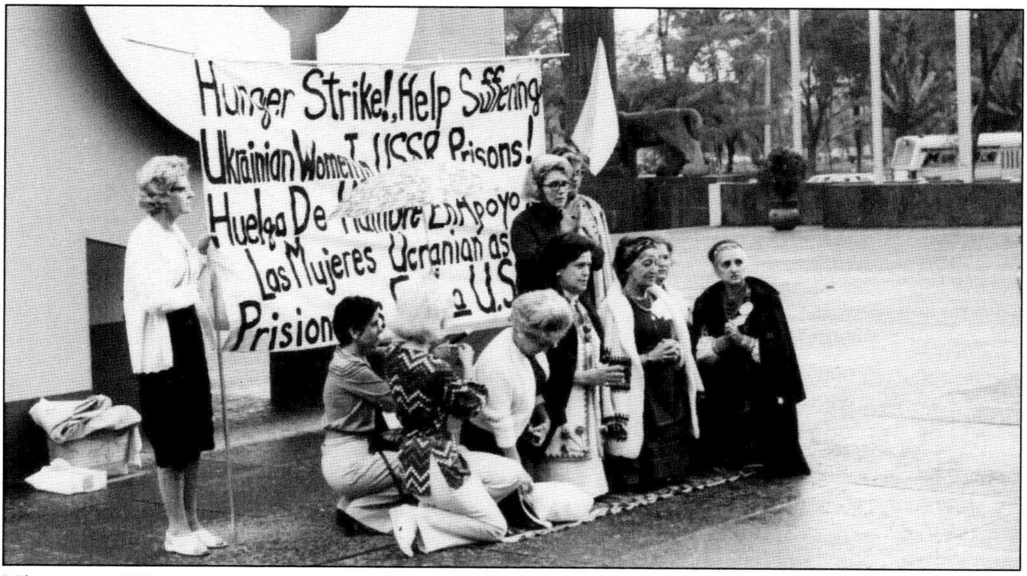

Ukrainian Women participate in a hunger strike demonstration at the International Women's Year 1975 Conference in Mexico City. Detroiters praying for the release of Ukrainian women in Soviet prisons are Marie Zarycky (third from left with camera) and Dr. Mary Beck (center). (Marie Zarycky.)

In 1985, the poignant story of Ukrainian sailor Miroslav Medvid prompted a desperate attempt by Ukrainians to intercede with the U.S. State Department to ensure his freedom in the port of New Orleans. His two attempts to jump a Soviet ship and plead asylum were unsuccessful. He was forcefully returned to Soviet custody despite many demonstrations across the United States, such as this in front of the federal building in Detroit. (Marie Zarycky.)

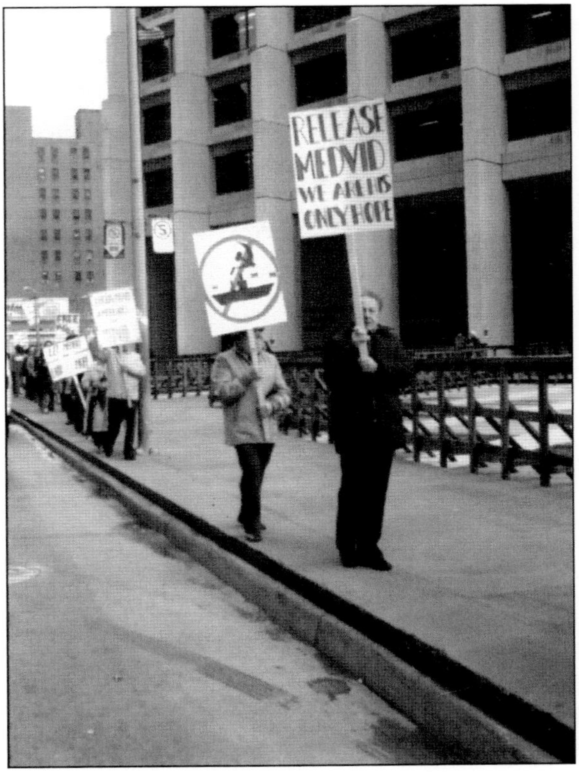

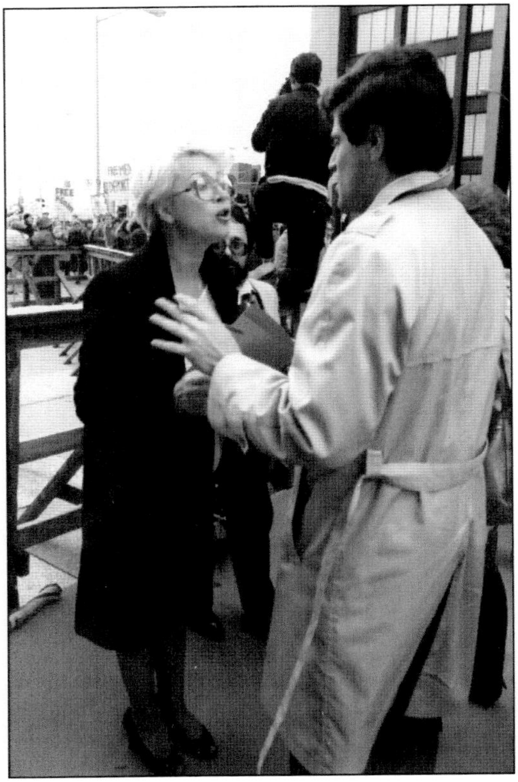

Activist Marie Zarycky provides details to a reporter in October 1985, during the Medvid Defense Rally. She was providing information that could be helpful in gaining asylum for Ukrainian sailor Miroslav Medvid. (Marie Zarycky.)

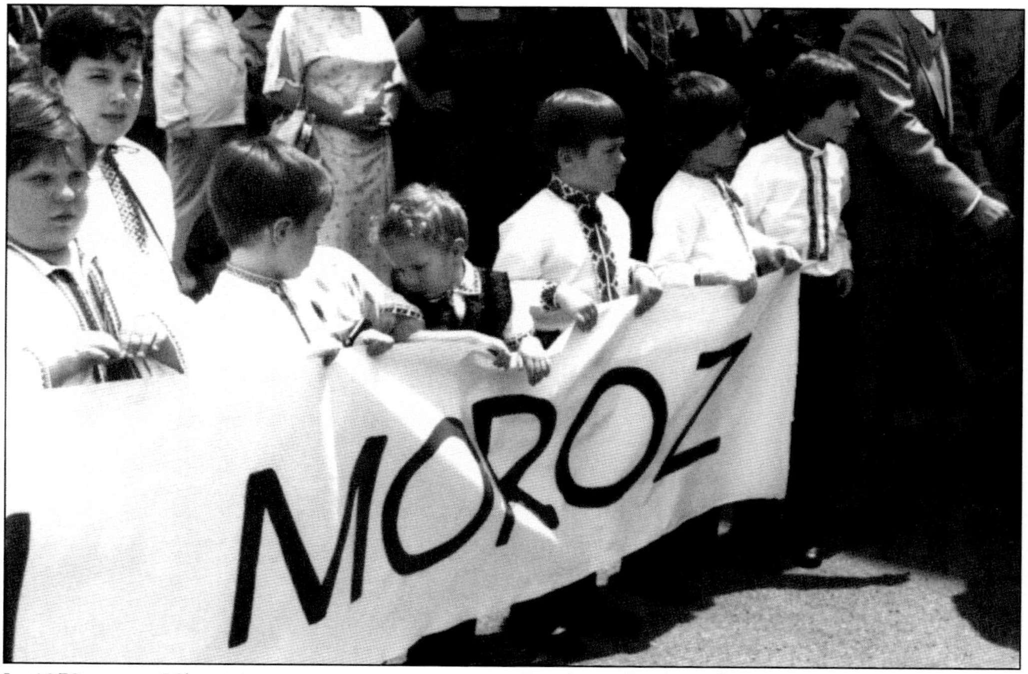

In 1979, young Ukrainian supporters greet recently released political prisoner Valentyn Moroz at a rally in Warren. (Roman Maziak.)

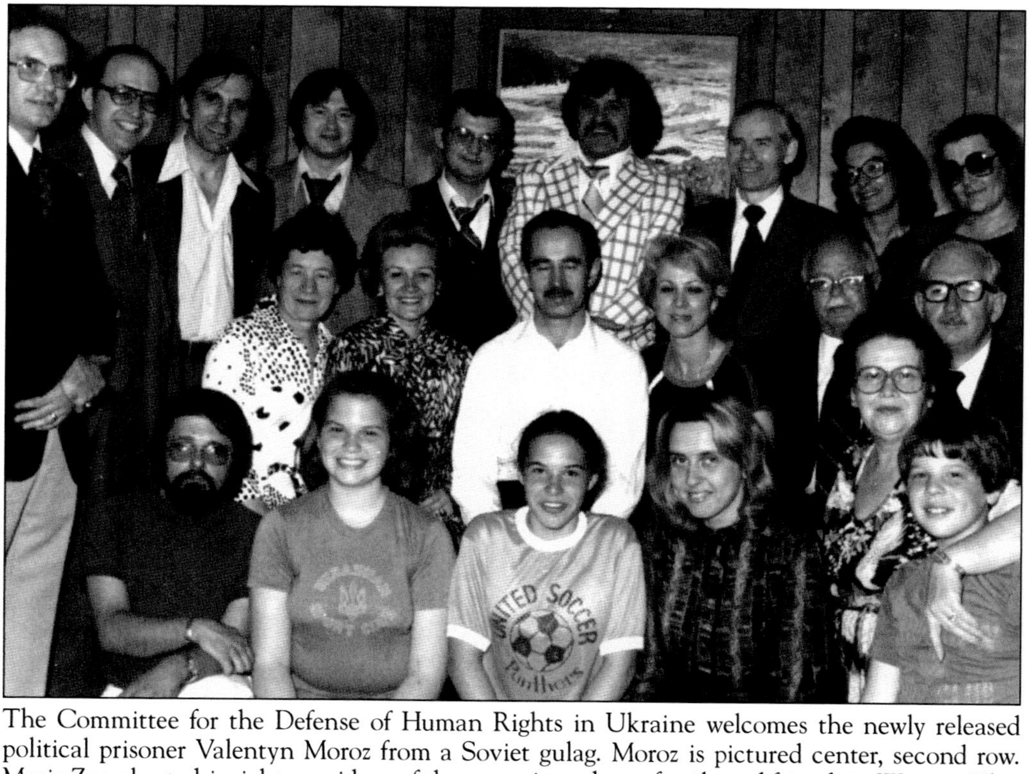

The Committee for the Defense of Human Rights in Ukraine welcomes the newly released political prisoner Valentyn Moroz from a Soviet gulag. Moroz is pictured center, second row. Marie Zarycky, to his right, president of the committee, hosts family and friends in Warren. This image is from 1979. (Marie Zarycky.)

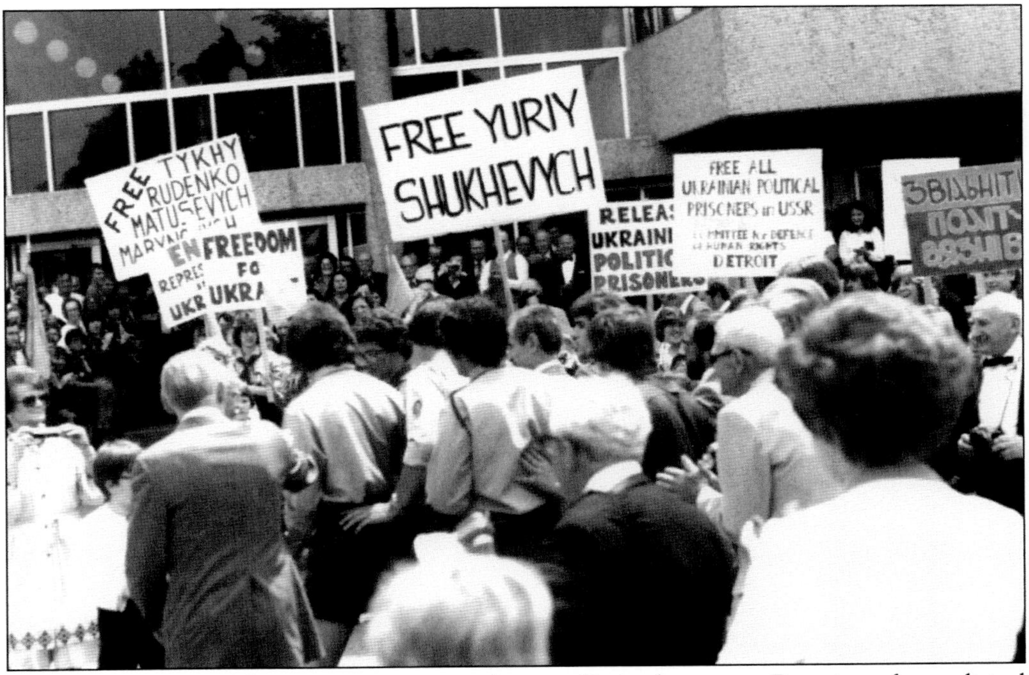

In this 1979 image, Ukrainian activists conduct a rally in downtown Detroit to free political prisoners in Ukraine. (Roman Maziak.)

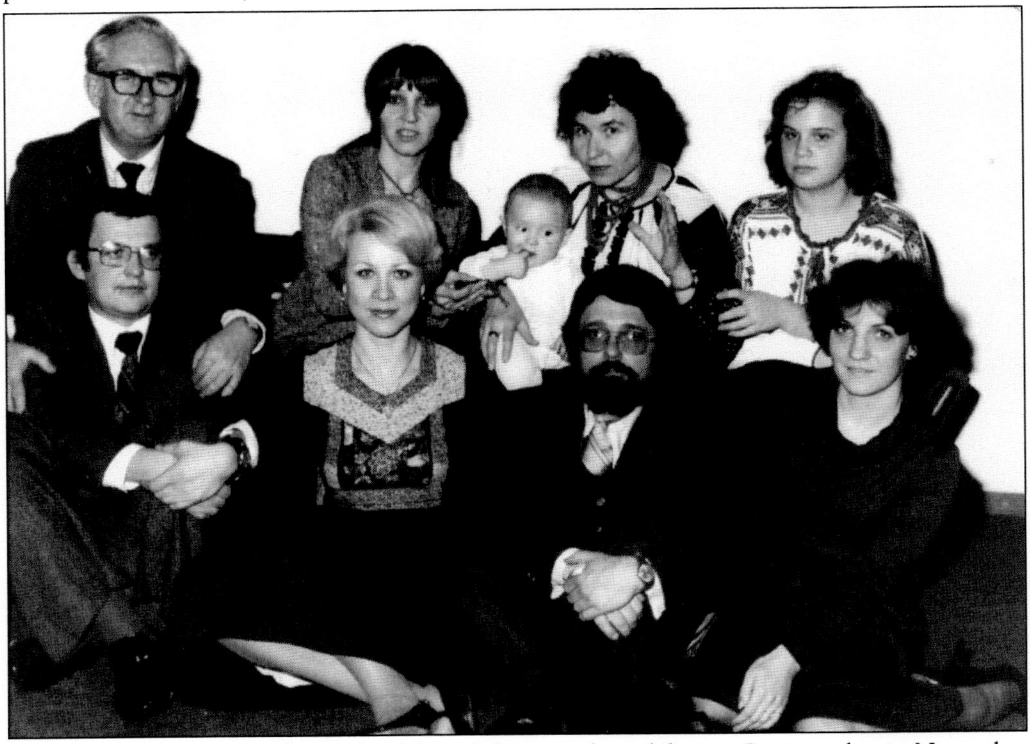

Nadia Switlychna, second row, third from left, was released from a Soviet gulag in November 1978 and was welcomed to the Detroit area by members of the Committee for the Defense of Human Rights in Ukraine. (Marie Zarycky.)

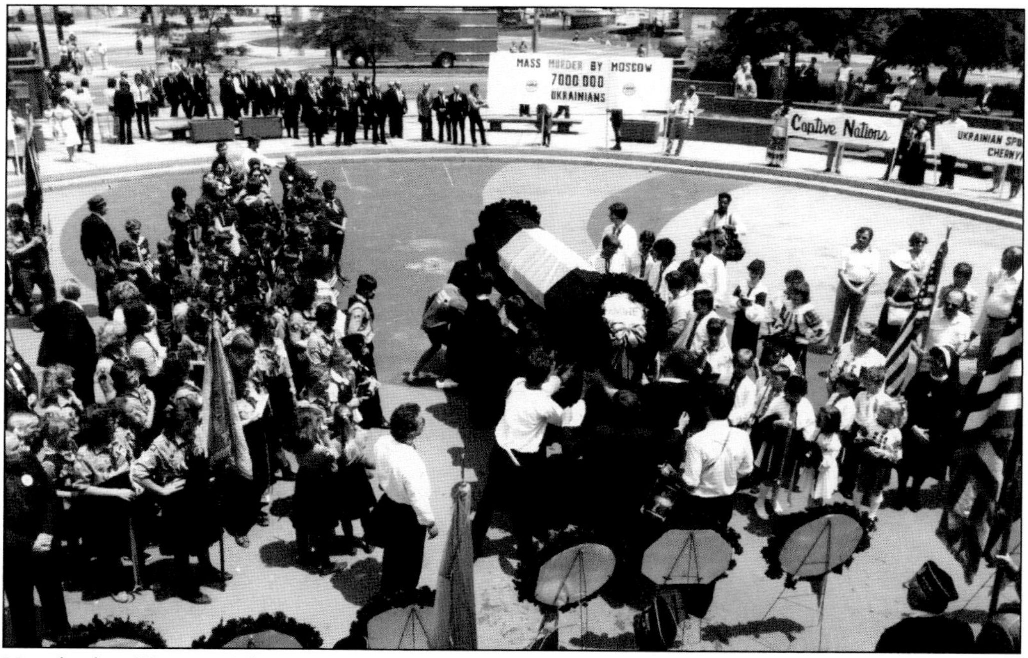

Hundreds of Detroit Ukrainians staged a massive march in remembrance of the seven million victims of the Holodomor (Famine) of 1932–1933 in Ukraine. At the conclusion of the demonstration, a coffin symbolizing the lost victims is lowered onto a temporary catafalque. This image is from 1983.

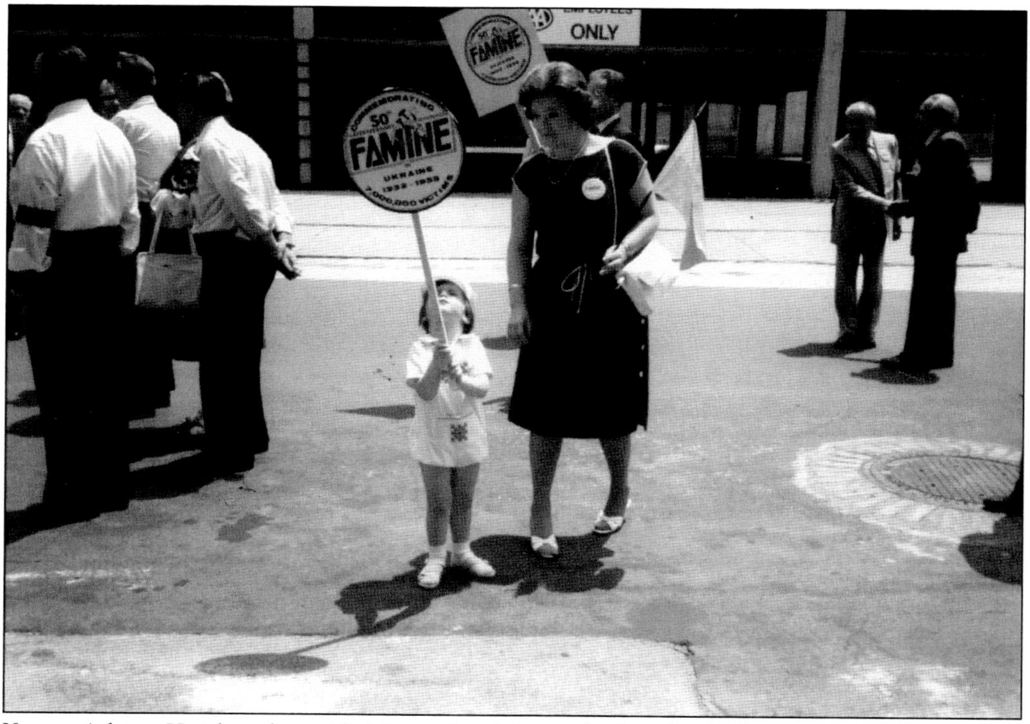

Young Adrian Kwitkowsky, with his mother Marta, displays his picket sign in support of the victims of the Holodomor in this 1983 image. (Marta Kwitkowsky.)

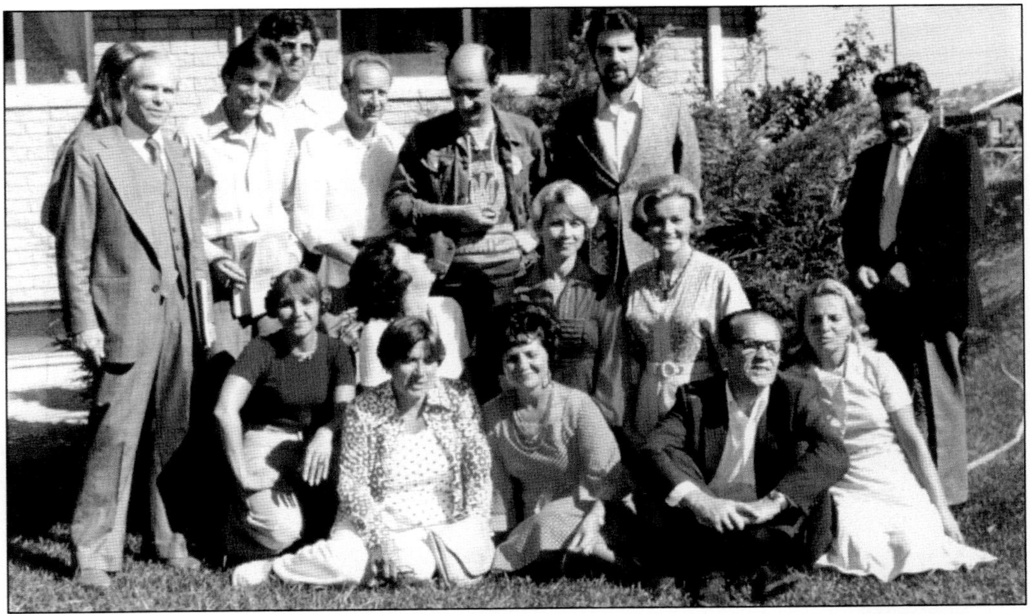

In 1977, the first political prisoner released from a Soviet psychiatric prison, Leonid Pliusch, top row center, is greeted by members of the Committee for the Defense of Human Rights in Ukraine at the home of Marie Zarychy in Warren. (Marie Zarycky.)

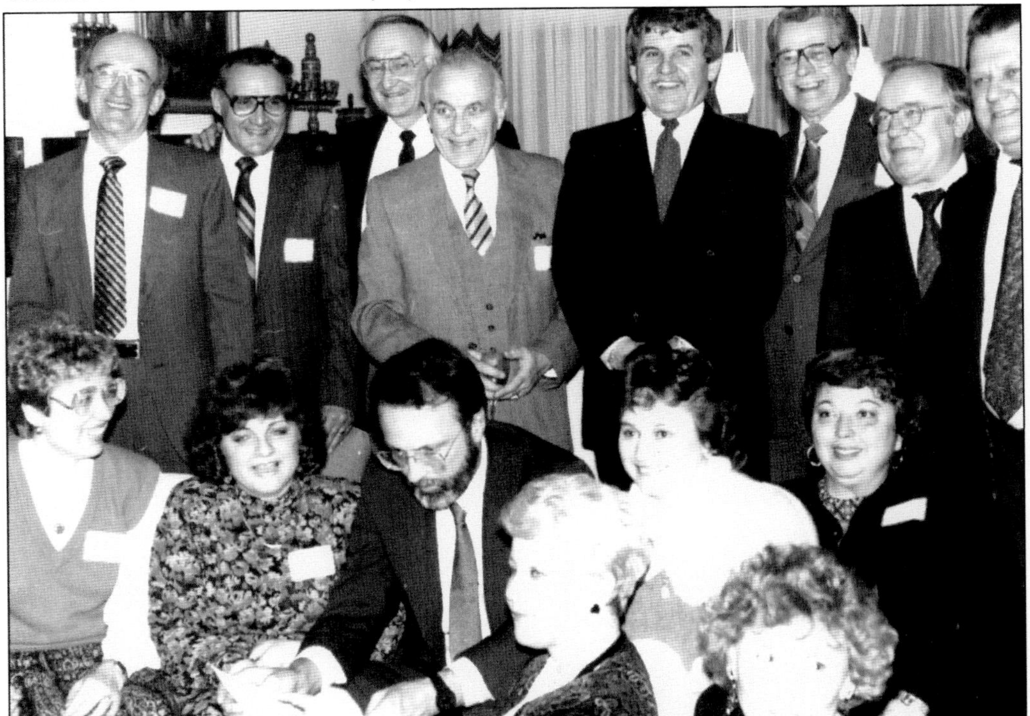

Kalyna and Nick Mykolenko host a reception for U.S. Congressman David Bonior at their Warren home in 1987. Members of Americans for Human Rights in Ukraine (AHRU) and the Ukrainian Veterans sought Congressman Bonior's support for religious and national rights for Ukrainians in the U.S.S.R. This image is from 1987. (Marie Zarycky.)

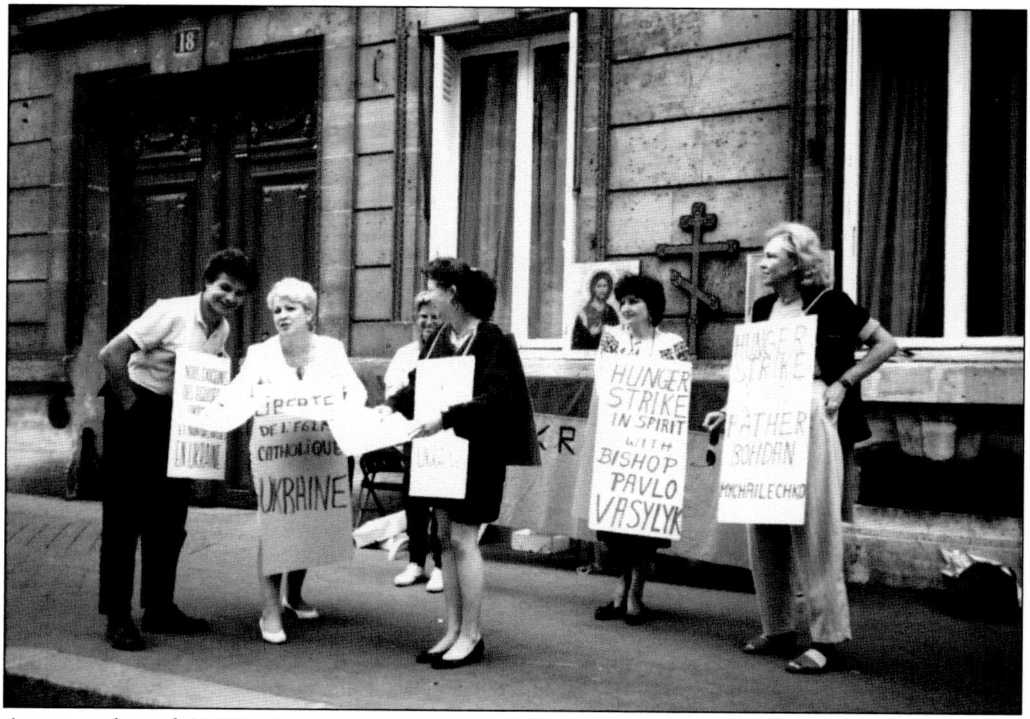

As a member of AHRU, Marie Zarycky, second from left, demonstrates with representatives of The World Federation of Free Ukrainians in front of the Sorbonne, in Paris, France. In 1988, the Helsinki Accords Conference reviewed the U.S.S.R.'s violations of its citizens' religious rights. Demonstrators appealed for reinstatement of the Ukrainian Catholic Church. (Marie Zarycky.)

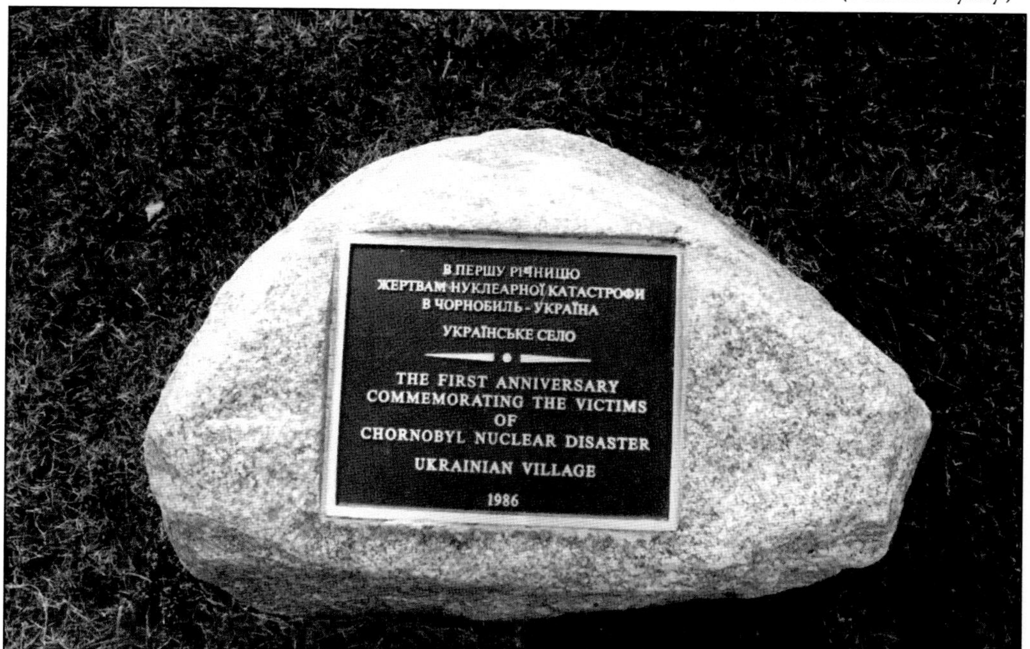

A memorial plaque sits on the grounds of the Ukrainian Village, a residency for seniors, commemorating the first anniversary of the victims of the Chernobyl nuclear disaster.

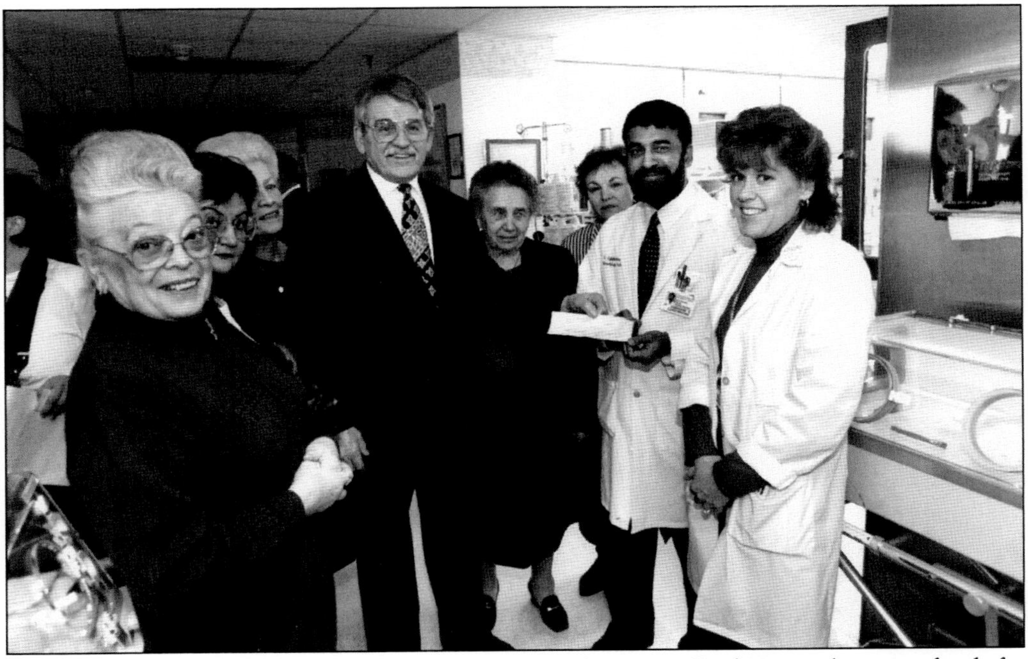

In 1999, Stephen M. Wichar initiated a project with the Henry Ford Hospital to raise funds for the first neonatal incubator for the Liviv Oblast Clinical Hospital in Ukraine. The members of his committee are, from left to right, Stefa Dub, Christine Shumayko, Justine Nelligan, (Stephen Wichar), Teklia Slywka, and Julianna Maziak. On the far right, Dr. Suddhaker Ezhutachan, head of neonatology at Henry Ford Hospital, and Christine Newman, neonatal nursing specialist, delivered the unit to the Ukrainian hospital and trained physicians how to use it.

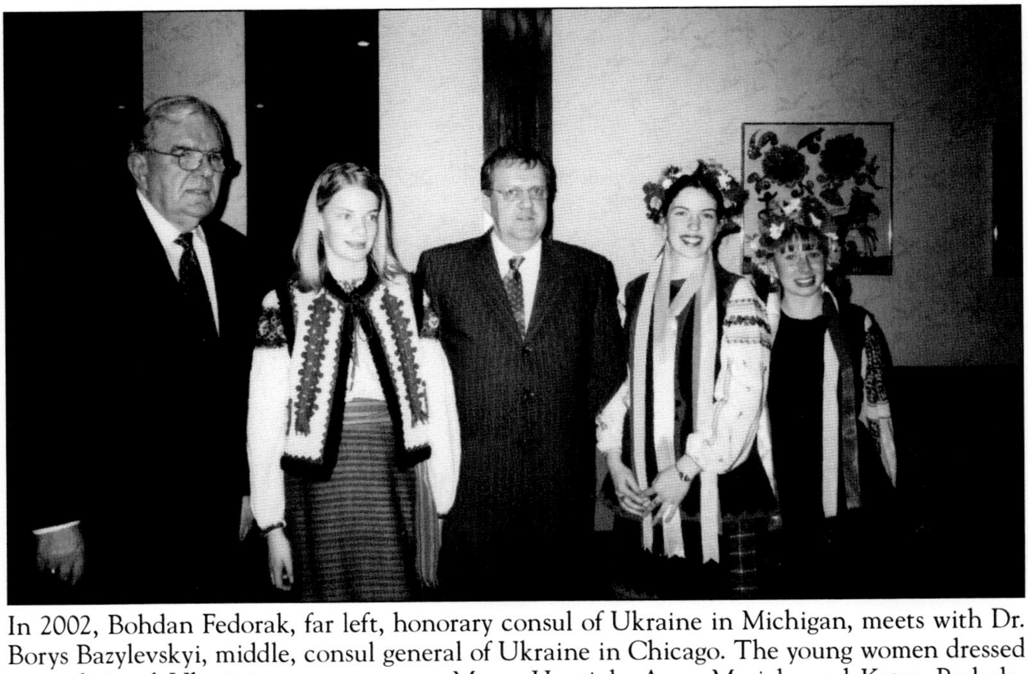

In 2002, Bohdan Fedorak, far left, honorary consul of Ukraine in Michigan, meets with Dr. Borys Bazylevskyi, middle, consul general of Ukraine in Chicago. The young women dressed in traditional Ukrainian costumes are Marta Hnatiuk, Anya Maziak, and Katya Prybula. (Roman Maziak.)

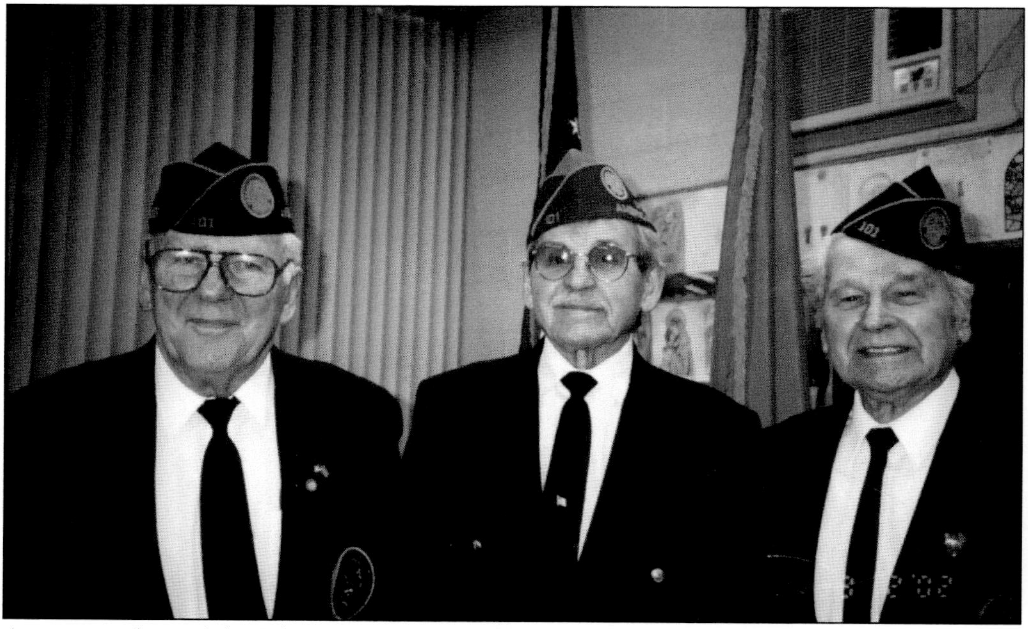

Active members of the Ukrainian American Veterans, Post 101, are Oleh Cieply, Stephen M. Wichar, and Joseph Elnick. This image is from 2000.

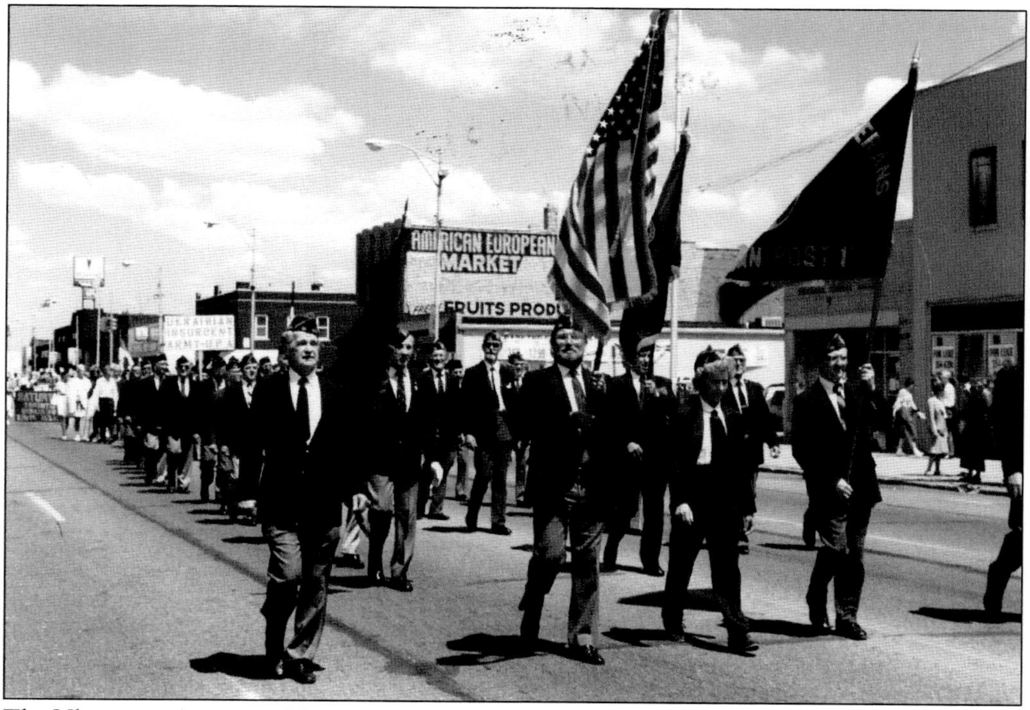

The Ukrainian American Veterans, Post 101, proudly display their flags in a Hamtramck parade. This image is from the 1990s. (Lydia Kolodchin.)

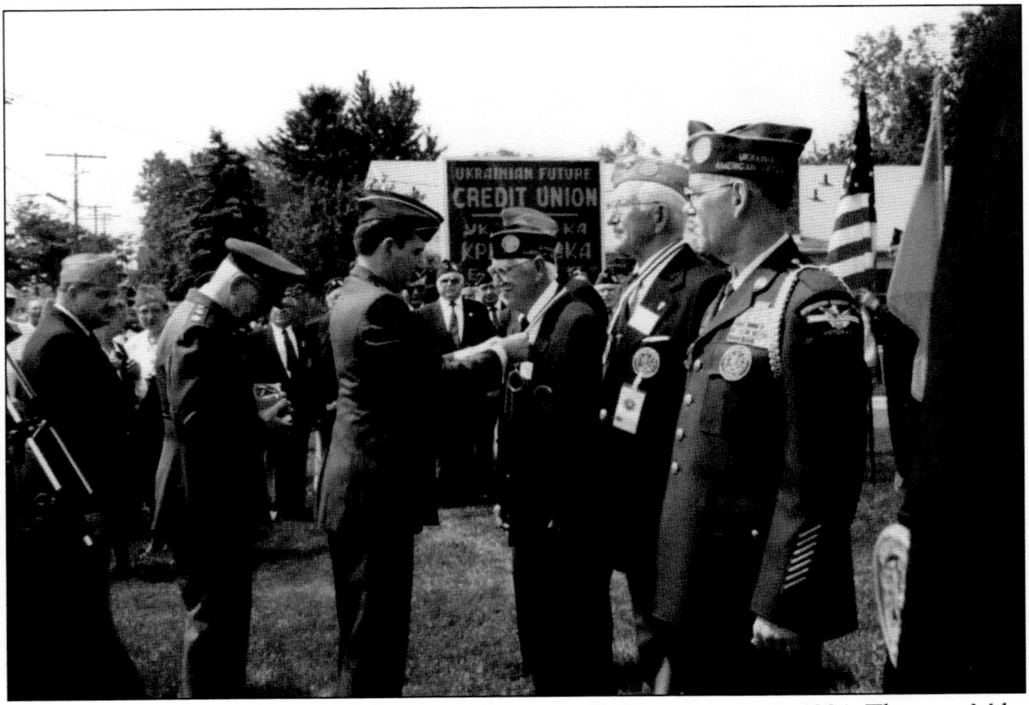

General Orest Kohut decorates Ukrainian American D-Day veterans in 1994. They are Mike Ogrodnik, Bohdan Bezkorowayny, and Sgt. Vasyl Barabash.

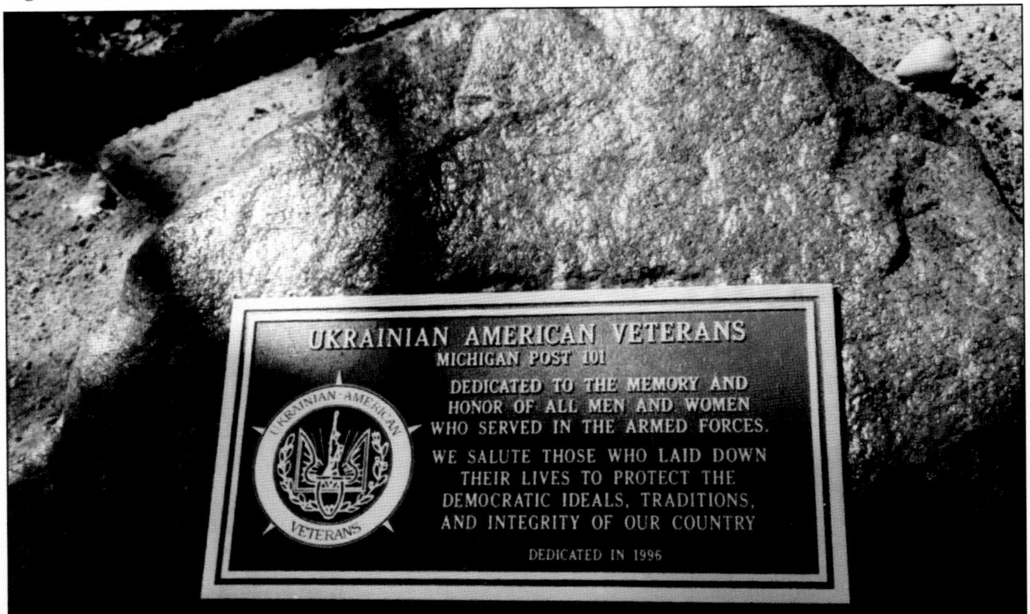

There have been numerous Ukrainian American veterans laid to rest at the Fort Custer National Cemetery in Augusta, Michigan. In honor of all United States veterans, Ukrainian Veterans, Post 101, established a memorial commemorating their service. It was dedicated in 1996.

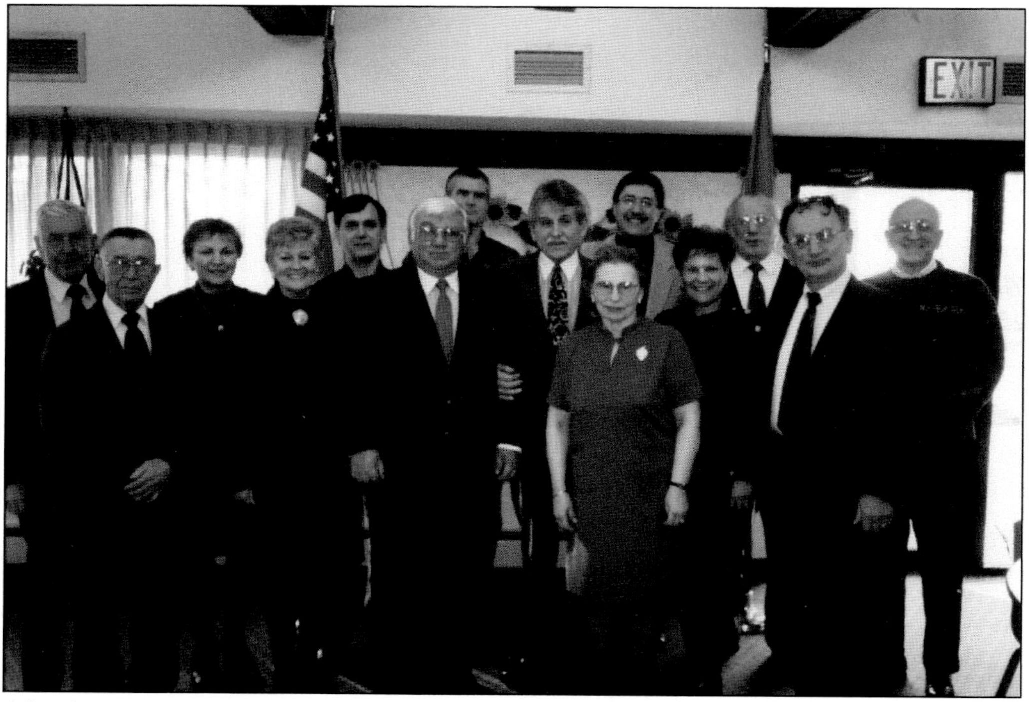

After being in existence for decades, the Ukrainian American Center was reorganized into the Ukrainian American Center Foundation (UACF). The foundation provides generous scholarships for young Ukrainian-American students as a tribute to the dedication of Ukrainian pioneers in Michigan. Pictured above are members of UACF in the 1990s.

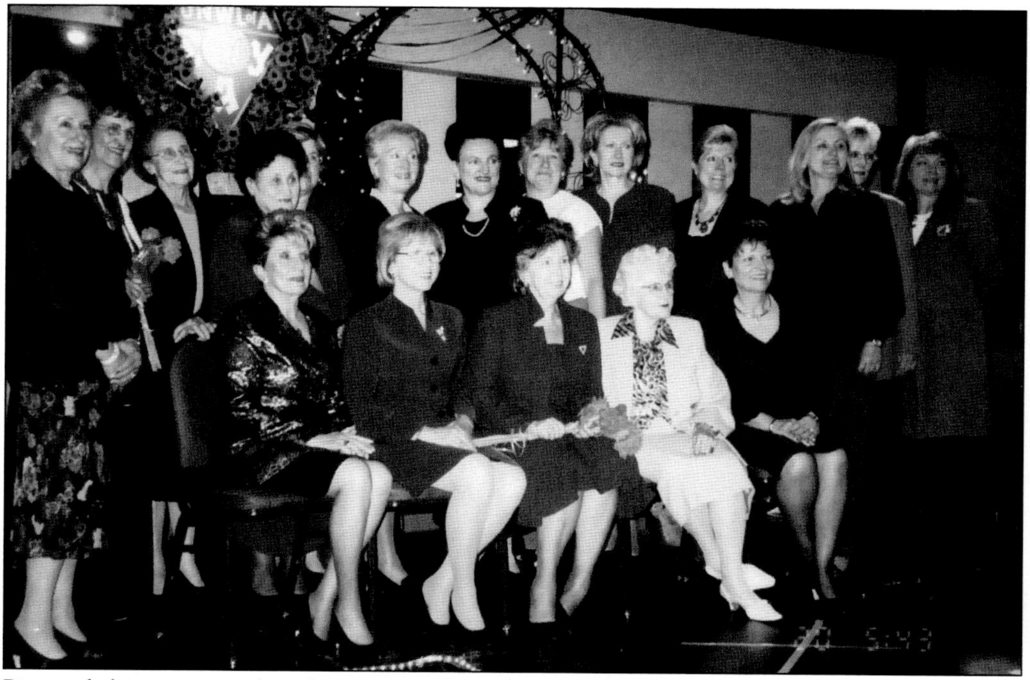

Pictured above are members from various branches of Detroit's UNWLA (Soyuz Ukrainok) with their national president Irene Kurowycky. (Roman Masiak.)

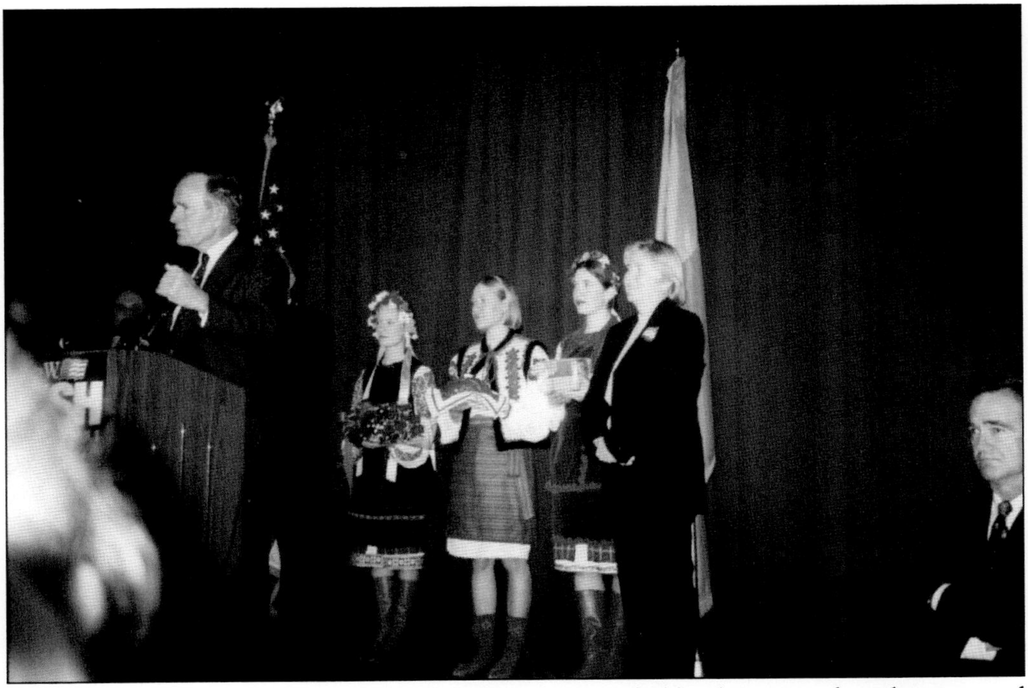

Young women, dressed in traditional Ukrainian costumes, hold welcoming gifts to be presented to former President George Bush, who visited the Ukrainian Cultural Center in Warren. He was there campaigning for his son George W. Bush in 2000. (Roman Maziak.)

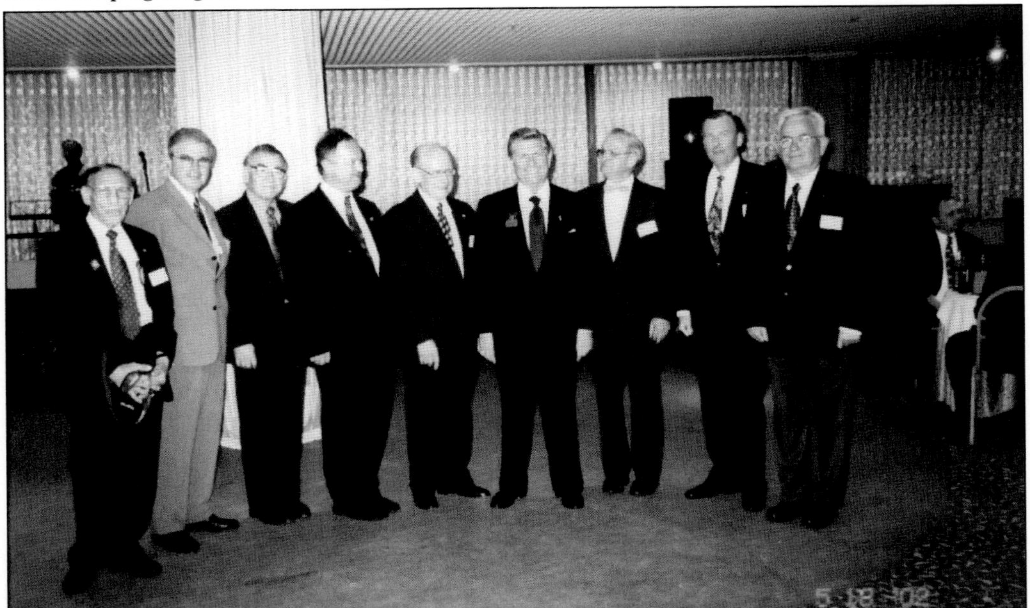

In 2002, Lubomyr Hewko, fifth from the right, of the Clarkston Rotary Club, and Richard King, fourth from the right, president of Rotary International, posed with a group of Rotarians at the tenth anniversary of the chartering of the first Rotary Club in Kyiv in post-Soviet Ukraine. Hewko was the initiator and sponsor of this club. The Clarkston Rotary Club has been extremely generous in humanitarian aid to Ukraine. (Lubomyr Hewko.)

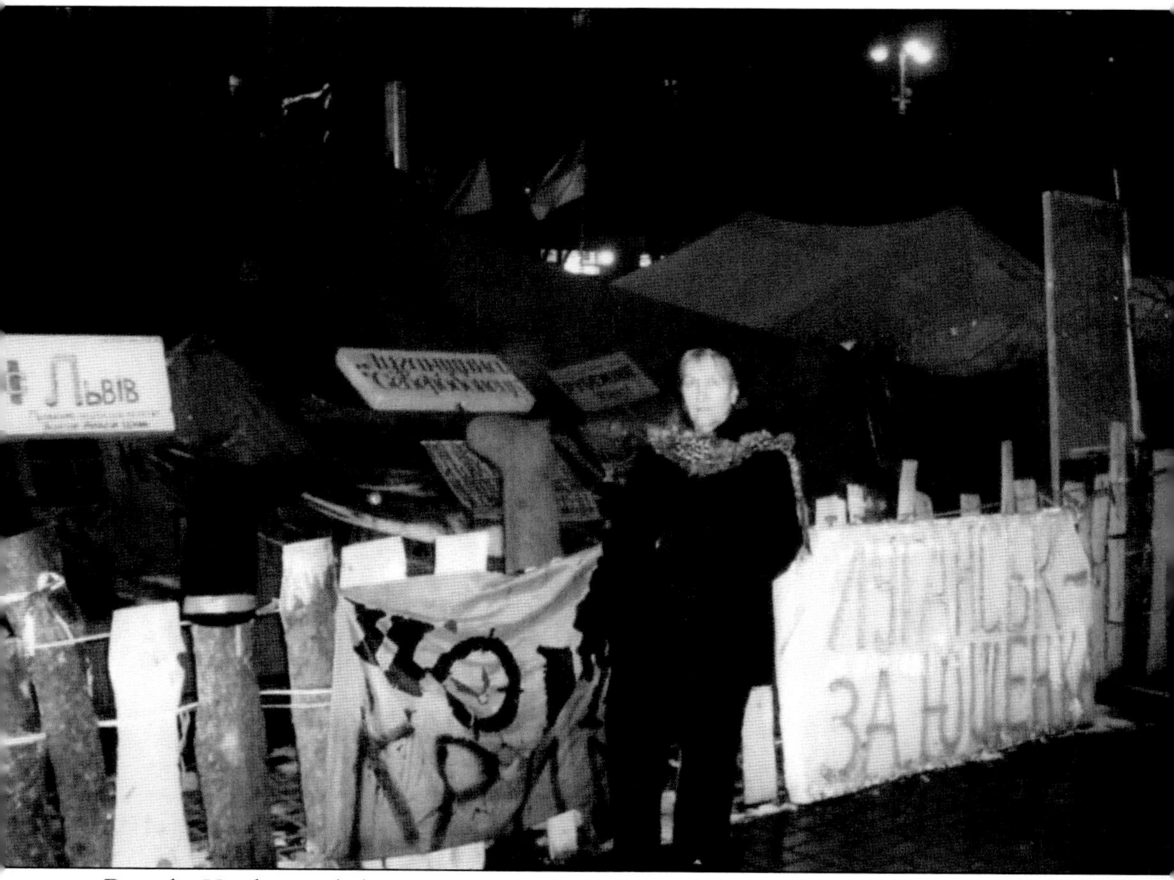

Dzvinka Hayda traveled to Kyiv as an election monitor in December 2004. She is standing in front of an Orange Revolution Protest Camp on Khryshtatyk Avenue. The Orange Revolution was in protest of widespread election fraud in the November 2004 presidential election. (Dzvinka Hayda.)

Five

Youth and Education

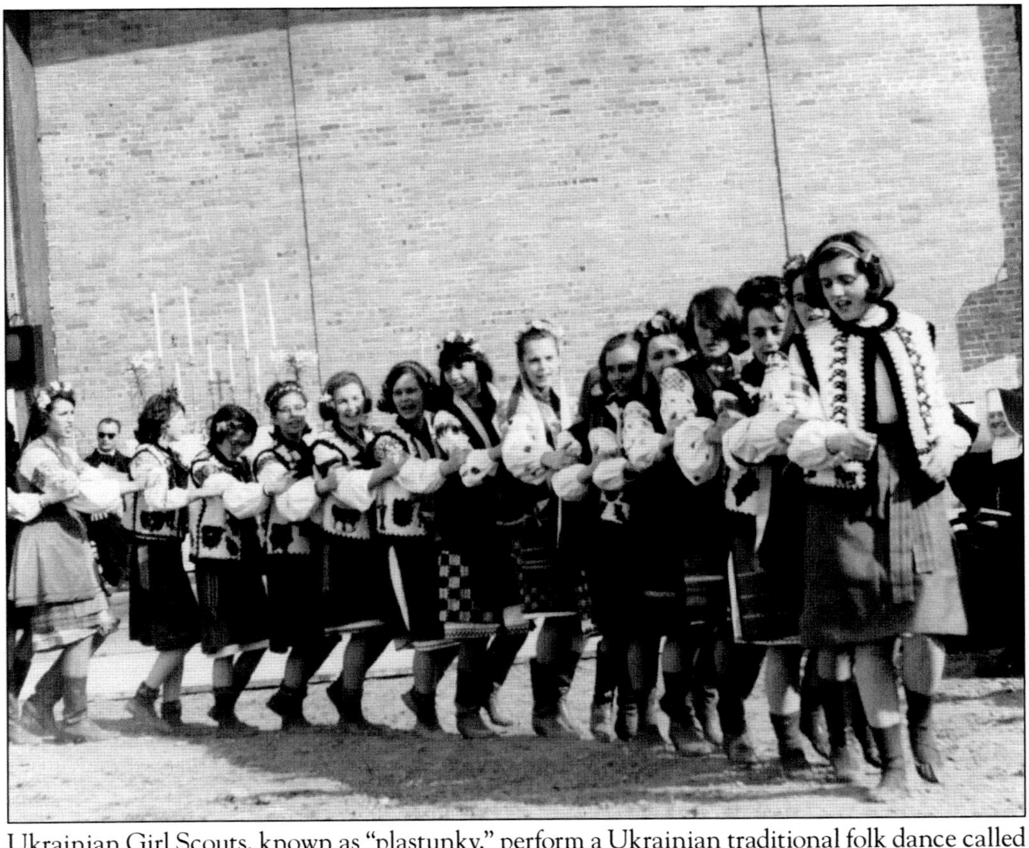

Ukrainian Girl Scouts, known as "plastunky," perform a Ukrainian traditional folk dance called the "Hahilky" at the 1966 dedication of the newly constructed St. Josaphat Ukrainian Catholic Church in Warren. (Lubomyr Hewko.)

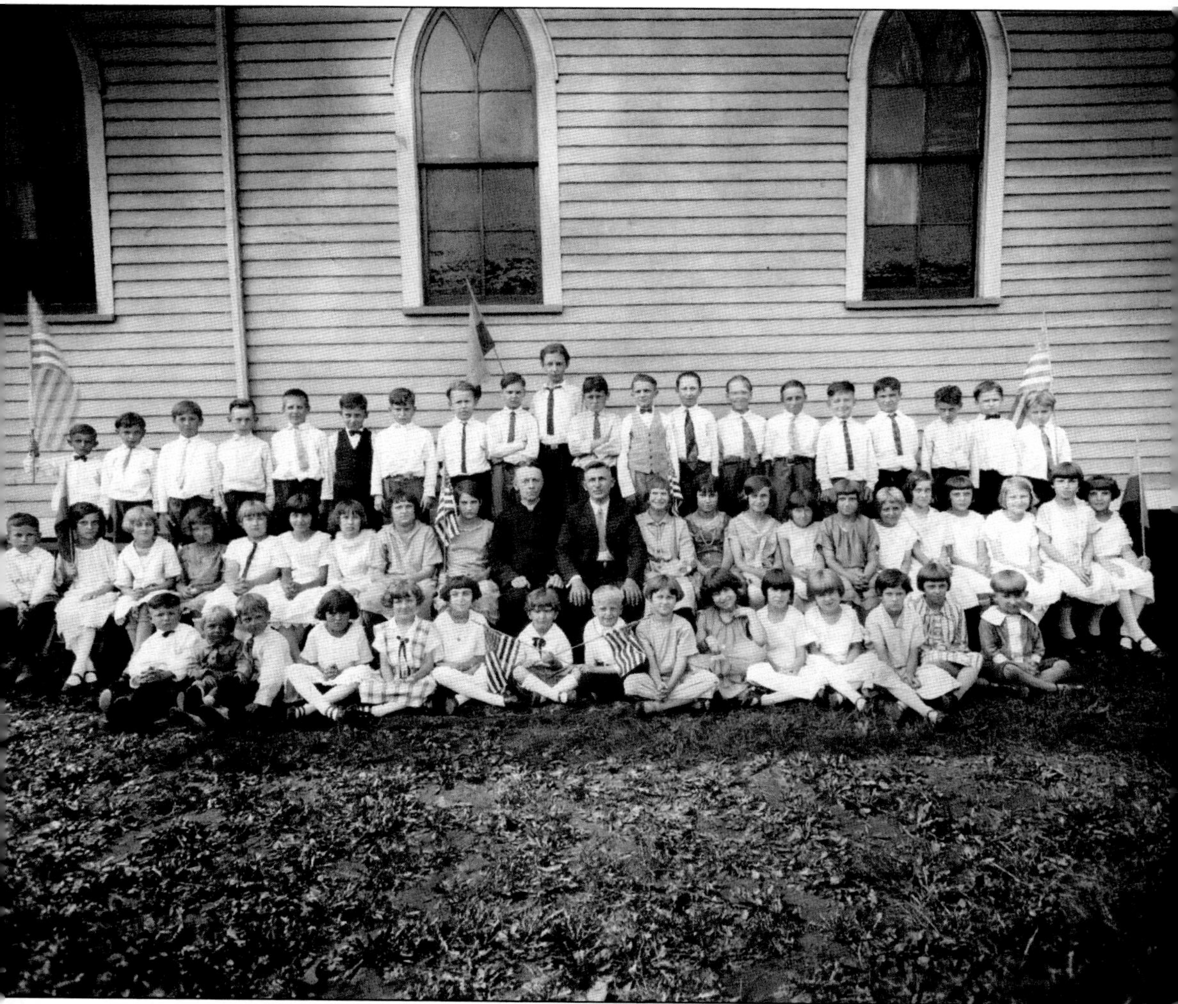

St. Johns Ukrainian Catholic School students pose with Father Pelechowych. They proudly hold up both Ukrainian and American flags honoring their heritage while displaying their American patriotism. St. John's primarily served families living on the west side of Detroit. This image is from around 1920. (Joseph Szafranski.)

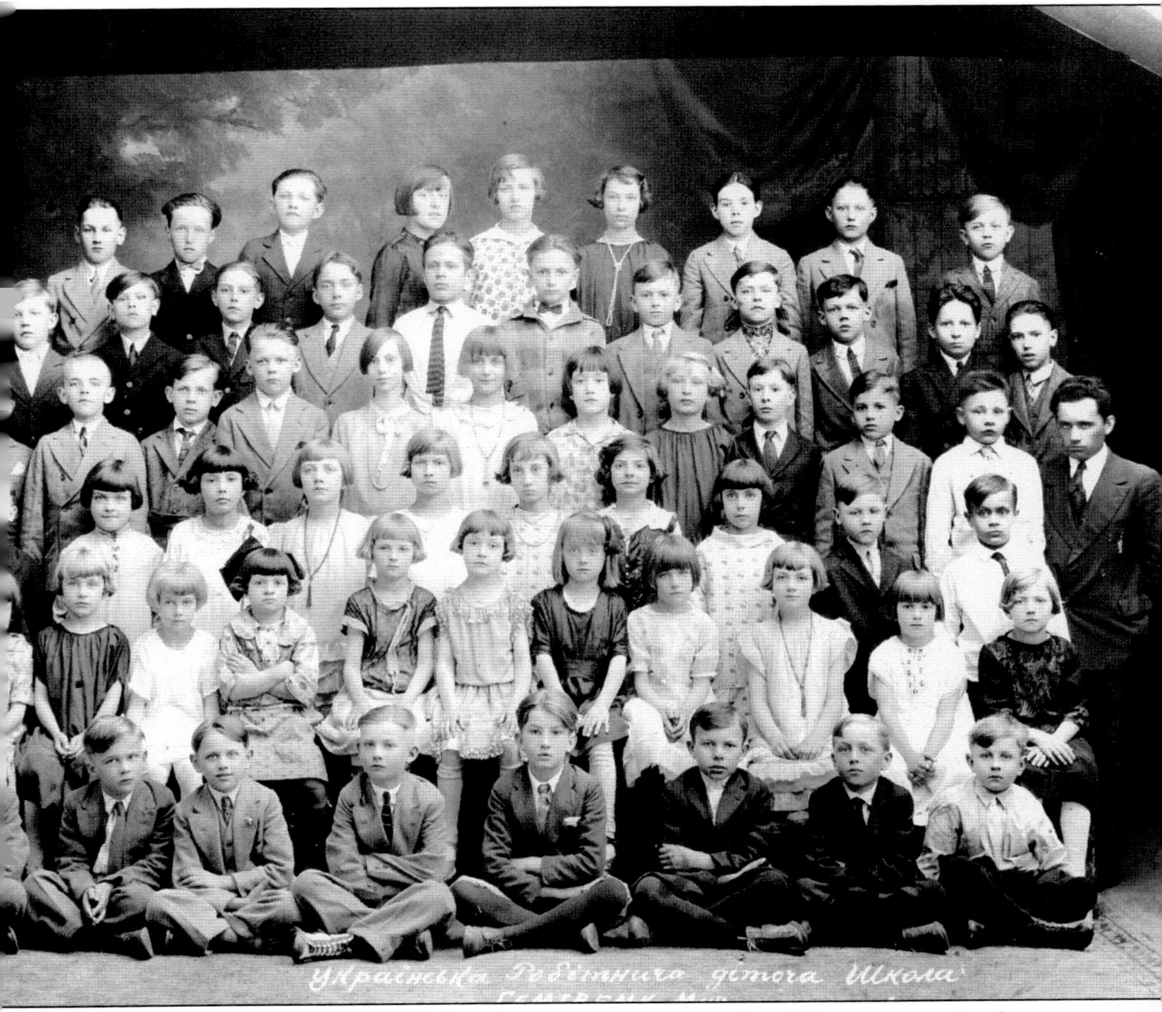

Education was such a priority within the Ukrainian community that following a regular day at school, the children then attended Ukrainian school several nights a week. In Ukrainian school, the focus was on learning the Ukrainian language and preserving the cultural heritage. The students pictured above primarily resided on the east side of Detroit and in Hamtramck. This image is from the 1920s.

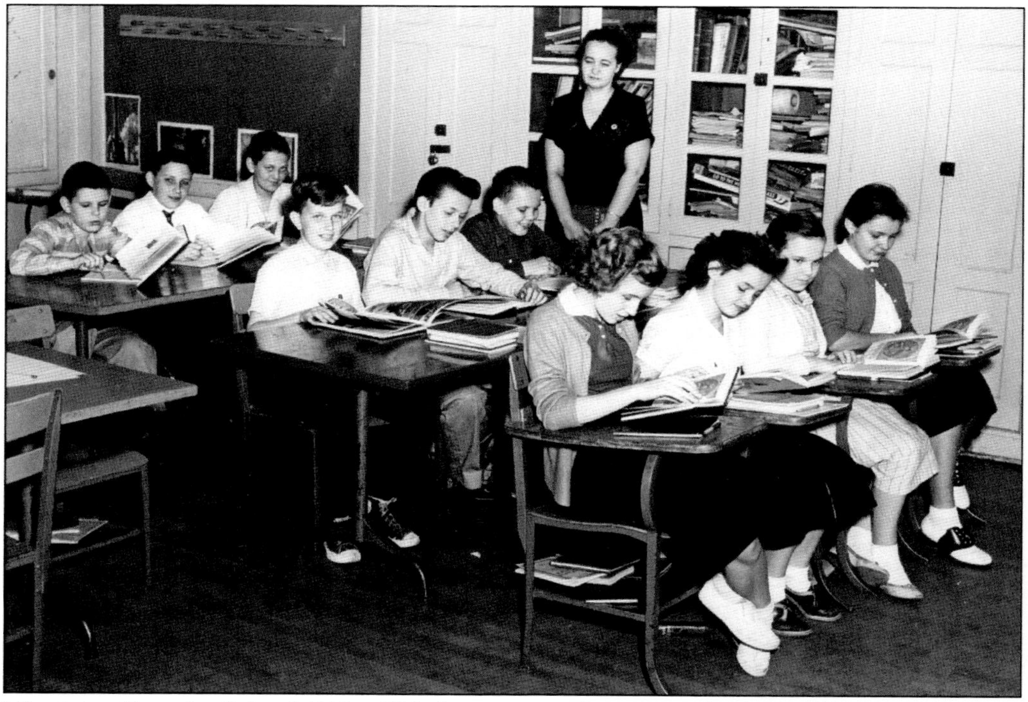

Ukrainian Saturday School, Ridna Shkola, was a regular routine for these fifth graders pictured in 1956. (Marta Kwitkowsky.)

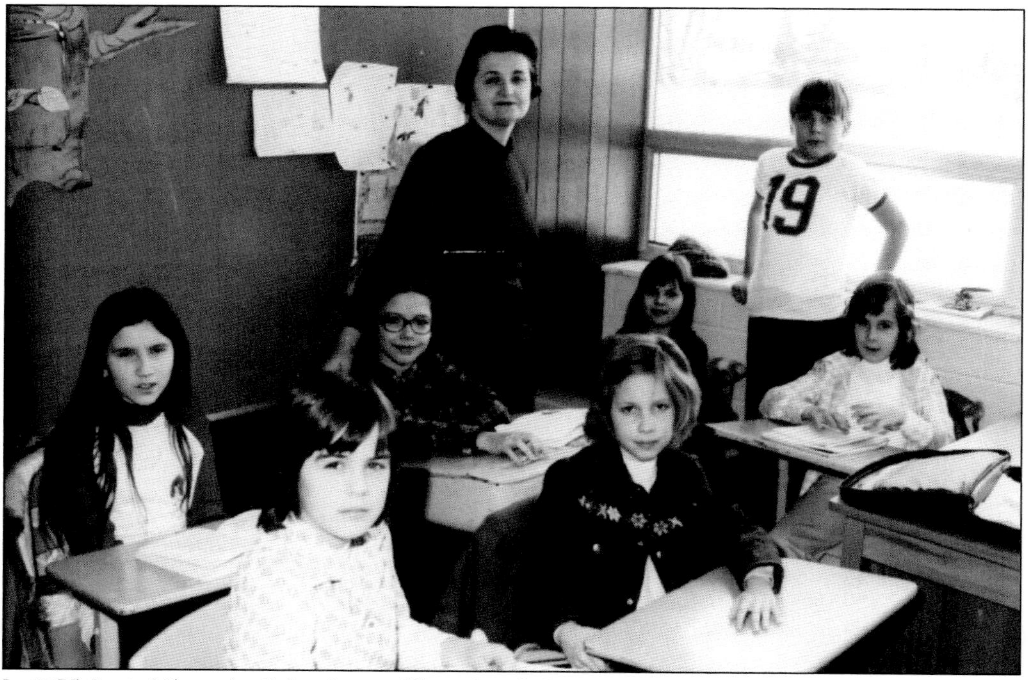

In 1975, Lesia Ukrainka School was affiliated with St. Mary's Ukrainian Orthodox Church. The fourth graders are, (first row) Natalka Prytula, Rita Starostenko, and Lisa Petrusha; (second row) Luba Melnichuk, Liza Symonenko, and Natalka Kowalenko; (third row) teacher Luba Zura and Alex Petrusha. (Elizabeth Symonenko.)

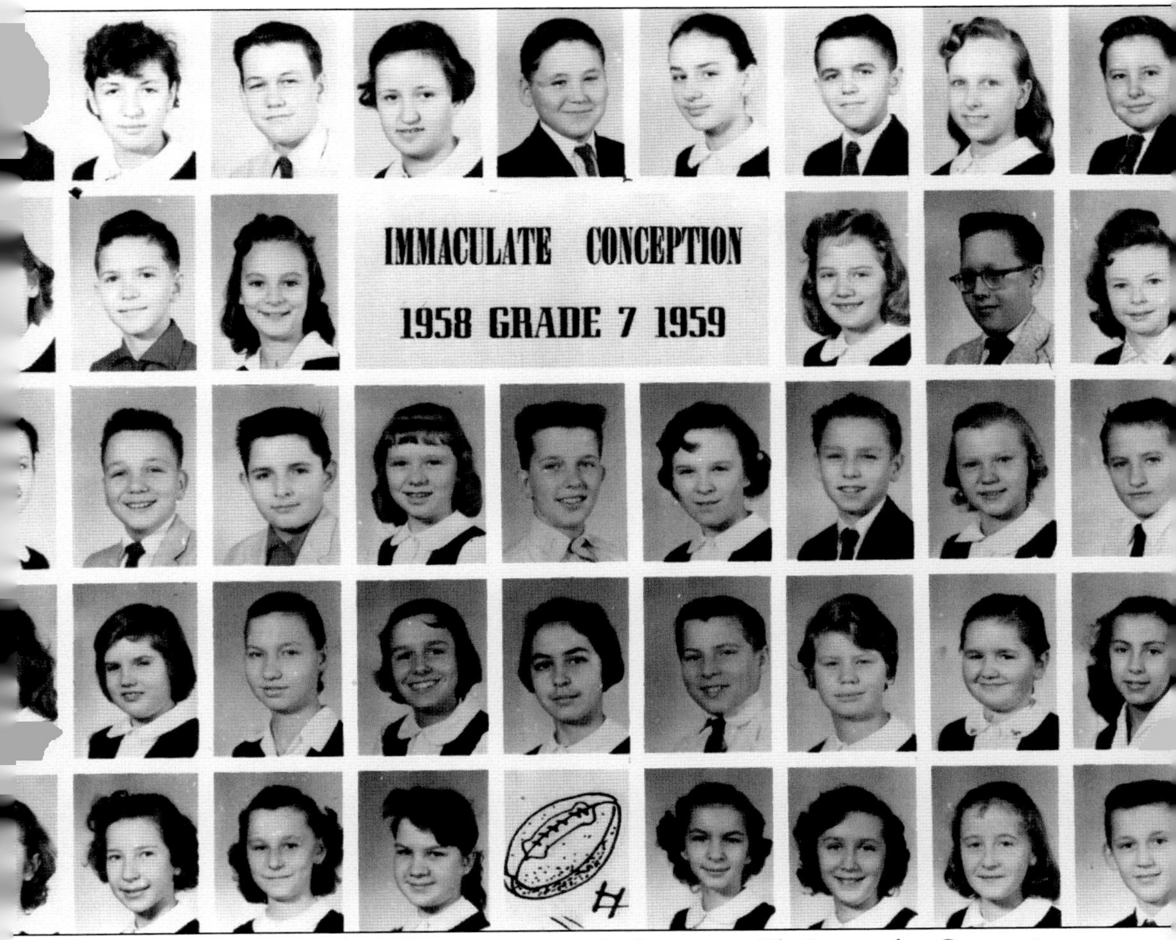

A typical class picture from the 1950s can conjure up fond memories. The Immaculate Conception Ukrainian Catholic School seventh grade class of 1958–1959 consists of (first row) Diane Bojcuniak, Rosemarie Krasicky, Alexandra Kindrat, Marlene Guy, Alexandra Hundich, Anna Bojduj, Irene Guran, and Bohdan Hrycaj; (second row) Sonia Kuchar, Alice Kozak, Oksana Bartkiw, Motria Kraus, Alexandra Klymyshyn, Michael Andriashko, Sharon Kaczor, Lydia Kazaniwsky, and Mary Kaczmar; (third row) Alice Jarecky, William Moskal, Alex Maritczak, Marie Karpinsky, Bohdan Kniahenycky, Marta Fedyshyn, Lubomyr Bartkiw, Irene Antoniak, and Bohdan Kowalyk; (fourth row) Luba Kocielko, Russell Jablinsky, Lennore Czarnonicz, Sandra Lucyk, Michael Lukasik, and Stephanie Gulczevsky; (fifth row) Mrs. Homynyk, Christine Kohut, Michael Hrynick, Roksolana Musztuk, Walter Maclowsky, Anna Kowalczuk, George Kazaniwsky, Nancy Kolocy, and Walter Chubatyj. (Marta Kwitkowsky.)

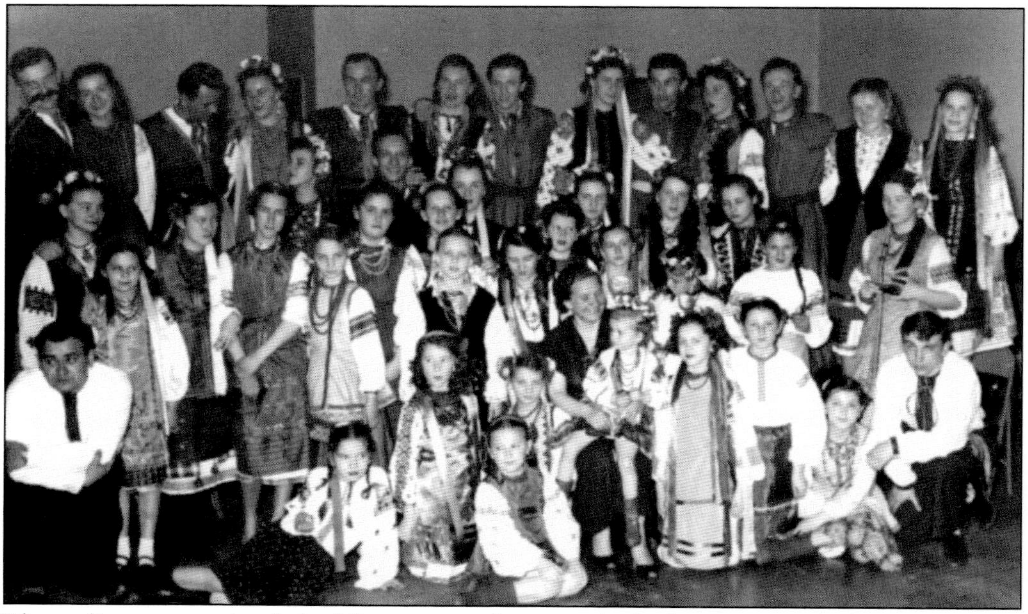

The audience appreciated the Ukrainian performance by both younger and older members of the community. This image is from 1952. (Tania Petryna.)

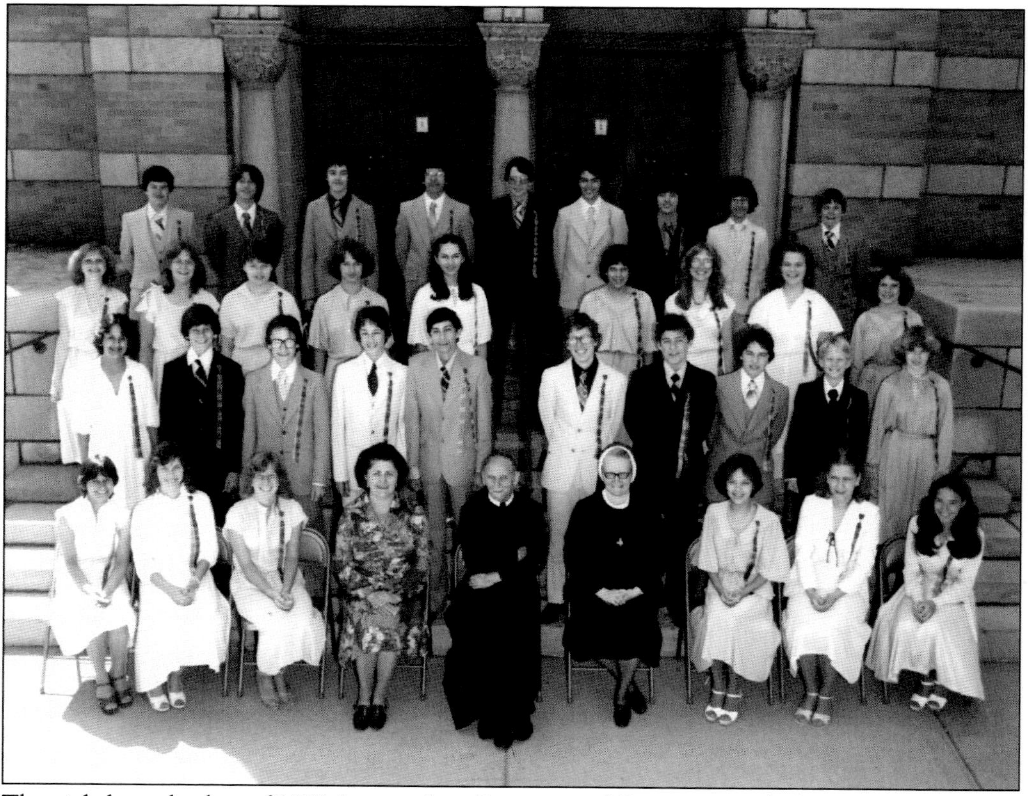

The eighth grade class of 1979, Immaculate Conception Ukrainian Catholic School, celebrates their graduation on the steps of the church with, first row center, Reverend I. Lotucky; fourth from left, Mrs. Jurek; and sixth from left, Sister Chrysostom. (Roman Maziak.)

Young women adorned in Hutzul costumes await their turn on stage for a Trembita dress rehearsal. (Roman Maziak.)

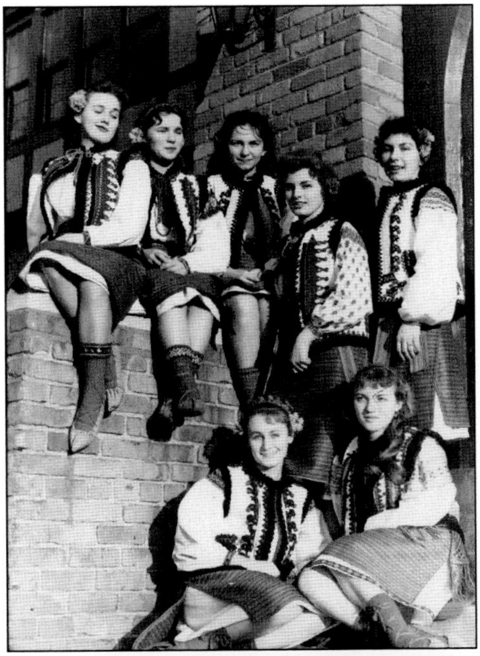

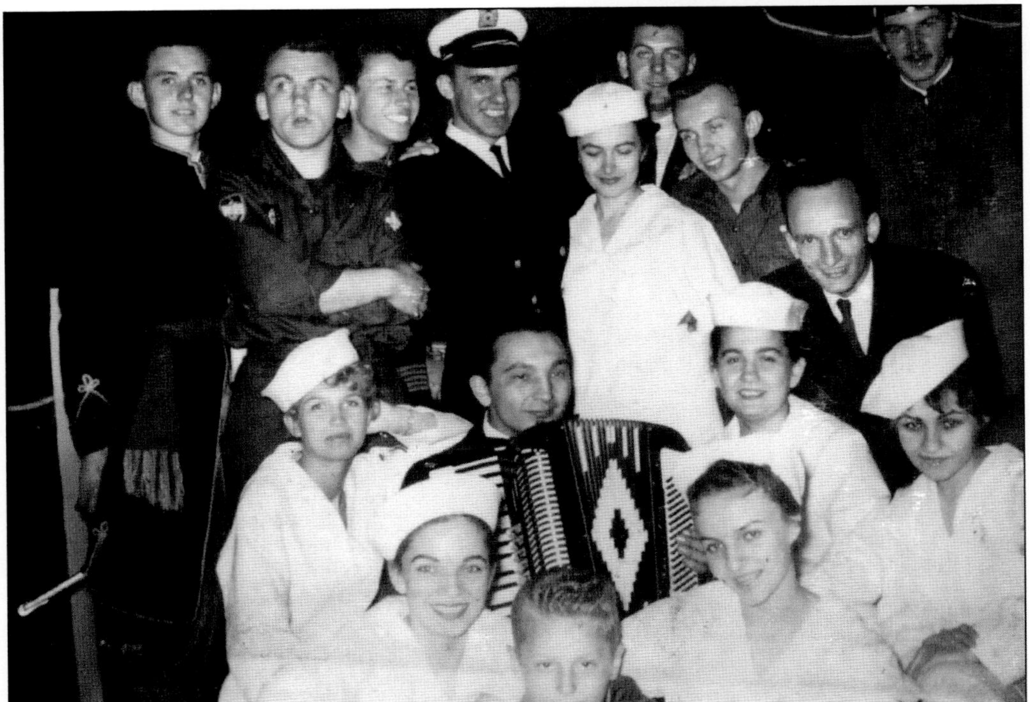

The Black Sea Scouts "Chornomorci" and "Khwylky" prepare to perform a scene in commemoration of raising the Ukrainian flag on the Black Sea Fleet. Seen here are (first row) Christina Lypeckj, Oles Fedorovych, and Myrosia Sawchuk; (second row) Gena Jurkiw, Richard Tomiak, Zirka Milanych, and Luba Sawchuk; (third row) Mykola Hryhorczuk, Ihor Iwanycky, Yuriy Boychuk, Steve Kohut, Oksana Korduba, Nestor Kolcid, Roman Masiak, and Yuriy Slusarchuk. This image is from the 1960s. (Roman Maziak.)

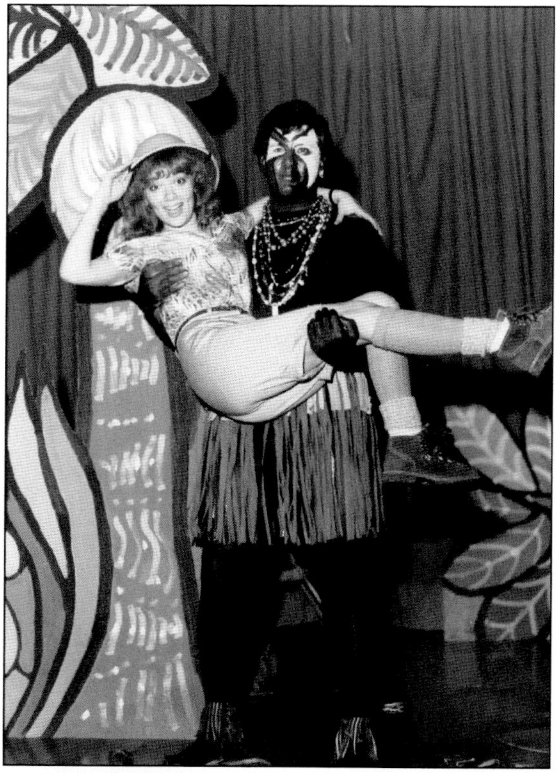

The Immaculate Conception Catholic High School play in 1983 was *Kwata Kuba* directed by Vera Andrushkiw. Donna Fedenko and Roman Los perform in a scene from the play. (Vera Andrushkiw.)

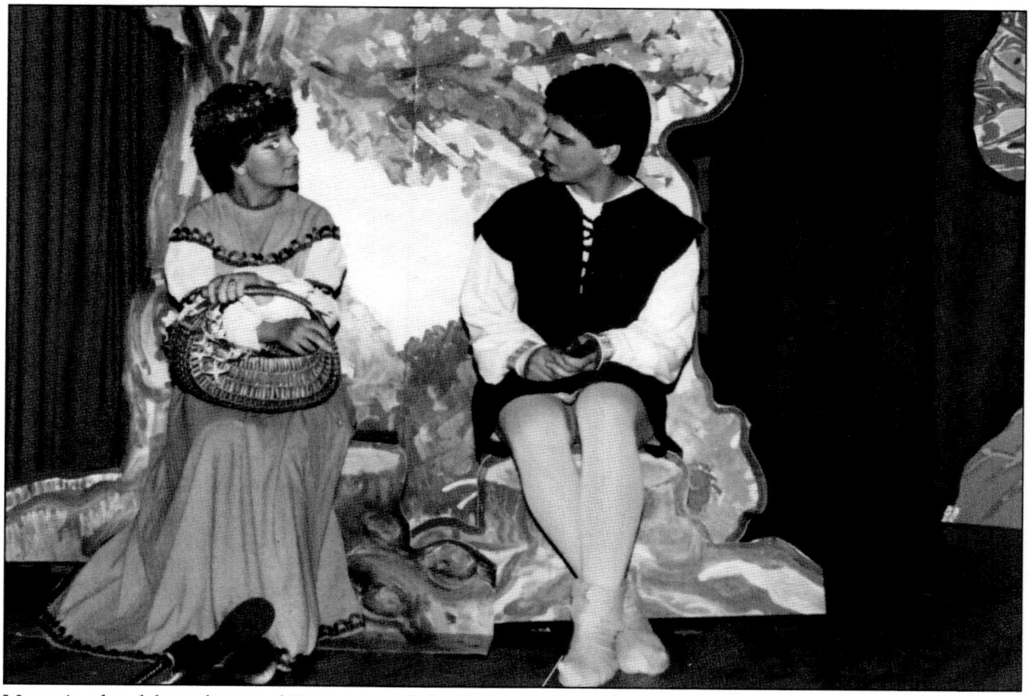

Vera Andrushkiw directed *Princess and the Pea* at Immaculate Conception Catholic High School in 1985. Christine Andrushkiw plays the part of the princess, and Andrew Zarycky plays the part of the prince. (Marie Zarycky.)

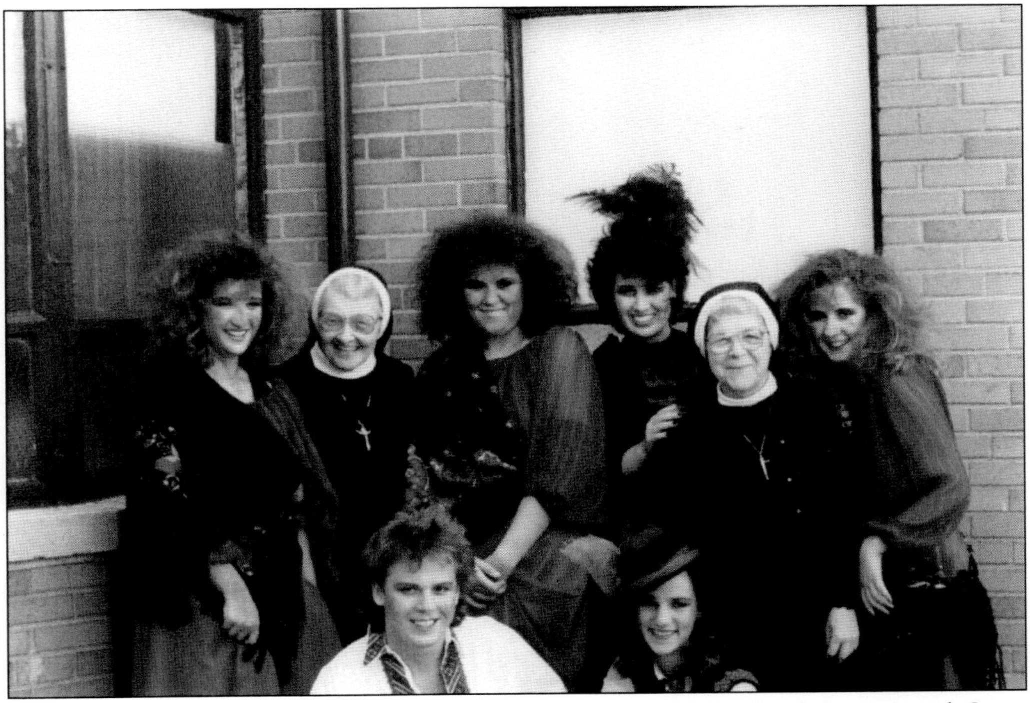

In 1986, cast members of an Immaculate Conception Catholic High School play pose with Sister Clement and Sister Vincent. (Vera Andrushkiw.)

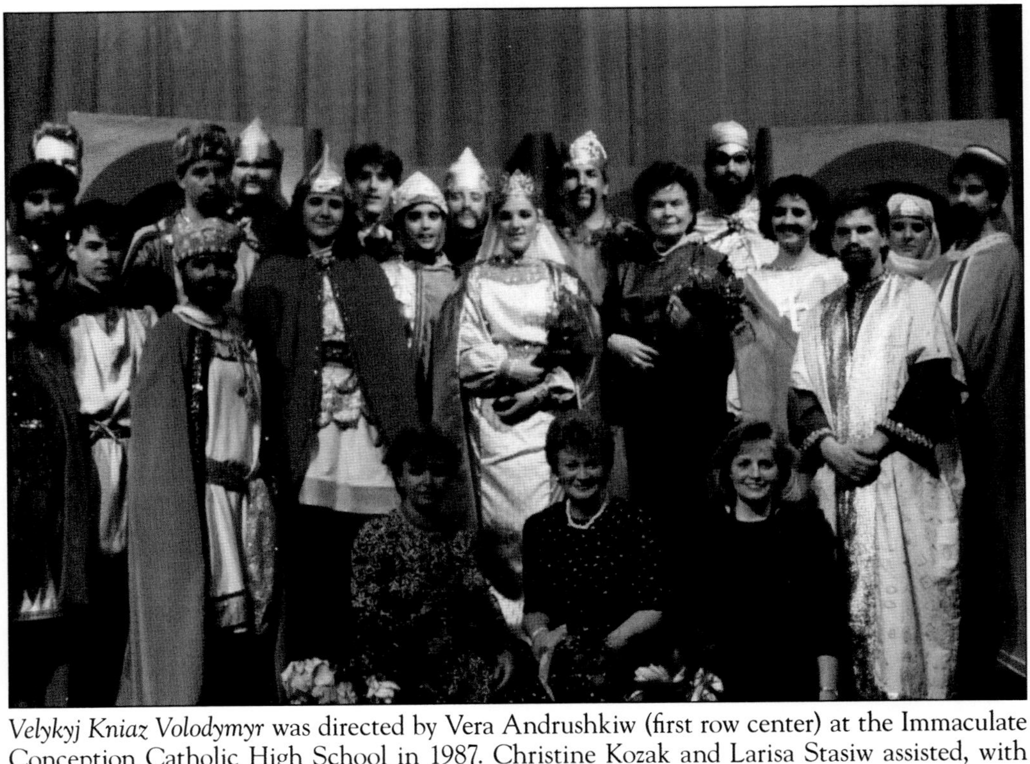

Velykyj Kniaz Volodymyr was directed by Vera Andrushkiw (first row center) at the Immaculate Conception Catholic High School in 1987. Christine Kozak and Larisa Stasiw assisted, with Maria Harasewych consulting. (Vera Andrushkiw.)

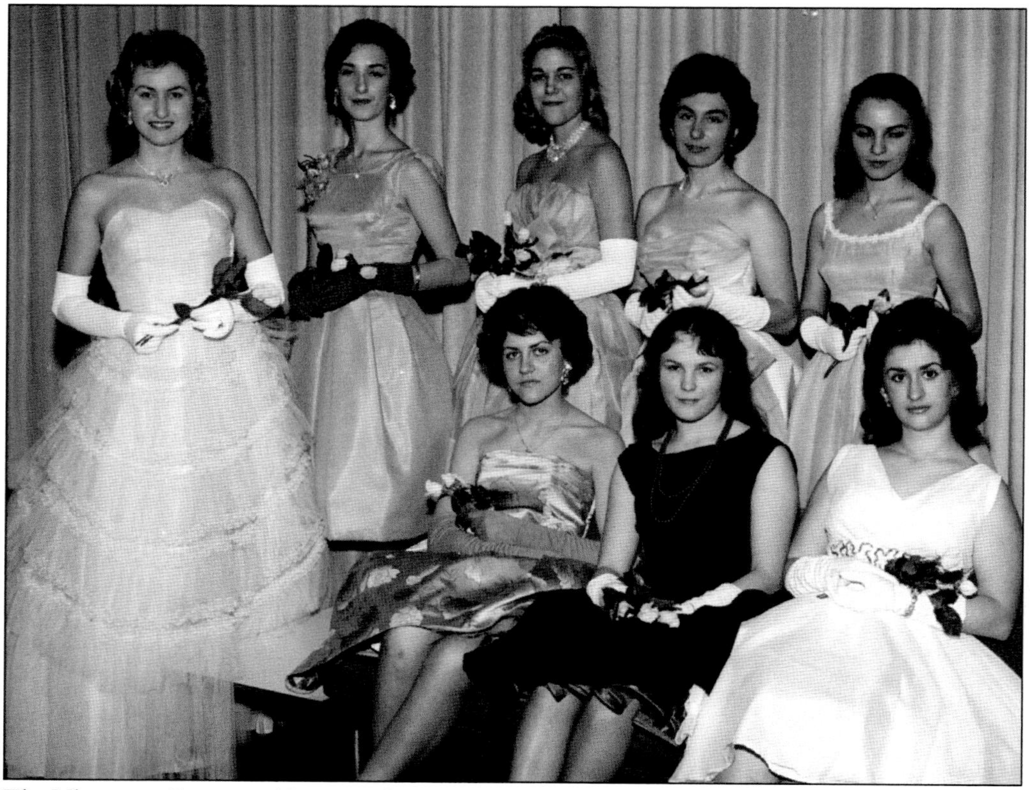

The Ukrainian Engineers' Society of America presents the debutantes of 1961. Seen here are (first row) Vera Treshnewsky, Ulana Shumylo, and Oksana Sena; (second row) Svitlana Lebedovych, Ulana Kunynsky, unidentified, Kwitka Diakiw, and Myrosia Sawchuk. (Roman Maziak.)

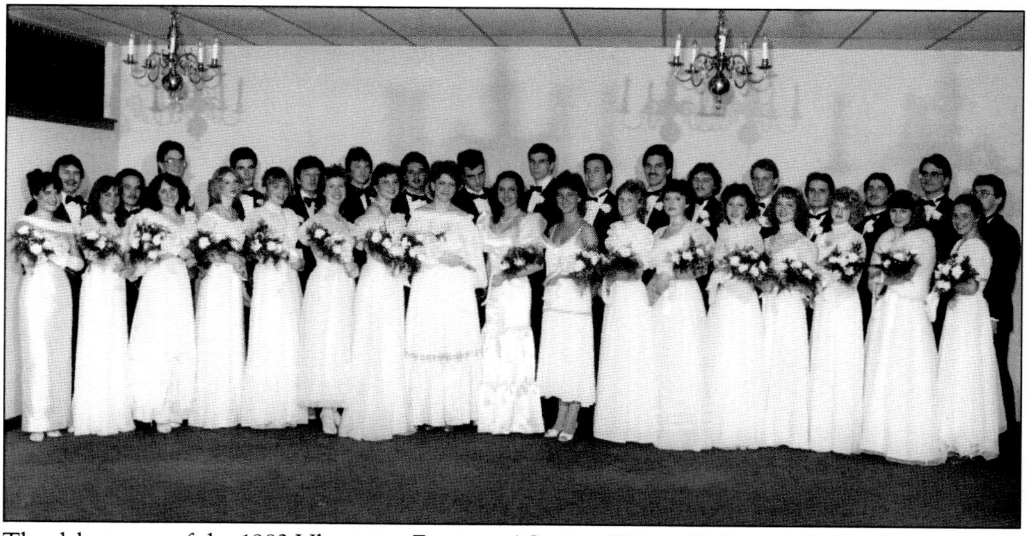

The debutantes of the 1983 Ukrainian Engineers' Society Winter Debutante Ball are presented at the Ukrainian Cultural Center in Warren. They are Patricia Ann Enright, Tessa Masyk, Joanna Markowycz, Mary Rachwal, Karen Neuman, Petra Hryshko, Christine Zarycky, Romana Remeniuk, Christina Renata Juzych, Christine Lash, Nadia Bluj, Lisa Bishyk, Tania Christina Sepell, Donna Fedenko, Natalia Kapitanec, Sonia Anna Prybula, and Oksana Hnatchuk. (Maria Zarycky.)

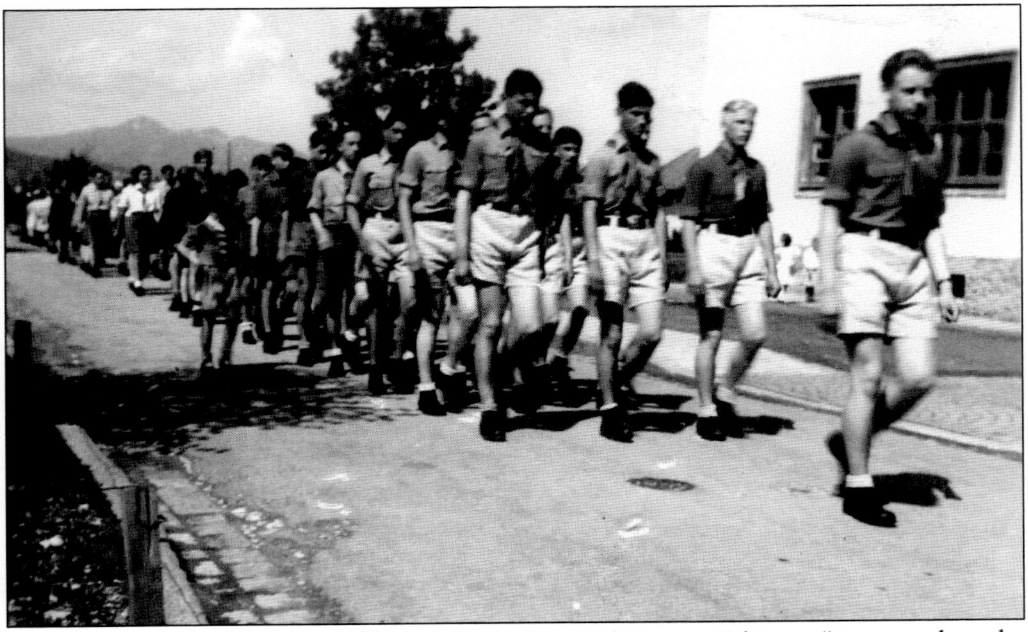

Lubomyr Hewko leads a group of Ukrainian Boy Scouts, known as "plastuny," in a parade at the displaced persons camp in Fussen, Germany, where he lived as a 17-year-old refugee after World War II, in 1946. He recalls that because of post-war extreme shortages of goods, the uniforms of the scouts were made from discarded bags, in which flour was sent to the camp by the American Refugee Relief Fund. (Lubomyr Hewko.)

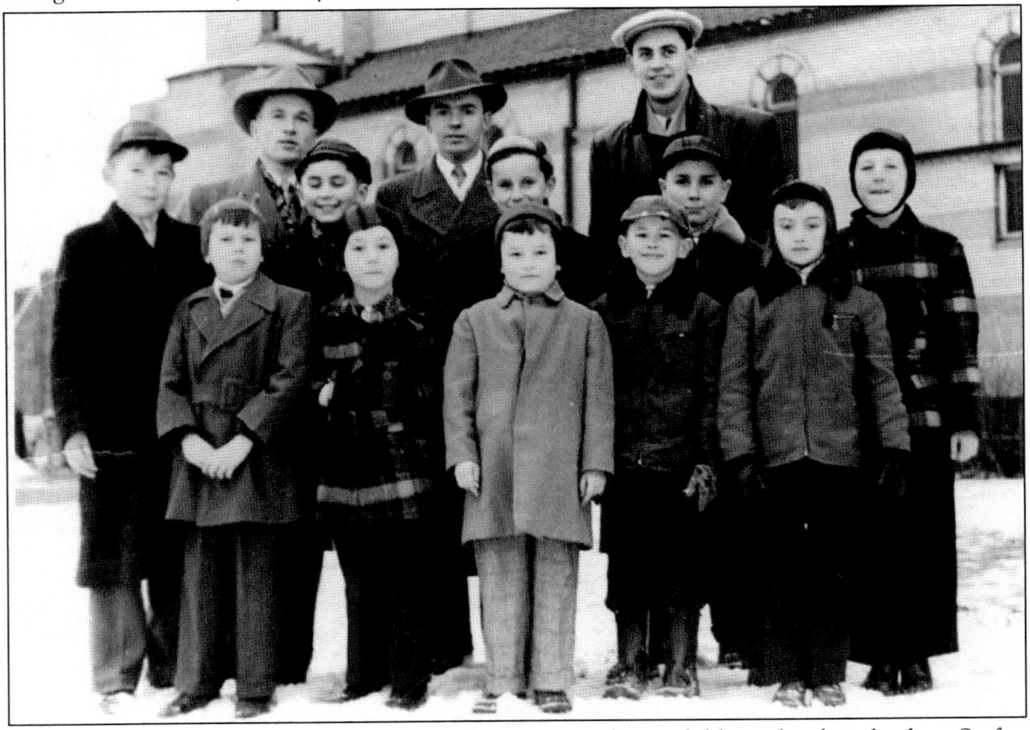

Young members of Plast (Ukrainian scouts) are escorted on a field trip by their leaders, Stefan Fedenko, Mykola Tataryn, and Bohdan Nehaniv, in the early 1950s. (Bohdan Nehaniv.)

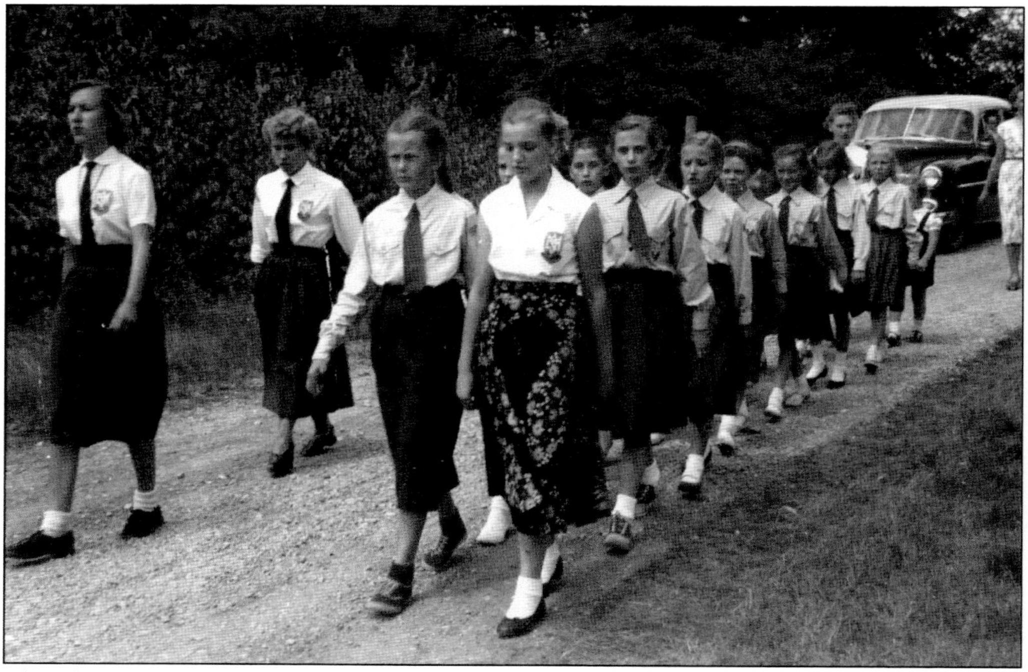

The Ukrainian Youth Group (Spilka Ukrajinskoji Molodi) marches in Dibrova (a local Ukrainian park) during a SUM-ZLET (multi-city gathering). This image is from 1956. (Dzvinka Hayda.)

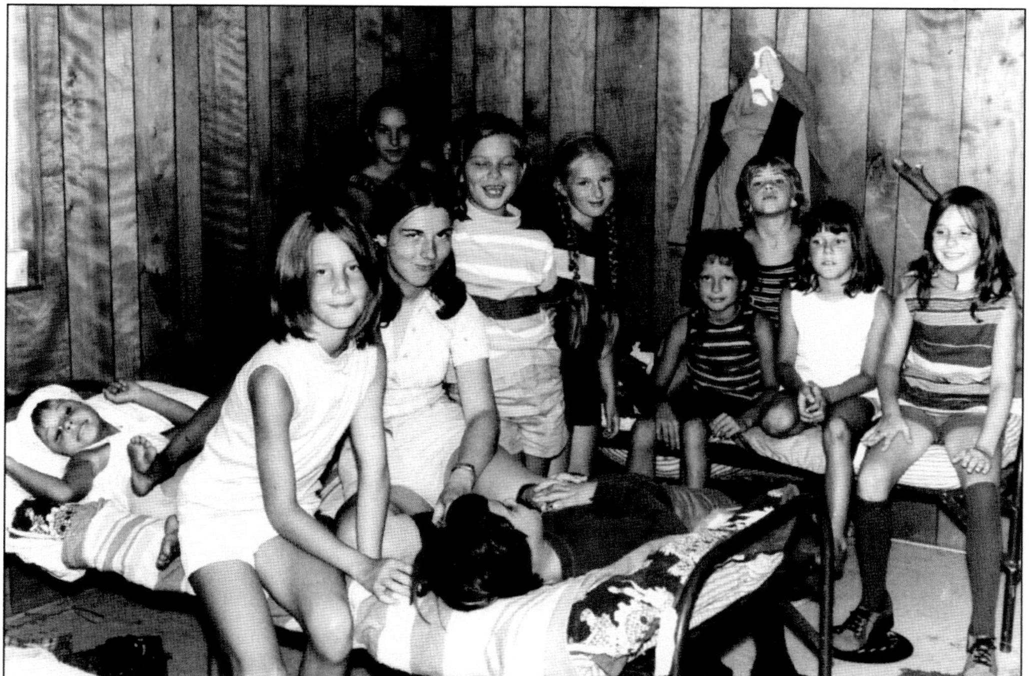

Plast Girl Scouts (novachky) relax in their cabin at Dibrova in 1975. Sitting are, from left to right, Natalia Monastyrsky, group leader Christine Woryk, Christine Zarycky, Nadia Bluj, Christine Barnych, Christine Boychuk, Lida Golavan, and Christine Hladysh. In the rear are Tessa Masyj and Renia Juzych. On the cot is Oksana Hnatchuk. (Marie Zarycky.)

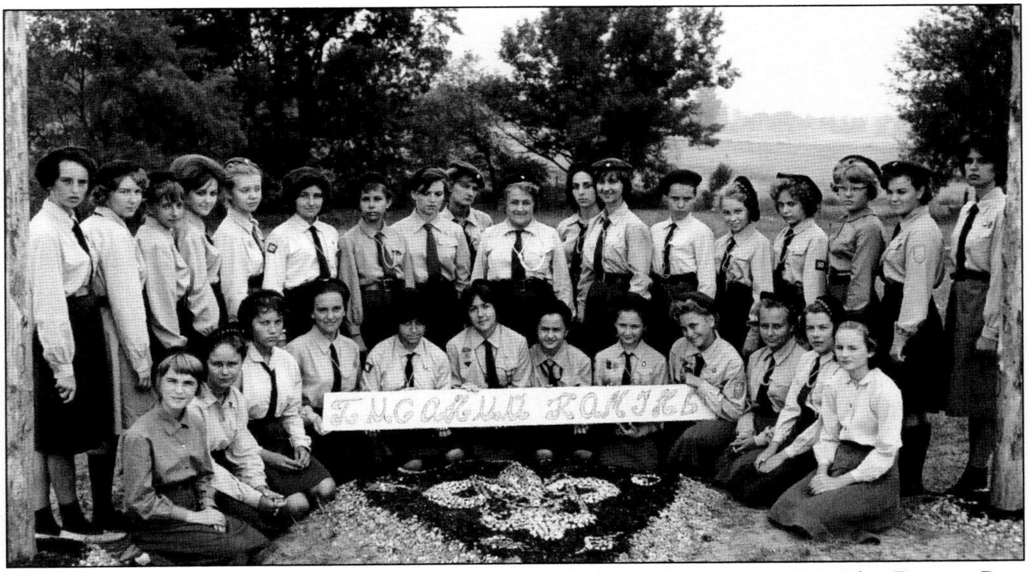

Plast, a Ukrainian scouting organization, was founded in Ukraine in 1911. The Detroit Post was founded in 1949. This youth group has been historically dedicated to the development of citizenship, character, and sound minds and bodies of its members through camping and sporting activities. The organization is open to both girls and boys. This image is from the 1960s.

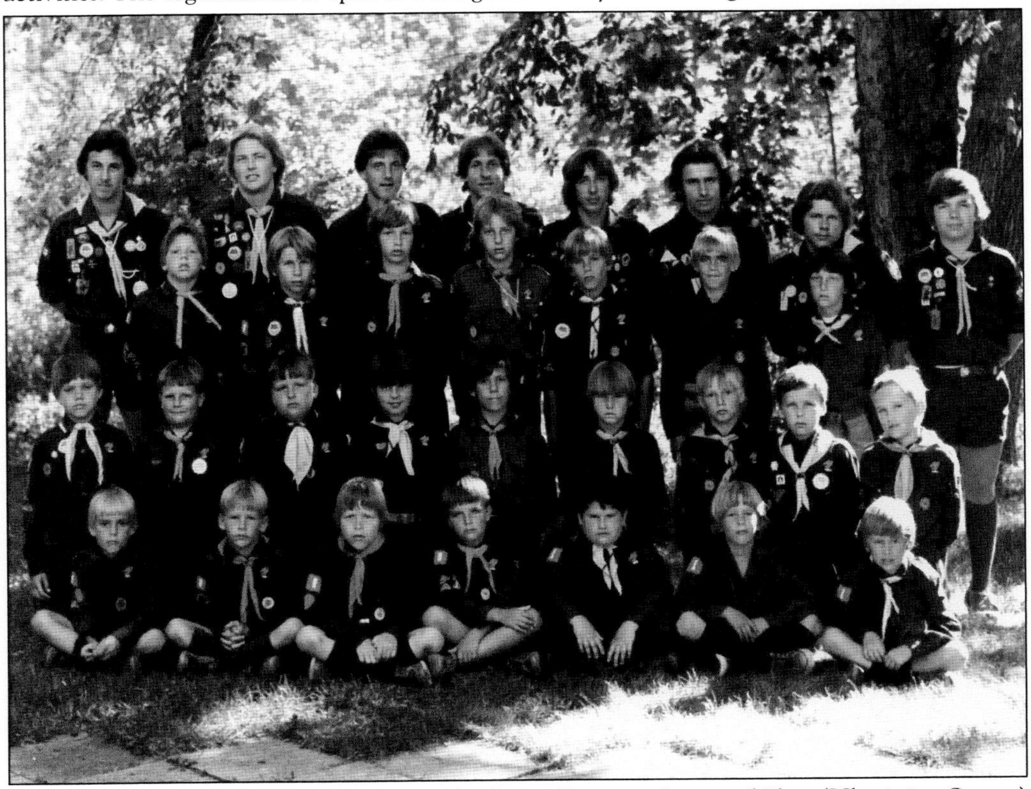

In 1954, the Detroit community purchased Dibrova Estate and granted Plast (Ukrainian Scouts) 16 acres of land for their camping needs. The organization has its headquarters in Warren. This image is from 1975. (Marie Zarycky.)

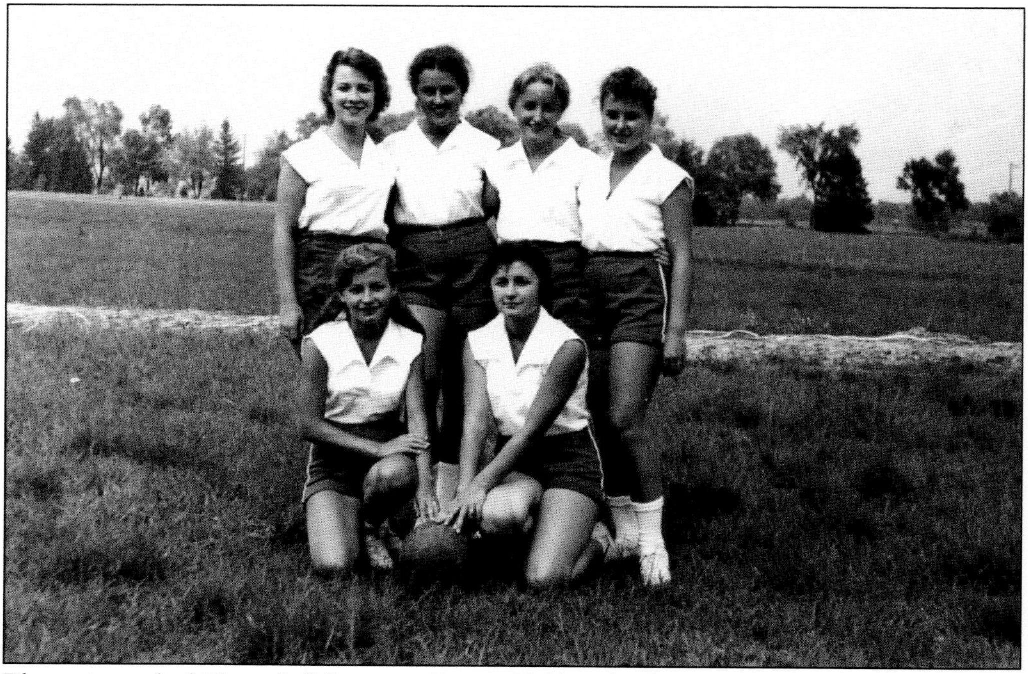

The main goal of Chernyk (Ukrainian Sports Club) is the formation and training in different sporting activities for the Detroit area Ukrainian youth. Pictured is the 1959 Chernyk Women's Volleyball Team on Dibrova in Brighton. (Roman Maziak.)

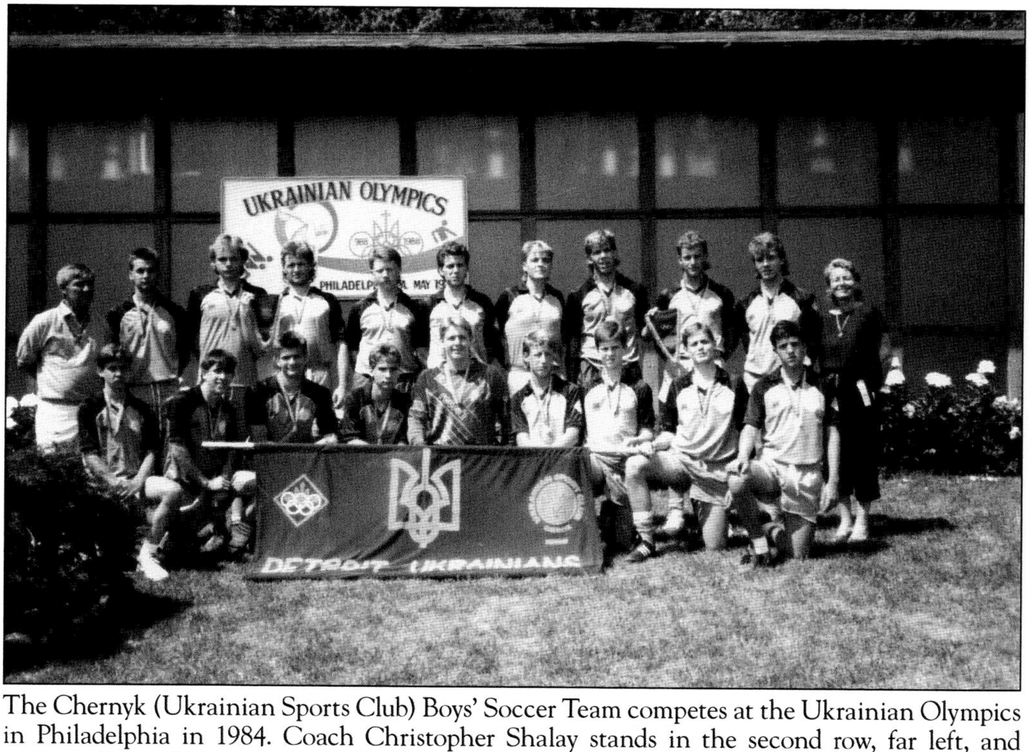

The Chernyk (Ukrainian Sports Club) Boys' Soccer Team competes at the Ukrainian Olympics in Philadelphia in 1984. Coach Christopher Shalay stands in the second row, far left, and manager Roma Kohut stands on the far right. (Lydia Kolodchin.)

Six

Ties to the Homeland

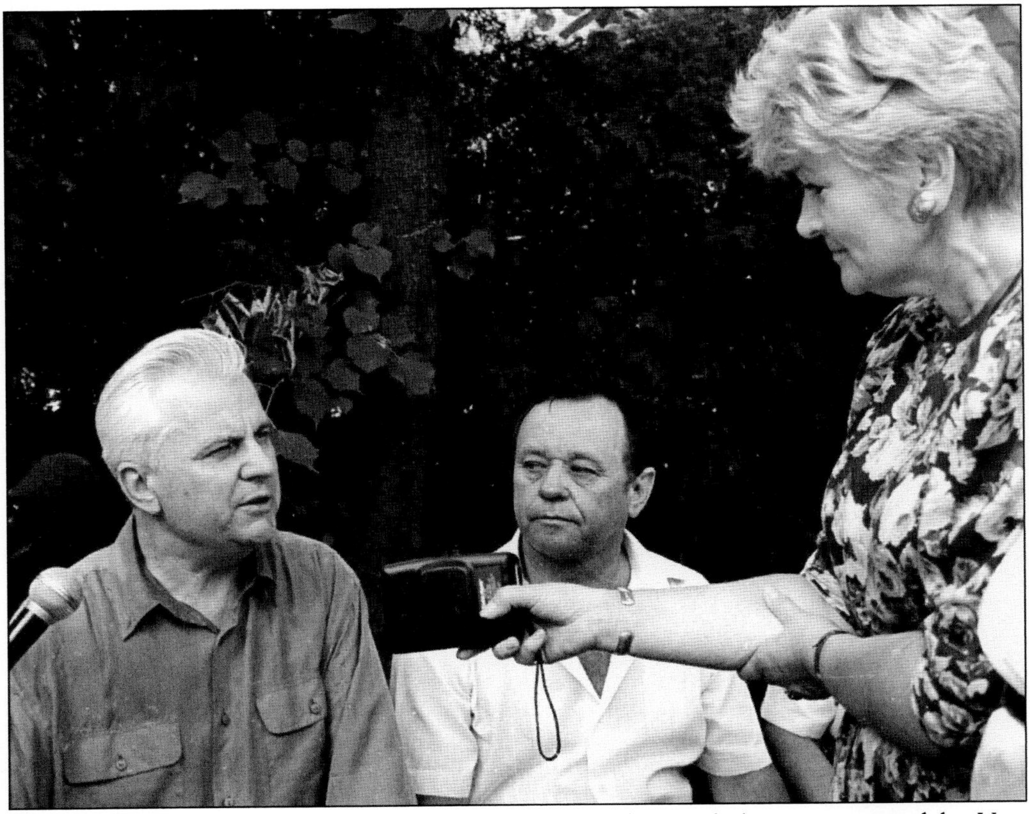

The first president of an independent Ukraine, Leonid Krawchuk, is interviewed by Vera Andrushkiw in Truskavets, Ukraine. Andrushkiw has represented the U.S.-Ukraine Foundation in the capacity of vice president of external relations and vice president of foreign relations. Her relationship with the foundation has given her responsibilities in dealing with Ukrainian issues both in the United States and in Ukraine. (Vera Andrushkiw.)

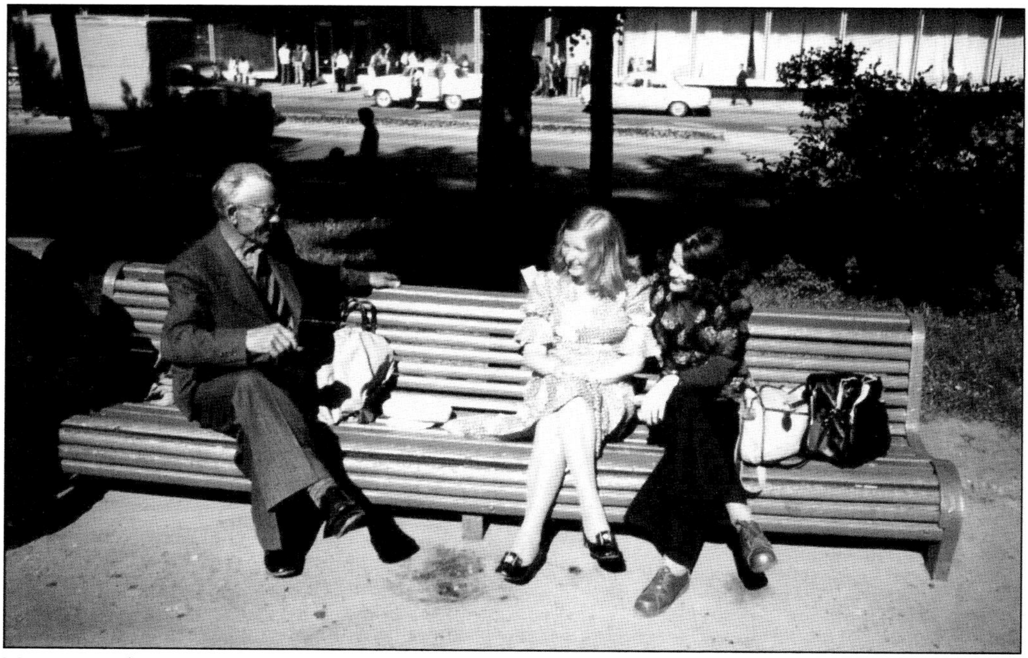

Nancy Wichar, on the far right, meets her Ukrainian relatives for the first time in the city of Lviv, Ukraine, in 1977. It was coincidental that her uncle, Stephen Wichar (on the left), would hold the same name as her father, and that her cousin (in the middle), Nadia Wichar, would hold the same name as her mother.

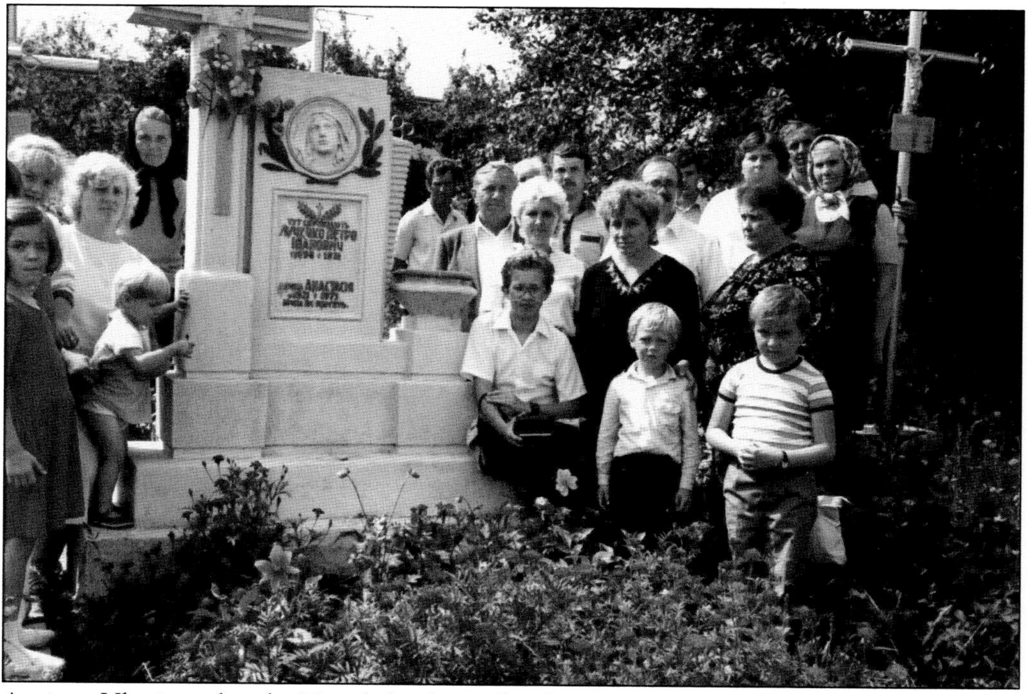

A trip to Ukraine takes the Maziak family to a local cemetery to visit the family gravesite. Their hearts were warmed to see their name had been added to the gravestone in appreciation for all their assistance. (Roman Maziak.)

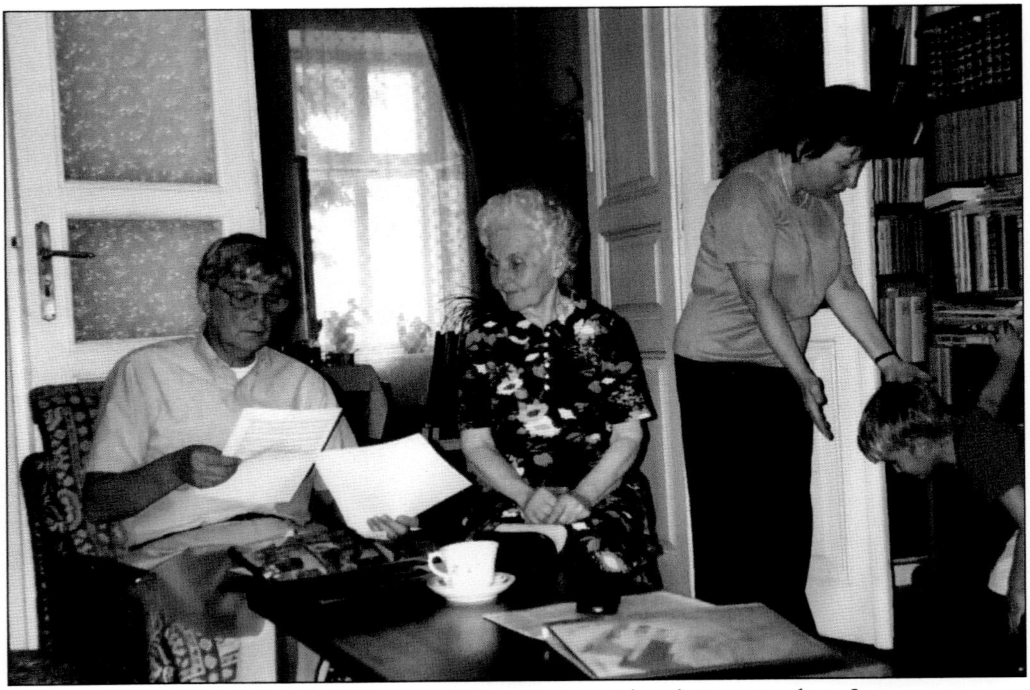

Andrew Petrina reads family papers and documents with relatives in their Lviv apartment. (Tania Petrina.)

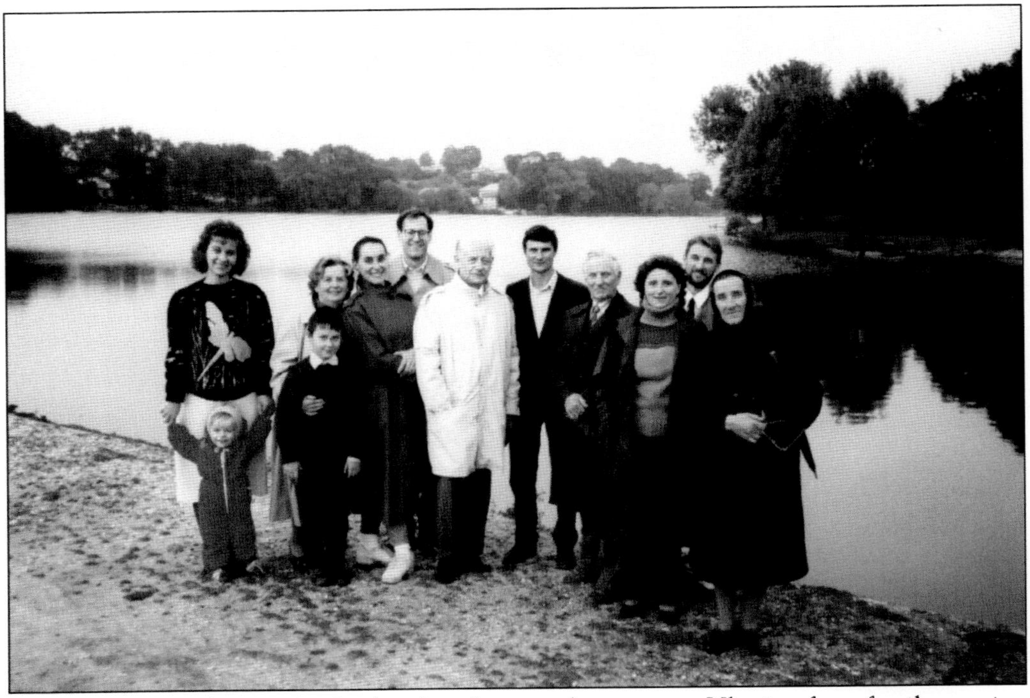

After 47 years, Lubomyr Hewko (in the white coat) returns to Ukraine for a family reunion in 1992. He stands by a pond with relatives near the family home near Zbarazh, Ukraine. (Lubomyr Hewko.)

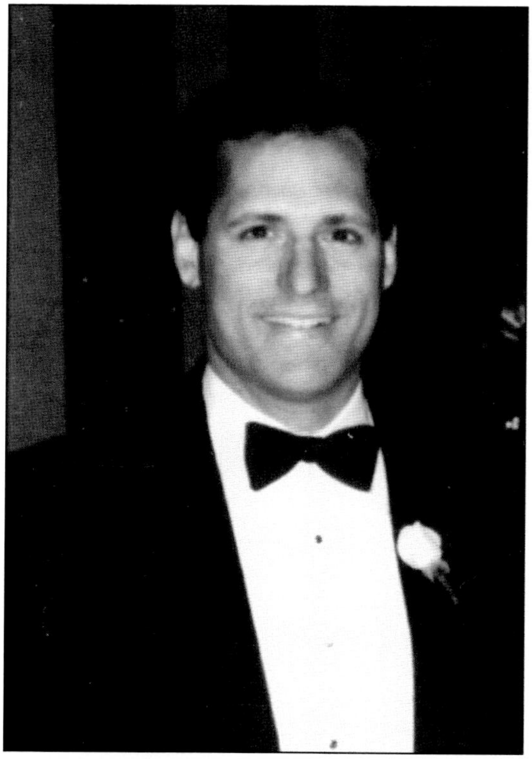

As a young lawyer, John Paul Hewko established a branch of the first western-type law firm in Kyiv, the capital of the newly independent Ukraine. He was also an executive secretary of the International Body of Constitutional Experts, which helped draft the first Ukrainian democratic constitution. This image is from the 1990s. (Lubomyr Hewko.)

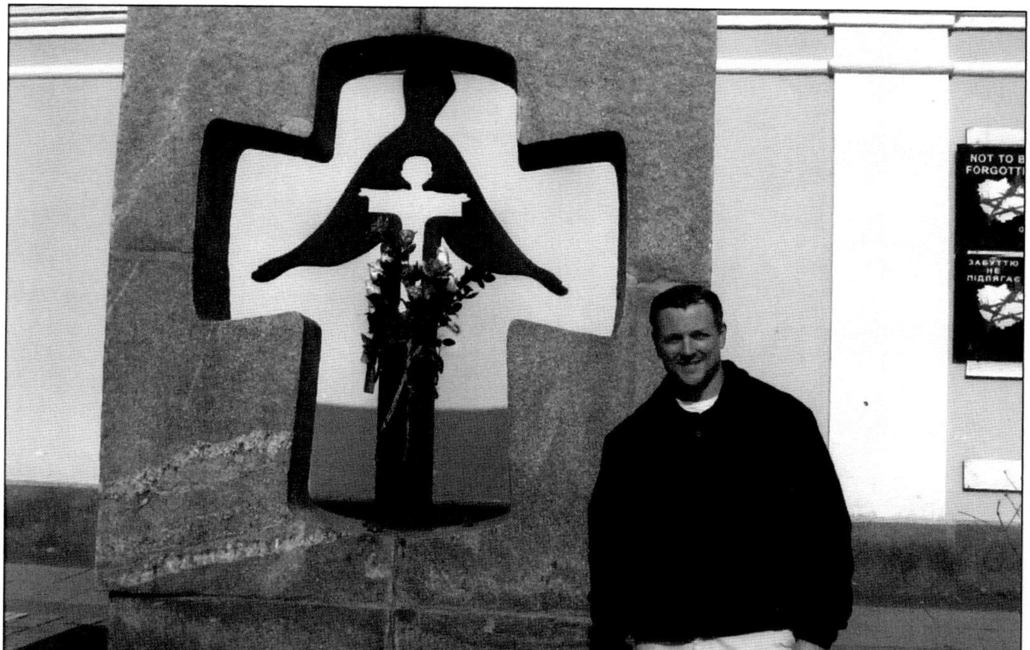

On his first trip to Ukraine, Michael T. Wichar, a third generation Ukrainian, visited Kyiv during Pres. George W. Bush's 2008 campaign to support Ukraine's effort to become part of the NATO alliance. He is pictured standing in front of the Kyiv Holodomor Memorial observing the 1932–1933 Soviet genocide/famine in Ukraine.

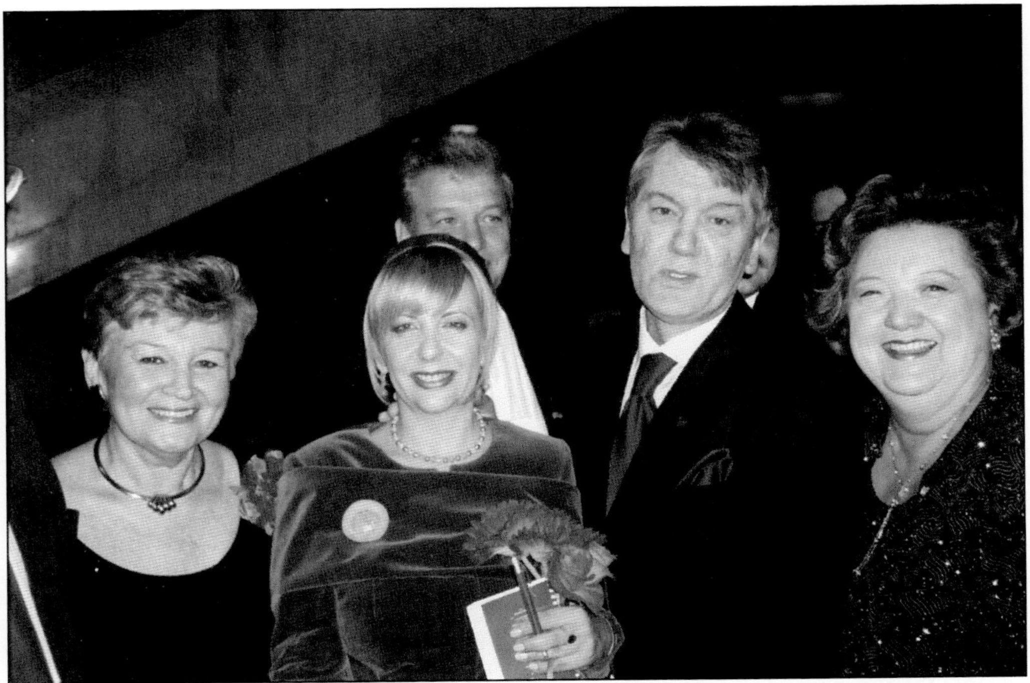

Vera Andrushkiw, far left, and Nadia McConnel, far right, of the U.S.-Ukraine Foundation, join Kateryna Chumachenko Yuschenko and Ukraine president Victor Yuschenko at the post-inaugural reception in Kyiv in 2005. (Vera Andrushkiw.)

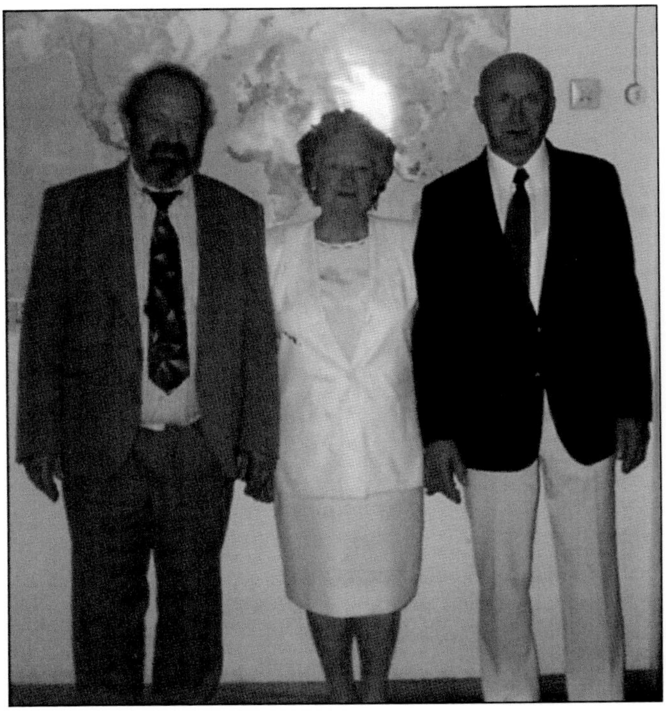

Vyacheslav Bryukhovetsky (left), president of Kyiv-Mohyla Academy in Ukraine, is pictured with Olga Duzyj (center) and Jaroslaw Duzyj (right) in 1996. Bryukhovetsky was present to accept a grant from the Duzyj Charitable Foundation. The oldest university in Ukraine, the Kyiv-Mohyla Academy has benefited from the endless hard work and fundraising of Mr. and Mrs. Duzyj. (Andrey Duzyj.)

Find Your Place in History.

www.arcadiapublishing.com

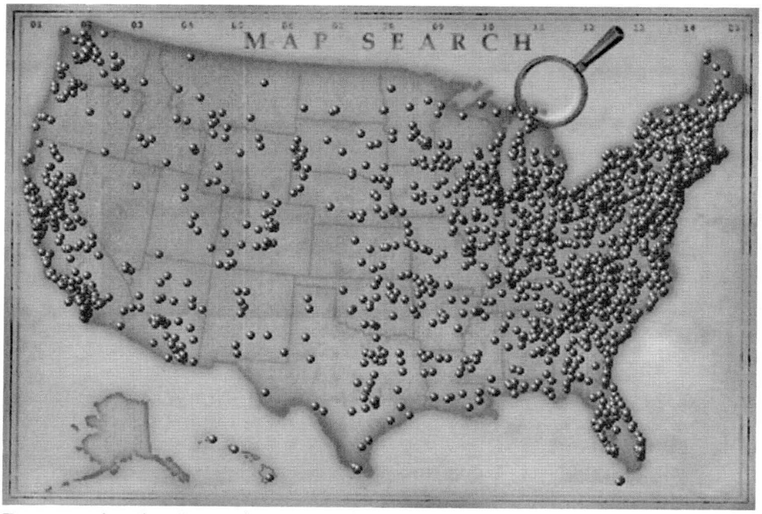

Discover books about the town where you grew up, the cities where your friends and families live, the town where your parents met, or even that retirement spot you've been dreaming about. Our Web site provides history lovers with exclusive deals, advanced notification about new titles, e-mail alerts of author events, and much more.

MADE IN THE USA

Arcadia Publishing, the leading local history publisher in the United States, is committed to making history accessible and meaningful through publishing books that celebrate and preserve the heritage of America's people and places. Consistent with our mission to preserve history on a local level, this book was printed in South Carolina on American-made paper and manufactured entirely in the United States.

This book carries the accredited Forest Stewardship Council (FSC) label and is printed on 100 percent FSC-certified paper. Products carrying the FSC label are independently certified to assure consumers that they come from forests that are managed to meet the social, economic, and ecological needs of present and future generations.

FSC
Mixed Sources
Product group from well-managed forests and other controlled sources

Cert no. SW-COC-001530
www.fsc.org